REVISE AQA GCSE (9–1)
Religious Studies A
CHRISTIANITY AND ISLAM

REVISION GUIDE

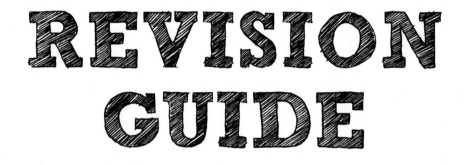

Series Consultant: Harry Smith

Author: Tanya Hill

- -

Also available to support your revision:

Revise GCSE Study Skills Guide   9781447967071

The **Revise GCSE Study Skills Guide** is full of tried-and-trusted hints and tips for how to learn more effectively. It gives you techniques to help you achieve your best – throughout your GCSE studies and beyond!

Revise GCSE Revision Planner   9781447967828

The **Revise GCSE Revision Planner** helps you to plan and organise your time, step-by-step, throughout your GCSE revision. Use this book and wall chart to mastermind your revision.

For the full range of Pearson revision titles across KS2, KS3, GCSE, Functional Skills, AS/A Level and BTEC visit:
www.pearsonschools.co.uk/revise

Published by Pearson Education Limited, 80 Strand, London, WC2R 0RL.

www.pearsonschoolsandfecolleges.co.uk

Copies of official specifications for all Pearson qualifications may be found on the website: qualifications.pearson.com.

Text and illustrations © Pearson Education Ltd 2018
Typeset and illustrated by Kamae Design
Produced by Out of House Publishing
Cover illustration by Eoin Coveney

The right of Tanya Hill to be identified as author of this work has been asserted by her in accordance with the Copyright, Designs and Patents Act 1988.

First published 2018

21 20 19 18

10 9 8 7 6 5 4 3 2 1

British Library Cataloguing in Publication Data
A catalogue record for this book is available from the British Library.

ISBN 978 1 292 20886 2

Acknowledgements
We are grateful to the following for permission to reproduce copyright material:

Photographs
(Key: T-top; B-bottom; C-centre; L-left; R-right)

123RF: Sergey Nivens 1 tl, Anna Tovkach 1tr, Joaquin Ossorio-Castillo 13 br, Jasminko Ibrakovic 19, bigevil600 29 cr, Marco Herrndorff 104 cl, blojfo 104 bl, epfop 125 tl, fredex8 93 tl, Alamy: Artimages 7cl, Peter Barritt 8, GoGo Images 10, Alistair Linford 13 tr, Prisma Archivo 22, Photosindia 29tl, Reuters 50,dpa picture alliance 51, The History Collection 61, Janine Wiedel Photolibrary 65, age fotostock 72, jozef sedmak 78 br, Alexandre Rotenberg 86, Zoonar GmbH 89, Pictorial Press Ltd 92, Science History Images 93, Michael Kemp 95, Jim West 101, Chandra Prasad 105 tl, Graham Prentice 110, See Li 124, Heritage Image Partnership Ltd 73, 131 cr,132 cr, SuperStock 132 cl, Chronicle 136,137, Granger Historical Picture Archive 140, Miriama Taneckova 144 cl, Roger Bamber 111 tr; Bridgeman Images: Bendixen, Siegfried Detler (1786–1864)/Private Collection/The Stapleton Collection 144 cr,Pictures from History 91; Catersnews: 43; Getty Images: Dea/G. Dagli ort 7 cr, AFP/NOAH SEELAM 47, Time Life Picture 78 cr, DEA/M. Seemuller 90, Yun Lu 93, CBS Photo Archive 97 cr, NurPhoto 113, AFP/Mahmoud Zayyat/Stringer 123, Corbis Historical/Stefano Bianchetti 131 tl, SuperStock 135, Alinari Archives 138; Shutterstock: graphixmania 1c, BroNrw 33, ZouZou 41, ArrowStudio 42,Monkey Business Images 46, Rashevskyi Viacheslav 57, Nickolay Khoroshkov 59, fizkes 62, phloxii 63, Facundo Arrizabalaga/Epa 97cl, Sergey Mironov 105cl, Billion Photos 111, ShaunWilkinson 125cl, Wipas Rojjanakard 125bl, Mordechai Meiri 141, Outer Space 54

All other images © Pearson Education

Text
p1–11,13, 14, 16–18, 36, 38, 40, 42, 44, 46, 48, 50, 54, 56, 58, 60, 62, 68, 70, 72, 74, 76, 80, 84, 86, 88, 90, 92, 94, 96, 100, 102, 104, 106, 108, 110, 112, 116, 118, 120, 122, 124, 126, 130, 131, 132, 134–148, 161, 166, 168, 170–174: Biblica Inc: Scripture taken from the Holy Bible, New International Version®, NIV® Biblica Inc (1973, 1978, 1984, 2011);

pp20, 22–26, 28–32, 34, 37, 41, 43, 45, 47, 49, 51, 55, 57, 59, 61, 63, 65, 67, 71, 75, 77, 79, 81, 85, 87, 89, 91, 93, 95, 97, 101, 103, 107, 109, 111, 117, 119, 121, 123, 125, 127, 165, 167, 171: The Qur'an Project Distribution Centre: 'The Qur'an Project (Saheeh International Translation), Maktabah Booksellers and Publishers (2010); p3, 11, 15: American Bible Society: Scripture taken from the Contemporary English Version (1991, 1992, 1995); p9: Cambridge University Press: Extracts from The Book of Common Prayer, the rights in which are vested in the crown, Cambridge University Press; p36, 42, 74, 104, 108: Cambridge University Press: Scripture quotations from The Authorised (King James) Version. Rights in the Authorised Version in the United Kingdom are vested in the Crown, Cambridge University Press; p120: Church of England: General Synod of the Church of England (1981); p5, 11: Church Society: 39 Articles IV, 39 Articles XXV, Church Society (2003); p14, 58, 108: Crossway Bibles: The Holy Bible, English Standard Version. ESV® Text Edition (2001); p58: Serrini, Father Lanfranco Christian Declaration on Nature – Assisi, 1986, an interfaith meeting to discuss ways of saving the natural world (1986); p92: Thomas Nelson: Scripture taken from the New King James Version® (1982); p56: Vatican Publishing Library: Apostles Creed © Libreria Editrice Vaticana; p120: Vatican Publishing Library: Catechism of the Catholic Church 2439, Libreria Editrice Vaticana; p64: Vatican Publishing Library: Humanae Vitae, Libreria Editrice Vaticana (1968); p6, 149: Vatican Publishing Library: Nicene Creed Copyright, Libreria Editrice Vaticana.

Contents

. . . .

A small bit of small print:

AQA publishes Sample Assessment Material and the Specification on its website. This is the official content and this book should be used in conjunction with it. The questions in *Now try this* have been written to help you practise every topic in this book. Remember: the real exam questions may not look like this.

The nature of God I

Christians believe in one god and understand him to have certain characteristics. Their belief in the nature of God influences other Christian beliefs as well as how Christians practise their religion.

God as omnipotent, loving and just

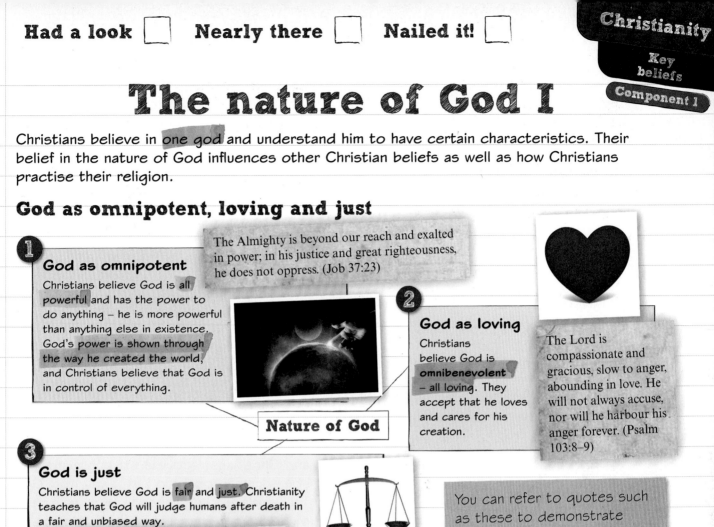

① God as omnipotent

Christians believe God is all powerful and has the power to do anything – he is more powerful than anything else in existence. God's power is shown through the way he created the world, and Christians believe that God is in control of everything.

The Almighty is beyond our reach and exalted in power; in his justice and great righteousness, he does not oppress. (Job 37:23)

② God as loving

Christians believe God is **omnibenevolent** – all loving. They accept that he loves and cares for his creation.

The Lord is compassionate and gracious, slow to anger, abounding in love. He will not always accuse, nor will he harbour his anger forever. (Psalm 103:8–9)

Nature of God

③ God is just

Christians believe God is fair and just. Christianity teaches that God will judge humans after death in a fair and unbiased way.

And the heavens proclaim his righteousness, for he is a God of justice. (Psalm 50:6)

You can refer to quotes such as these to demonstrate what Christians believe about the nature of God.

- -

The problem of evil and suffering

The presence of evil and suffering in the world can cause problems for Christians, as the diagram below shows. It is known as the 'inconsistent triad' because it is difficult to accept the nature of God and explain the presence of evil and suffering in the world.

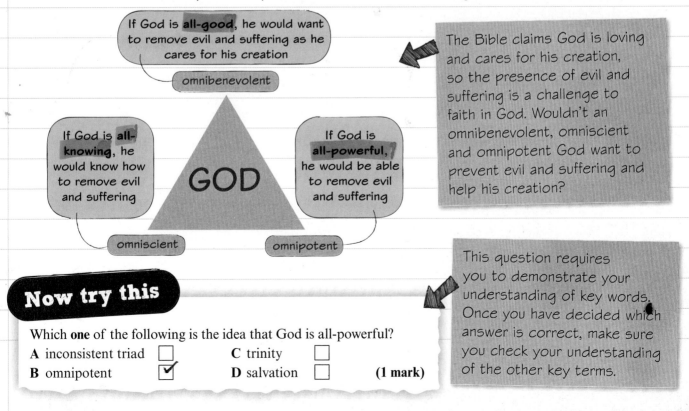

If God is **all-good**, he would want to remove evil and suffering as he cares for his creation

omnibenevolent

GOD

If God is **all-knowing**, he would know how to remove evil and suffering

omniscient

If God is **all-powerful**, he would be able to remove evil and suffering

omnipotent

The Bible claims God is loving and cares for his creation, so the presence of evil and suffering is a challenge to faith in God. Wouldn't an omnibenevolent, omniscient and omnipotent God want to prevent evil and suffering and help his creation?

This question requires you to demonstrate your understanding of key words. Once you have decided which answer is correct, make sure you check your understanding of the other key terms.

Now try this

Which **one** of the following is the idea that God is all-powerful?

A inconsistent triad ☐   C trinity ☐
B omnipotent ☑   D salvation ☐   **(1 mark)**

Had a look ☐ Nearly there ☐ Nailed it! ☐

Evil and suffering

The existence of evil and suffering in the world challenges the Christian belief in an all-loving and all-powerful God. Christians respond to this challenge in a number of ways, with some maintaining that God did not create evil.

What does the Bible say about evil and suffering?

- ✓ Genesis says that God created a perfect world.
- ✓ The Fall: Adam and Eve used their free will in the Garden of Eden to disobey God (the Fall), which allowed evil and suffering to enter the world.
- ✓ Christians believe God sent Jesus to Earth to overcome the evil in the world and die for the sins of humanity on the cross.
- ✓ Some Christians accept that evil came into the world through the devil, for example when the devil tempted Adam and Eve in the Garden of Eden.

Christian responses to the problem of evil and suffering

1 **Book of Psalms** – this offers reassurance that evil and suffering have a purpose in the world: that they give people the opportunity to follow the example set by Jesus in order to live as God intended.

> God is our refuge and our strength. (Psalm 46:1)
>
> Teach me knowledge and good judgement, for I trust your commands. Before I was afflicted I went astray, but now I obey your word. (Psalm 119:66–67)

2 **Job** – the Bible describes how Job endured many examples of suffering, including physical pain and losing his family, yet he did not lose his faith. He trusted in God and believed that suffering was part of God's plan for him. Christians believe that they may not understand why they suffer, but they need to trust in God and will be rewarded for doing so.

> In all this, Job did not sin by charging God with wrongdoing. (Job 1:22)

3 **Free will** – God gave people free will and Christians recognise that humans sometimes choose to turn away from God. This explains the presence of many acts of moral evil. Theories such as this are contained in St Augustine's *Theodicy*.

4 **Vale of soul-making** – this is the idea that evil and suffering have a purpose, even if we do not know what it is. Suffering can make a person stronger and help them appreciate the good things in their life. So evil may not always be a bad thing. The philosopher John Hick put forward this theory.

5 **Prayer** – many Christians respond to evil in the world by prayer, so that God will give them the strength to cope with the problems they are facing. Christians believe that even if their prayers are not answered in the way that they want, God has a plan for everyone.

6 **Charity** – many Christians have been inspired by the suffering in their own lives to try to help others. For example, Chad Varah established the Samaritans as a result of the suffering he witnessed in his community as a priest working in London.

Now try this

There are 3 SPaG marks available on this paper.

'It is not possible to believe in God and accept evil and suffering in the world.'
Evaluate this statement. In your answer you should:
- refer to Christian teaching
- give reasoned arguments to support the statement
- give reasoned arguments to support a different point of view
- reach a justified conclusion.

(12 marks plus 3 SPaG marks)

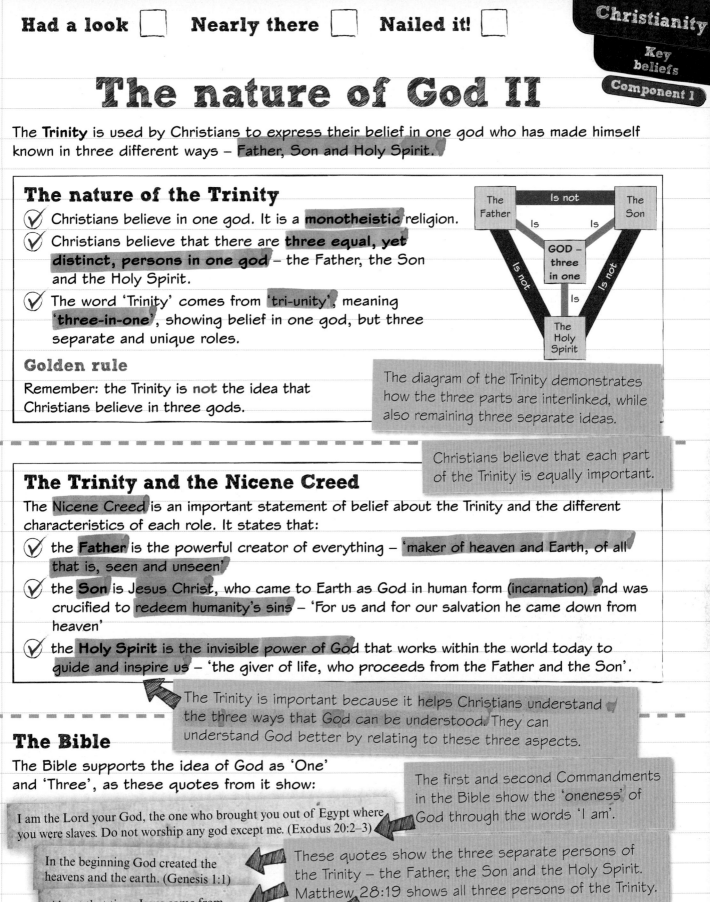

The nature of God II

The **Trinity** is used by Christians to express their belief in one god who has made himself known in three different ways – Father, Son and Holy Spirit.

The nature of the Trinity

✓ Christians believe in one god. It is a **monotheistic** religion.

✓ Christians believe that there are **three equal, yet distinct, persons in one god** – the Father, the Son and the Holy Spirit.

✓ The word 'Trinity' comes from 'tri-unity', meaning 'three-in-one', showing belief in one god, but three separate and unique roles.

Golden rule

Remember: the Trinity is **not** the idea that Christians believe in three gods.

The Father — Is not — The Son
Is — Is
Is not — GOD – three in one — Is not
Is
The Holy Spirit

The diagram of the Trinity demonstrates how the three parts are interlinked, while also remaining three separate ideas.

Christians believe that each part of the Trinity is equally important.

The Trinity and the Nicene Creed

The Nicene Creed is an important statement of belief about the Trinity and the different characteristics of each role. It states that:

✓ the **Father** is the powerful creator of everything – 'maker of heaven and Earth, of all that is, seen and unseen'

✓ the **Son** is Jesus Christ, who came to Earth as God in human form (incarnation) and was crucified to redeem humanity's sins – 'For us and for our salvation he came down from heaven'

✓ the **Holy Spirit** is the invisible power of God that works within the world today to guide and inspire us – 'the giver of life, who proceeds from the Father and the Son'.

The Trinity is important because it helps Christians understand the three ways that God can be understood. They can understand God better by relating to these three aspects.

The Bible

The Bible supports the idea of God as 'One' and 'Three', as these quotes from it show:

The first and second Commandments in the Bible show the 'oneness' of God through the words 'I am'.

I am the Lord your God, the one who brought you out of Egypt where you were slaves. Do not worship any god except me. (Exodus 20:2–3)

In the beginning God created the heavens and the earth. (Genesis 1:1)

About that time, Jesus came from Nazareth in Galilee, and John baptised him in the Jordan River. (Mark 1:9)

These quotes show the three separate persons of the Trinity – the Father, the Son and the Holy Spirit. Matthew 28:19 shows all three persons of the Trinity.

Go to the people of all nations and make them my disciples. Baptise them in the name of the Father, the Son, and the Holy Spirit. (Matthew 28:19)

Now try this

1 Give **two** Christian beliefs about the Trinity. **(2 marks)**
2 Explain **two** Christian teachings about the Trinity.
Refer to sacred writings or another source of Christian belief and teaching in your answer. **(5 marks)**

Creation

Christians may have different understandings of the Christian Creation story. For example, Christians may interpret the story in a literal or a non-literal way.

Fundamental Christians

Fundamental Christians, also known as Literalists or Creationists, believe that:

- the Creation story as it is told in the Bible is **literally true**, because the Bible is the literal 'word of God'

- God made the world in six 24-hour days.

Literalists do not accept scientific explanations about the creation of the universe, such as the Big Bang theory or the theory of evolution. They think these scientific explanations are wrong. For more on the Big Bang theory, see page 54. Turn to page 60 to find out more about the theory of evolution.

> In the beginning was the Word, and the Word was with God, and the Word was God. (John 1:1)

This Bible passage introduces the idea that the universe was created at a command from God – at his 'Word'.

Liberal Christians

Liberal Christians, also known as non-literalists, believe that:

- God created the world but **not exactly** how the story in the Bible says – they see the Bible story as **metaphorical** (not literally true but more story-like). For example, they view the Genesis story of Creation as more myth than fact – the word 'day' in the Creation story is a **metaphor** for a much longer period

- science and religion together explain Creation. There is no conflict between religious and scientific explanations – the Bible explains **why** Creation happened and science explains **how**.

> In the beginning God created the heavens and the earth. Now the earth was formless and empty, darkness was over the surface of the deep, and the Spirit of God was hovering over the waters. (Genesis 1:1–2)

This biblical quote shows the power of God in creating the universe and the role of the Spirit of God.

Worked example

Explain **two** ways in which Christians may understand the account of Creation in the Bible.   **(4 marks)**

Fundamentalist Christians may understand the account of Creation in a literal way, believing that as the Bible is the Word of God, it must be true. They will accept that God created the world in six 24-hour days and reject all scientific discoveries such as the Big Bang, as these are not mentioned in the Bible.

Liberal Christians will understand the account of Creation in a metaphorical way, believing that science and religion together can explain Creation. They believe God created the world but science helps us to understand that he did this through the Big Bang and evolution.

The first part of this student answer identifies one way in which the Christian account of Creation can be understood, then develops this by further explaining what this understanding involves.

The student then identifies a second way in which the Christian account of Creation can be understood and develops it in the same way as the first.

Now try this

'The Bible provides a complete answer to how the universe was created.'
Evaluate this statement. In your answer you should:

- refer to Christian teaching
- give reasoned arguments to support the statement
- give reasoned arguments to support a different point of view
- reach a justified conclusion.   **(12 marks plus 3 SPaG marks)**

You can argue the fundamentalist and liberalist viewpoints for this question, developing each argument fully. You need to reach a final overall judgement in conclusion; think about using a three-paragraph structure – Agree, Alternative view, Conclusion.

The afterlife

Belief in the afterlife means accepting that life continues after death. Christians believe there is an afterlife for those who believe in God. This belief influences how they try to live their lives.

Christian beliefs about:

1 Resurrection

Christians believe that death is not the end. They believe that the **resurrection** of Jesus – when he came back to life from the dead – proves life after death.

> I am the resurrection and the life. The one who believes in me will live, even though they die. (John 11:25)

2 Judgement

Christians accept God is just and it is God who will decide the destination of every human's soul after death. They believe that Jesus is also involved in judgement and will offer every human the opportunity of salvation. Those who refuse will face the 'Last Judgement'.

> For we must all appear before the judgement seat of Christ, so that each of us may receive what is due us for the things done while in the body, whether good or bad. (2 Corinthians 5:10)

3 Heaven

Heaven is mentioned in the Bible, yet it is rarely described. Some Christians believe heaven is a physical place, but most think it is a spiritual state of being united with God for eternity. The Bible teaches there is no sin, sadness or suffering in heaven.

> He will wipe away every tear from their eyes. There will be no more death or mourning or crying or pain. (Revelation 21:4)

> For we know that if the earthly tent we live in is destroyed, we have a building from God, an eternal house in heaven, not built by human hands. (2 Corinthians 5:1)

4 Hell

The Bible teaches that hell is where unrepentant sinners go after death if they have not accepted God's offer of forgiveness and salvation through Jesus. It is a place of pain and suffering, without God.

> Do not be afraid of those who kill the body but cannot kill the soul. Rather, be afraid of the One who can destroy both soul and body in hell. (Matthew 10:28)

5 The soul

- Death is only the end of the body; the soul is immortal.
- Souls that have been saved either go to heaven or to **purgatory** (which is the idea of a 'waiting room', where souls go to be cleansed before entering heaven).
- Souls that have not achieved salvation will go to hell.

The 39 Articles of Religion

The 39 Articles of Religion, drawn up in 1563, are statements from the Church of England to make clear the position of the Church on key teachings.

> Christ did truly rise again from death, and took again his body, with flesh, bones, and all things appertaining to the perfection of Man's nature; wherewith he ascended into Heaven, and there sitteth, until he return to judge all Men at the last day. (39 Articles IV)

Divergent understandings

All Christians accept the belief in life after death. However, some Christians:

- ✓ understand heaven and hell as physical places, whereas others accept them as spiritual ideas
- ✓ believe members of all faiths have a place in the 'Kingdom of God', whereas others believe those without faith who have lived good lives will be rewarded
- ✓ believe in the Second Coming or return of Jesus from heaven to Earth.

Some Christians see life as a test for the final judgement, whereas others see belief in God as more important.

Now try this

Explain **two** ways in which belief about heaven and hell influences Christians today.   **(4 marks)**

Jesus as the Son of God

The word 'incarnation' means 'becoming flesh'. Christians use the term to explain how God took human form through Jesus and lived and experienced life as a human.

The importance of Jesus today

Jesus is seen by Christians as the incarnate **Son of God** and is given great importance within Christianity.

- His birth fulfilled the prophecy of **Christ** coming to Earth as the **Saviour** who was promised by God – so God took human form to be present within the world.

- Jesus is the 'Son' part of the three ideas (the **Trinity**) that are the Christian understanding of God, and is part of the Nicene Creed.

Gospels in the New Testament

✓ Information about the life of Jesus is found in the Bible in the first four books of the **New Testament** – Matthew, Mark, Luke and John. These books are known as the Gospels.

✓ Accounts in the New Testament describe Jesus' birth, life and death.

The Word became flesh and made his dwelling among us. (John 1:14)

He appeared in the flesh, was vindicated by the Spirit, was seen by angels, was preached among the nations, was believed in the world, was taken up in glory. (1 Timothy 3:16)

We believe in one Lord, Jesus Christ, the only Son of God ... he came down from heaven: and was incarnate by the Holy Spirit of the Virgin Mary, and was made man. (Nicene Creed)

Jesus as Divine

Though Jesus was human, he was **divine**, which means he was God. Christians believe the Bible shows us examples of how Jesus is divine.

1. Jesus is **omnipotent** (Matthew 28:18) and **omniscient** (John 21:17).
2. Jesus **forgave sins** (Mark 2:5–7).
3. Jesus **performed miracles** (for example, John 21:25).
4. People **worshipped** and **prayed to** Jesus (Matthew 2:11).
5. Jesus was **resurrected** after death (Mark 16:1–20).

Jesus as human

It is easier for Christians to understand and relate to Jesus, as he was human and experienced the same problems they do.

1. He was **born to a human** mother – Mary – as a 'normal' baby (Luke 2:7).
2. He had a **human body** (Luke 24:39).
3. Jesus got tired (John 4:6), thirsty (John 19:28) and hungry (Matthew 4:2).
4. He showed **human emotions** such as amazement (Matthew 8:10) and sorrow (John 11:35).
5. He **prayed** to God (John 17).
6. He **died** (Romans 5:8).

Worked example

Give **two** examples of how the Bible shows Jesus as divine.   **(2 marks)**

The Bible showed Jesus as divine when he performed miracles and was resurrected after death.

Here you are asked to state **two** correct examples. You are **not** required to develop these ideas, simply identify them in your answer.

Now try this

1 Which **one** of the following means God took human form through Jesus?

A divine ☐   B omnipotent ☐
C saviour ☐   D incarnation ☐   **(1 mark)**

2 Explain **two** Christian teachings about the Incarnation. Refer to sacred writings or another source of Christian belief and teaching in your answer.   **(5 marks)**

Crucifixion, resurrection and ascension

Jesus is an important figure for Christians, and the last few days of his life – including his crucifixion, resurrection and ascension – are key events.

The Last Supper

Jesus shared his last meal with his disciples, where bread was broken and wine drunk. Jesus predicted that one disciple would betray him.

'… I will not eat it again until it finds fulfillment in the kingdom of God.' (Luke 22:16)

Betrayal and arrest

Soldiers came for Jesus while he was in the Garden of Gethsemane. Judas had betrayed him by telling the soldiers where he could be found.

Then Jesus went with his disciples to a place called Gethsemane … (Matthew 26:36)

While he was still speaking, Judas, one of the Twelve, arrived. With him was a large crowd armed with swords and clubs. (Matthew 26:47)

Jesus

Ascension

The resurrected Jesus ascended to heaven 40 days after his resurrection.

After the Lord Jesus had spoken to them, he was taken up into heaven and he sat at the right hand of God. (Mark 16:19)

Resurrection

Jesus was brought back to life three days after his crucifixion.

… the men said to them, 'Why do you look for the living among the dead? He is not here; he has risen!' (Luke 24:5–6)

Crucifixion

Jesus was sentenced to death on a cross as he was accused of blasphemy, tried and found guilty.

Carrying his own cross, he went out to the place of the skull (which in Aramaic is called Golgotha). (John 19:17)

The importance of these events

- These events provide **evidence** that Jesus was the Son of God and came to Earth in human form. They show that Jesus was special and is worthy of respect and obedience.
- They demonstrate the Christian belief in **life after death**, which offers hope to Christians.
- They show the relationship between God and Jesus. Christians believe that through the death of Jesus, **God saved or redeemed humanity**, and it is through following Jesus' example that God can forgive them.
- They help Christians to understand the **sacrifice** Jesus made and reinforce the importance of Jesus within Christianity.

Now try this

This question tests your recall of knowledge – you need to state **two** pieces of accurate information, each in a short sentence.

1 Which of the following terms is used to describe Jesus rising from the dead?
  A resurrection ☐   **B** crucifixion ☐   **C** ascension ☐   **D** salvation ☐   **(1 mark)**

2 Give **two** reasons why the crucifixion and resurrection of Jesus are important in Christianity. **(2 marks)**

Salvation and atonement

Salvation for Christians refers to being saved from sin and being admitted to heaven, which happens through their belief in Jesus. **Atonement** is the idea that humans are reconciled to and forgiven by God through the death of Jesus.

Original sin

Sin is behaviour that is against God's laws or principles of morality.

Original sin refers to the traditional Christian belief that human nature is flawed, and so humans act against God. Fundamental or literalist Christians believe this was passed down from Adam and Eve when they first disobeyed God in the Garden of Eden.

Atonement

Christians understand atonement to be the mending of the relationship between God and humanity, which was broken when Adam and Eve disobeyed God in the Garden of Eden.

Salvation

Christians believe that to achieve salvation they must follow the laws of God.

The grace of God is shown through God's unconditional and generous love for his people, even if they do not deserve it.

> For God so loved the world that he gave his one and only Son, that whoever believes in him shall not perish but have eternal life. (John 3:16)

The role of Christ in salvation

Christians believe that through God sending Jesus to Earth, the sins of humanity are forgiven. Jesus, who was perfect and without sin, offered redemption for humans through sacrificing his life.

> Jesus is 'the stone you builders rejected, which has become the cornerstone.' Salvation is found in no one else, for there is no other name under heaven given to mankind by which we must be saved. (Acts 4:11–12)

Different understandings of atonement

- ✓ Jesus' death as a divine sacrifice represents God's love for humanity.
- ✓ Jesus' death was a sacrifice – an offering to God to mend the broken relationship.
- ✓ Jesus' death is the victory of good over evil, as Jesus was used as ransom to stop the devil having any hold over humanity.
- ✓ Jesus' death represents the price being paid for the forgiveness of humanity.

Significance of atonement and salvation for Christians today

Atonement and salvation are important because they:

- ✓ restore the relationship between God and humanity
- ✓ confirm belief in an all-powerful and loving God
- ✓ allow humans to understand the importance of being reconciled with other humans
- ✓ give humans hope that they can follow the example of Jesus, to be rewarded in the eternal afterlife.

Now try this

You are being asked to explain **two different** ways in which Christians understand the idea of atonement. Make sure you explain each point that you make.

Explain **two** contrasting ways that Christians understand the idea of atonement. **(4 marks)**

Forms of worship

Worship in Christianity is when Christians show respect and adoration towards God. It can take different forms, including liturgical and non-liturgical as well as informal and private. Different denominations (different groups) in Christianity worship in different ways.

Liturgical worship

Liturgical worship is when Christians worship according to a set pattern on a regular basis, for example on a Sunday. There will be set prayers and readings, led by the priest or minister, often using the Book of Common Prayer. Catholics and Anglicans often follow liturgical worship patterns.

Non-liturgical worship

Non-liturgical worship is less formal than liturgical worship, as it does not follow a set pattern and can involve more unscripted or improvised forms of worship. Methodism and Pentecostalism are denominations that have more non-liturgical worship services.

Come, let us bow down in worship, let us kneel before the Lord our Maker! (Psalm 95:6)

... the true worshipers will worship the Father in the Spirit and in truth, for they are the kind of worshipers the Father seeks. (John 4:23)

It is very meet, right, and our bounden duty, that we should at all times, and in all places, give thanks unto thee, O Lord, Holy Father, Almighty, Everlasting God. (Book of Common Prayer)

Informal worship

Some Christians prefer spontaneity in their style of worship, having no fixed nature.

Charismatic worship is an informal worship often held by Pentecostal churches. It may involve:

- clapping, dancing and music to emphasise the importance of spreading the Gospel
- speaking in tongues. This form of worship represents being filled with the Holy Spirit.

Private worship

Private worship is spending time alone considering one's faith or connecting to God. It can be:

- a person spending time alone
- simply reading the Bible
- meditation on God
- praying quietly as a group
- a retreat, where Christians withdraw to focus on prayer.

Examples of Christian worship

1 **Eucharist/Holy Communion/Mass** – most Christians have a formal liturgical service each Sunday, when bread and wine (representing the **body and blood of Jesus Christ** as stated at the Last Supper) are distributed among the congregation. There will be hymns, a Bible reading and a sermon.

2 **The Bible** – a key feature used in Christian worship, the Bible will be used in liturgical services as well as by individual Christians in private study. The study of the Bible in small groups may also take place, to share the message from God and understand it more fully.

3 **Silence** – some Christians, such as the Quakers (the Religious Society of Friends), follow **no set pattern of worship** or services. Instead, followers sit in silence for significant periods of time. It is not understood to be private worship, as they are collectively sharing worship together. Some may feel prompted to speak, read aloud or share personal experiences.

Now try this

Explain **two** contrasting ways that Christians worship.

(4 marks)

Prayer

Prayer is when a Christian communicates with or talks to God. In Christianity, there are different types of prayer, including traditional set prayers, spoken prayers and silent prayers.

Nature and purpose of prayer

There are four main purposes of prayer for Christians:

1 to get closer to God and communicate with him

2 to praise God or thank him for what he has done

3 to ask for God's help

4 to say sorry to God when a person feels they have done something wrong.

Christian children are brought up to pray. They will often be taught the Lord's Prayer and traditionally pray with their hands together and eyes closed, although today Christians may also hold their hands up or hold hands with each other.

What the Bible teaches about prayer

Therefore I tell you, whatever you ask for in prayer, believe that you have received it, and it will be yours. (Mark 11:24)

But when you pray, go into your room, close the door and pray to your Father, who is unseen. Then your Father, who sees what is done in secret, will reward you. (Matthew 6:6)

The Lord's Prayer

Our Father in Heaven, hallowed be your name, your kingdom come, your will be done, on earth as it is in heaven. Give us today our daily bread. And forgive us our debts, as we also have forgiven our debtors. And lead us not into temptation, but deliver us from evil. (Matthew 6:9–13)

Set prayers

Some Christians have a prayer book that is used in their Sunday services of worship. Many prayers reflect key Christian beliefs, which may praise or thank God for what he has done and provided.

Types of prayers

Informal prayer

This is when people pray by themselves privately. It can include praying silently or aloud. Sometimes Christians use the Bible to help them understand the prayer they are offering to God.

The Lord's Prayer

This is the most famous prayer, which it is believed Jesus taught to his followers. It contains many of the key Christian beliefs about God.

The significance of different types of prayers

Christians feel different prayers, and indeed forms of worship, suit different occasions.

- Set prayers may be easier to follow.
- Informal prayer may allow a Christian to feel more connected to God.

- Individuals can choose the type of prayer that suits them best.
- Worshipping with others gives a sense of community, and there is someone leading the prayers.

Now try this

'It is better for Christians to worship privately than publically.'
Evaluate this statement. In your answer you should:
- refer to Christian teaching
- give reasoned arguments to support this statement
- give reasoned arguments to support a different point of view
- reach a justified conclusion.   **(12 marks)**

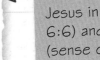

Consider the benefits of both private prayer (a personal connection to God; advised by Jesus in Matthew 6:6) and public prayer (sense of community).

Baptism

A **sacrament** is a rite of passage that Christians understand as something physical done to the body that has a permanent effect on the soul. It is seen as an outward and visible sign of an invisible and spiritual grace. Sacraments recognise important milestones in the life of a Christian – for example, **baptism** recognises a person becoming part of the Church community.

Most **Protestant Churches** recognise two sacraments (baptism and the Eucharist).

Some **non-conformist Churches** recognise two sacraments; some recognise none.

Sacraments ordained of Christ be not only badges or tokens of Christian men's profession, but rather they be certain sure witnesses, and effectual signs of grace, and God's good will towards us. (39 Articles XXV)

Different views of the sacraments

Catholics recognise seven sacraments: baptism, confirmation, penance and reconciliation, Eucharist, ordination, marriage, and anointing of the sick (extreme unction).

The 39 Articles state that the sacraments are important as evidence of being a Christian.

Baptism

The sacrament of baptism is a way of becoming a member of the Church and shows that they accept Jesus.

I baptise you in the name of the Father, the Son, and the Holy Spirit.

These words are used in the sacrament of baptism, which is based on the following Bible quotes.

Practices in Christian denominations may differ.

- Some Churches (Anglican, Roman Catholic, Presbyterian and Orthodox Christian) practise infant baptism.
- Other Churches (Baptist and Pentecostal) prefer a dedication ceremony to mark the birth of a baby, and support adult or believer's baptism.

Then Jesus came from Galilee to the Jordan to be baptised by John. (Matthew 3:13)

Go and make disciples of all nations, baptising them in the name of the Father and of the Son and of the Holy Spirit. (Mathew 28:19)

Infant baptism

Most Christian groups have a ceremony to welcome a baby into the Christian faith – a christening or baptism.

- Parents and godparents make promises on behalf of the child.
- A sign of the cross is made on the baby's forehead and water is poured on their head from the font in the church.
- A lighted candle is given to represent the light of Jesus.

Believer's/adult baptism

Some non-conformist Churches, e.g. the Baptist Church, prefer adult baptism as they feel only an adult can fully make the choice of belonging to the Church.

- Each candidate is asked questions about their faith and states why they wish to become a Christian.
- They are baptised through full immersion – fully put under the water.

Infant baptism is believed to remove the baby from original sin – when Adam and Eve disobeyed God in the Garden of Eden.
Adult baptism is seen as a gift of grace from God to wash away sins (not original sin).

Now try this

1 Which **one** of the following is **not** part of an infant baptism ceremony?
  A full immersion ☐   **B** godparents ☐
  C lighted candle is given ☐   **D** happens at the font ☐   **(1 mark)**
2 Give **two** reasons why some Christians may prefer believer's baptism to infant baptism.   **(2 marks)**

Eucharist

The sacrament of the Eucharist, also known as Holy Communion, is a re-enactment of the Last Supper Jesus shared with his disciples.

Eucharist

- Eucharist literally means 'thanksgiving'.
- It celebrates Jesus' sacrifice through his death and resurrection. Christians give thanks to God for his creation of the world and the life, death and resurrection of Jesus.
- Each denomination has its own name for the service.
  - Catholics call it 'Mass'.
  - The Church of England calls it 'Eucharist' or 'Holy Communion'.
  - Baptists call it 'The Lord's Supper'.

Teachings on the Eucharist

[Jesus] took some bread in his hands. Then after he had given thanks, he broke it and said, 'This is my body, which is given for you. Eat this and remember me.' After the meal, Jesus took a cup of wine in his hands and said, 'This is my blood, and with it God makes his new agreement with you. Drink this and remember me.' (1 Corinthians 11:23–25)

Celebration of the Eucharist

Church of England	Prayers of preparation and penitence; Liturgy of the Word – Bible readings; sermon from the vicar; Apostle's Creed; Liturgy of the sacrament – consecrated (blessed) bread is broken; baptised members of the congregation receive bread and wine kneeling at the altar; children receive a blessing.
Orthodox Christians	Use candles and incense; priest is behind royal doors; Gospel is read – the Divine Liturgy; the Nicene Creed is recited; bread is broken into four parts; consecrated bread and wine is given to the congregation; prayers of thanksgiving; unconsecrated bread is given out to be taken home as a sign of being part of the Christian community.
Catholics	Liturgy of the Word – three Bible readings; Liturgy of the Eucharist – bread and wine brought to the altar; people receive this from a priest – a wafer of bread and red wine is given from a single chalice; bread and wine is stored in the tabernacle; blessing using the words 'Go in peace'.
Non-conformist (e.g. Baptist)	Use a communion table, not an altar; minister or layperson takes the service; two Bible readings; anyone can take communion (even children); communion handed out while worshippers kneel at table or is passed around; wine is non-alcoholic or may be grape juice.

Significance

1. It is a sacrament – an outward sign of an inward grace.

2. It remembers the Last Supper when Jesus gave instructions to his disciples to remember him through the wine and bread.

3. It marks the sacrifice made by Jesus through his death.

4. It brings the Christian community together in worship.

Different interpretations

- **Catholics** believe in **transubstantiation** – the bread and wine become the actual body and blood of Jesus. Christ's presence in them is known as 'the real presence'.
- **Orthodox Christians** accept the Eucharist as a sacrament though it is not possible to explain the transubstantiation as it is a divine mystery.
- **Most Protestants** accept bread and wine as symbolic of the body and blood of Jesus.
- **Baptists** accept bread and wine as a remembrance of the suffering of Jesus.
- **The Salvation Army** and **Quakers** do not practice or observe the Eucharist in any form.

Now try this

Explain **two** contrasting ways in which Christians understand the Eucharist (Holy Communion) service.

(4 marks)

Pilgrimage

A pilgrimage is a journey religious people make to a special or holy place. Pilgrimage is understood as an act of worship that shows devotion to God, although some Christians feel this is a personal choice in faith.

A history of Christian pilgrimage

- Christian pilgrimage has its roots in Jewish pilgrimage. Jews used to travel for religious festivals such as Passover.

  > Every year Jesus' parents went to Jerusalem for the Festival of the Passover. When he was twelve years old, they went up to the festival, according to the custom. (Luke 2:41–42)

- Christian pilgrimage was first seen when early Christians visited places of historical significance related to the life of Jesus – Bethlehem (his birth) and Jerusalem (his death).

- Other popular sites of pilgrimage are those with which saints are associated or where visions supposedly occurred. Lourdes and Iona are examples of places Christians visit.

  > Pilgrims are able to take time out from their normal everyday lives in order to concentrate on their religion.

Lourdes, France

1 Millions of Christian pilgrims, especially Catholics, visit to see the site of a famous vision experienced by Bernadette Soubirous and to be healed by its miraculous waters.

2 Bernadette is reported to have had visions of Mary, the mother of Jesus, many times. During one of these occasions, Bernadette was asked to drink at the spring beneath her feet even though this area was muddy. The following day, on this spot, the ground flowed with clear water.

3 Pilgrims visit this site believing it will cleanse their sins and cure illness. In 2018, the Catholic Church had recognised the 70th miracle of this kind.

Pilgrims at Lourdes:

- visit and pray in the Sanctuary of Our Lady of Lourdes
- take part in a torchlight procession every evening
- attend a service of Mass in the grotto where the vision occurred
- drink the water from the spring or collect some to take home
- spend time in prayer and reflection.

The Sanctuary of Our Lady of Lourdes

Iona, Scotland

1 Iona is a place of pilgrimage for Christians, as it is where saints are believed to have lived and prayers have been answered.

2 Iona has a monastic history and is considered to be a spiritual place.

Pilgrims at Iona:

- spend time in reflection and prayer
- join the 'pilgrimage walk', which happens every week around the island, stopping at places of historical and religious significance such as St Martin's Cross and the nunnery
- worship in the abbey church on the island.

Now try this

1 Give **two** reasons why Christians feel pilgrimage is important. **(2 marks)**
2 Explain **two** contrasting examples of Christian pilgrimage. **(4 marks)**

> Develop each example by giving further information or an example.

Celebrations

Celebration of festivals is important in Christianity. Festivals mark and remember important events in the history of the religion and bring followers of the religion together.

Christmas celebrates the **Incarnation** and **birth of Jesus** – when God's son came to Earth in human form. It is celebrated on 25 December, although this is not believed to be Jesus' actual birth date.

The festival of **Advent** marks the beginning of the Christian year and the **countdown to Christmas**. It takes place four Sundays before Christmas and is a period of preparation. Advent calendars and candles are used to count down the days.

Christmas

Cards and presents are given, houses are **decorated** and special **church services** such as Midnight Mass are held. Carols are sung and nativity plays put on. Families come together to share a **special meal** and Christians attend a special Christmas Day service.

Many Christians express the **meaning of Christmas** by helping others and sharing with them. It brings people together, even in a secular society.

Teachings on Christmas

And she gave birth to her firstborn, a son. She wrapped him in cloths and placed him in a manger, because there was no guest room available for them. (Luke 2:7)

And going into the house, they saw the child with Mary his mother, and they fell down and worshipped him. Then, opening their treasures, they offered him gifts, gold and frankincense and myrrh. (Matthew 2:11)

The story of Jesus' birth is found in the Gospels of Matthew and Luke, but with key differences. For example, Luke mentions the shepherds, and Matthew describes the Wise Men.

Easter is the festival that remembers the **crucifixion** and celebrates the **resurrection** of Jesus. Good Friday is when Jesus was crucified and then on Easter Sunday the sadness at the death of Jesus is forgotten and his resurrection is celebrated.

Holy Week is the final week of Lent, leading up to Easter. It commemorates the last week of Jesus' life, from when he entered Jerusalem on Palm Sunday to the Last Supper and crucifixion.

Easter

Special services are held. There may be a re-enactment of the crucifixion on Good Friday, and hot cross buns may be eaten to remind people of Jesus' death on the cross. Cards and presents may be given on Easter Sunday, along with Easter eggs to represent the empty tomb of Jesus after his resurrection.

The story of Jesus' resurrection helps Christians find **faith in eternal life** and confirms their beliefs about God.

Teachings on Easter

Jesus said to her, 'I am the resurrection and the life. The one who believes in me, will live, even though they die.' (John 11:25)

But if it is preached that Christ has been raised from the dead, how can some of you say that there is no resurrection of the dead? (1 Corinthians 15:12)

These Bible quotes show the importance of Easter in confirming Christian beliefs about the afterlife.

Now try this

1 Give **two** reasons why Christians feel it is important to celebrate Easter today. **(2 marks)**

2 'Christmas is still important today.'
Evaluate this statement.
In your answer you should:
- refer to Christian teaching
- give reasoned arguments to support this statement
- give reasoned arguments to support a different point of view
- reach a justified conclusion.

(12 marks)

The church in the local community

The local church has always held an important role within society – it is more than just a building where Christians worship. In the past, the church was where key messages were communicated and information was shared. Today, it helps to bring people together within local communities and support them.

Role and importance

The local church community is important because it:

1 unites the local community

2 provides support and comfort when needed

3 can give advice from sources of authority, such as the minister or vicar

4 gives identity and belonging to people in a community.

> Love your neighbour as yourself. (Matthew 22:39)
>
> For where two or three gather in my name, there am I with them. (Matthew 18:20)
>
> When I was hungry, you gave me something to eat, and when I was thirsty, you gave me something to drink. When I was a stranger, you welcomed me, and when I was naked, you gave me clothes to wear. (Matthew 25:35–36)

These quotes show the importance of supporting each other and working together – as local churches do.

---

1 Centre of Christian identity

The local church will organise events to bring together people in the community and create a sense of Christian identity. These include:

- clubs for children, such as Sunday School or youth groups, to educate them in the Christian faith
- social groups, such as coffee mornings, to create opportunities for Christians to share in their faith
- Bible study groups, where Christians can discuss their faith.

How the local church community helps

2 Food banks

Many local communities run their own food banks – a place where stocks of food, typically basic provisions, are supplied to those in need. These may be run by an organisation such as the Trussell Trust or a local church that wants to support those in the local community. They:

- provide emergency food, support and help to people in crisis in the UK
- are founded on principles seen in the Parable of the Sheep and the Goats (Matthew 25).

Non-perishable food is donated and sorted by volunteers before people who are in need are identified and issued with a food voucher.

4 Worship through living practices

The local church community will celebrate special events, including festivals such as Christmas and Easter and rites of passage such as baptisms, marriages and funerals. These help to mark important milestones in the lives of those within the community.

3 Outreach work

Many Christians choose either to volunteer or to work in positions that involve them going out into the local community, which is known as outreach work. For example, street pastors:

- are groups of trained volunteers who work on the streets
- are often seen on Friday and Saturday nights providing support and guidance to those in crisis or needing help, to build community relationships and work for safer streets
- work in local schools to support young people
- provide support and care in a crisis (response pastors).

Now try this

1. Give **two** ways that the local church helps in the community. **(2 marks)**
2. Explain **two** ways that food banks put Christian teachings into action.
   Refer to sacred writings or another source of Christian belief and teaching in your answer. **(5 marks)**

Sharing faith

Many Christians feel they have a responsibility to share their faith with others and provide a ministry of service through education, medical work or social justice.

Missionary and evangelical work

- Christians who undertake missionary or evangelical work are sent into an area to share their faith and the message of the Bible by preaching and teaching, and to provide a service to others.
- There is a long history of missionary work within Christianity. Prominent Christian missionaries include William Carey (1761–1834) and Eric Liddell (1902–45).
- Many Christians feel that by completing missionary or evangelical work they enable people to be saved from their sin through Jesus.

A **missionary** is a person who is 'sent out' on a religious mission to spread the Gospel, – the good news about Jesus. **Evangelical work** refers to the spreading of faith or preaching of the Gospel done by missionaries.

Bible teachings

Go and make disciples of all nations, baptizing them in the name of the Father and of the Son and of the Holy Spirit. (Matthew 28:19)

Go into all the world and preach the gospel to all creation. (Mark 16:15)

Jesus said, 'Peace be with you! As the Father has sent me, I am sending you.' (John 20:21)

'Come, follow me,' Jesus said, 'and I will send you out to fish for people.' (Matthew 4:19)

The first quote tells Christians to share their faith through missionary and evangelical work. The second states that they should share the Gospel. The third shows the presence of the Holy Spirit in the world. In the fourth, Jesus asks fishermen to help him save people by telling them God's message.

Locally, nationally and globally

Locally	Nationally	Globally
• Local churches fund projects to spread God's word, e.g. via grants to community projects. • Events open the Church to non-believers. • Local churches are involved in **ecumenical** work – they all work together to serve the community. • Local churches provide community support, e.g. through local food banks or events for children. • Alpha courses introduce people to the Christian faith.	• Many churches may be linked across the country and involved in national faith-based events, e.g. summer camps for children or charity events. • Special event days may be held where Christians from different denominations share their faith. • Many churches in different areas may work together on community projects. • Organisations such as the Church Army work in local communities to spread the Gospel and run projects such as homeless shelters.	• There may be opportunities to study or create links with Christians in different countries and to be involved in spreading the Christian message globally through missionary projects. • People can choose to go to underdeveloped areas and help with building work or education. • Televangelism with channels such as God TV broadcast Christian shows including conferences and concerts.

The Church also makes use of modern technologies such as social media, which enables messages to be shared.

Now try this

1 Which **one** of the following means a person who is 'sent out' to preach the message of the Gospel?
   A reconciliation ☐   **B** evangelism ☐   **C** church growth ☐   **D** missionary ☐   **(1 mark)**

2 Explain **two** Christian teachings about evangelism.
   Refer to sacred writings or another source of Christian belief and teaching in your answer.   **(5 marks)**

Importance of the worldwide Church I

Although Christians worship in many denominations and many individual churches across the world, they are all united by the fact that they are part of the worldwide Christian Church. Collectively they believe it is important to work together and support each other.

Reconciliation

Reconciliation is the process of restoring harmony after relationships between people have broken down. The worldwide Church recognises **reconciliation** as one of its goals:

> A new command I give you: Love one another. As I have loved you, so you must love one another. (John 13:34)
>
> ... if you hold anything against anyone, forgive them. (Mark 11:25)
>
> But I tell you, love your enemies and pray for those who persecute you. (Matthew 5:44)

Examples of working for reconciliation

1 **Quaker reconciliation projects** include:

- going into schools to educate children about peace
- working in places of conflict, for example Northern Ireland, to provide safe places for people to meet
- working in war-torn areas such as Palestine
- assisting in countries such as Kenya and Rwanda to reconcile groups in conflict with each other.

2 **Coventry Cathedral reconciliation ministry** was founded following the destruction of the cathedral in 1940, when a commitment was made to forgiveness and reconciliation rather than revenge. It provides partnerships in many countries working for peace and reconciliation in communities.

Persecution

Throughout history, and continuing today, Christians have faced judgement, punishment, poor treatment and even death, including:

- physical or verbal abuse
- stopping them practising their faith
- making them feel isolated.

Christians believe they should work to overcome persecution and break down barriers between people. The worldwide Church emphasises the shared nature of faith to unite all Christians.

How churches respond to persecution

1 Organisations such as the Barnabas Fund work to identify places in the world where Christians are being persecuted and organise projects to challenge this persecution.

2 Some Christian churches are forced into hiding when persecuted, for example churches in the former USSR were forbidden from practising Christianity between 1922 and 1991.

3 Some Christians, such as those in Iraq, have been forced to leave their homes and become refugees. They may be cared for by organisations in other countries.

4 Churches in different countries can support each other with the persecution they are facing – for example, UK churches support those in Nigeria and Kenya.

5 Churches educate others about Christianity to bring reconciliation and to break down barriers.

6 Churches pray for those being persecuted.

Now try this

Make sure you can explain what reconciliation projects do. Link why they do this to Bible teachings.

1 Give **two** ways in which Christian churches respond to persecution. **(2 marks)**

2 Explain **two** Christian teachings about reconciliation.
   Refer to sacred writings or another source of Christian belief and teaching in your answer. **(5 marks)**

Importance of the worldwide Church II

Charity is a key Christian practice of caring for all Christians in the world. A charity is usually an organisation set up to raise money and support for a good cause.

Christian teachings about charity

For I was hungry and you gave me something to eat, I was thirsty and you gave me something to drink, I was a stranger and you invited me in. (Matthew 25:35)

The Parable of the Sheep and the Goats shows how humans will be judged by God according to how they helped others.

Love your neighbour as yourself. (Mark 12:31)

Christianity teaches compassion and the importance of treating other people fairly. Jesus also taught about helping others: e.g. the Parable of the Good Samaritan (Luke 10:25–37).

God created mankind in his own image. (Genesis 1:27)

Christians believe God made all humans in his image so all people should have equality and dignity.

Love is patient, love is kind. It does not envy, it does not boast, it is not proud. It does not dishonour other, it is not self-seeking, it is not easily angered, it keeps no record of wrongs. (1 Corinthians 13:4–5)

Agape love – unconditional love towards everyone – is how Christians believe they should treat others.

The work of charities

Christian charities believe that they have a duty to help others and that they should treat others with compassion and be accountable for their actions. They work to help people around the world to live in dignity and peace, and fight for human rights such as food, water and shelter.

 Catholic Agency For Overseas Development (CAFOD)

- It helps those living in poverty in their own communities and campaigns for global justice.
- It provides food, water and shelter during times of emergency crisis.
- It works in communities across Africa, Asia, Latin America and the Middle East.
- Example projects: health clinics in Kenya, refugees' crisis support, emergency appeals.

2 Christian Aid

- It works globally to end poverty.
- It campaigns against injustice and seeks to change government policy.
- It works in communities across South America, the Caribbean, the Middle East, Africa and Asia.
- Example projects: safe farming in Ghana, medical programmes for HIV, emergency appeals.

Christian charities

3 Tearfund

- It works to reduce the effects of poverty and disaster in Latin America, the Caribbean, Africa and Asia.
- It supports poor communities, marginalised groups, vulnerable adults and children.
- Example projects: speaking out against exploitation in Nepal, emergency disaster relief, promoting reconciliation in Rwanda.

Now try this

Explain **two** ways that a Christian charity helps people across the world. **(4 marks)**

The six articles of faith in Sunni Islam

There are many schools of Islam. These schools agree on most beliefs and practices within the Islamic faith, although there are some differences. One of the main schools is Sunni. The **six articles of faith** are accepted by **Sunni Muslims.**

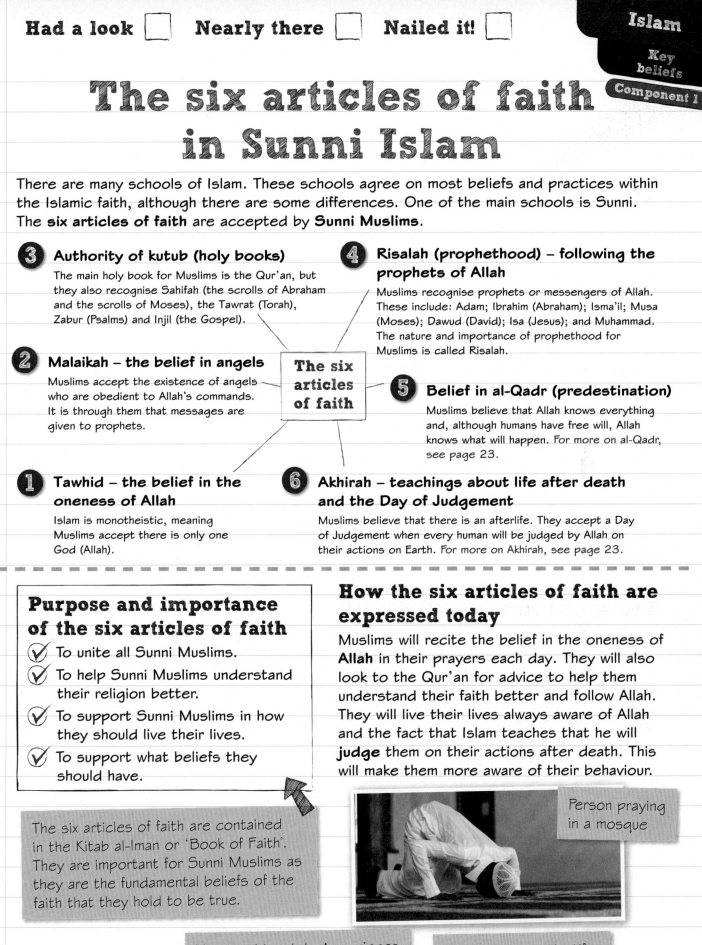

3 Authority of kutub (holy books)

The main holy book for Muslims is the Qur'an, but they also recognise Sahifah (the scrolls of Abraham and the scrolls of Moses), the Tawrat (Torah), Zabur (Psalms) and Injil (the Gospel).

2 Malaikah – the belief in angels

Muslims accept the existence of angels who are obedient to Allah's commands. It is through them that messages are given to prophets.

The six articles of faith

1 Tawhid – the belief in the oneness of Allah

Islam is monotheistic, meaning Muslims accept there is only one God (Allah).

4 Risalah (prophethood) – following the prophets of Allah

Muslims recognise prophets or messengers of Allah. These include: Adam; Ibrahim (Abraham); Isma'il; Musa (Moses); Dawud (David); Isa (Jesus); and Muhammad. The nature and importance of prophethood for Muslims is called Risalah.

5 Belief in al-Qadr (predestination)

Muslims believe that Allah knows everything and, although humans have free will, Allah knows what will happen. For more on al-Qadr, see page 23.

6 Akhirah – teachings about life after death and the Day of Judgement

Muslims believe that there is an afterlife. They accept a Day of Judgement when every human will be judged by Allah on their actions on Earth. For more on Akhirah, see page 23.

Purpose and importance of the six articles of faith

- ✓ To unite all Sunni Muslims.
- ✓ To help Sunni Muslims understand their religion better.
- ✓ To support Sunni Muslims in how they should live their lives.
- ✓ To support what beliefs they should have.

The six articles of faith are contained in the Kitab al-Iman or 'Book of Faith'. They are important for Sunni Muslims as they are the fundamental beliefs of the faith that they hold to be true.

How the six articles of faith are expressed today

Muslims will recite the belief in the oneness of **Allah** in their prayers each day. They will also look to the Qur'an for advice to help them understand their faith better and follow Allah. They will live their lives always aware of Allah and the fact that Islam teaches that he will **judge** them on their actions after death. This will make them more aware of their behaviour.

Person praying in a mosque

Now try this

You need to state **two** pieces of accurate information, each in a short sentence.

Make sure you identify **two** ways and explain each point you make.

1   Name **two** of the six articles of faith accepted by Sunni Muslims.   **(2 marks)**
2   Explain **two** ways that the six articles of faith may influence Muslims today.   **(4 marks)**

The five roots of Usul ad-Din in Shi'a Islam

Another major branch of Islam is Shi'a. Shi'a Muslims accept the five roots of Usul ad-Din, which are their foundations of faith.

Shi'a who believe there were 12 imams after the death of Muhammad are known as **Twelvers**. Shi'a who believe there were seven are known as **Seveners**.

The five roots of Usul ad-Din

1 Tawhid – the oneness of God
The idea of one god called Allah.

2 Adalat – justice
Allah is understood to be fair and just in the way he treats everything.

3 Nubuwwah – **prophethood**
The belief that Allah appointed prophets or messengers to pass his message on to humanity.

4 Imamate – successors to Muhammad
The belief that Allah appointed imams or leaders to guide humanity and be a source of authority.

5 Mi'ad – the **Day of Judgement** and the **Resurrection**
The belief that all humans will be judged by Allah on their actions after death.

The basis of the five roots of Usul ad-Din

Say: He is Allah, [who is] One, Allah , the Eternal Refuge. He neither begets nor is born, Nor is there to Him any equivalent. (Surah 112:1–4)

The five roots are all based around the central idea – Tawhid, the oneness of God. This is explained in the Qur'an.

Key similarities and differences

The six articles of faith in Sunni Islam and the five roots of Usul ad-Din in Shi'a Islam:

Similarities	Differences
✓ Both include and recognise the importance of Tawhid – the oneness of God. ✓ Both share the concepts of prophethood (Allah has messengers) and the idea of a Day of Judgement (an afterlife). ✓ Their central beliefs, summarised by the six articles and the five roots, affect how both live their lives. ✓ Their beliefs unite and support them in their faith.	✗ Shi'a Muslims place greater emphasis on the idea that Allah is completely fair and just through the concept of justice, or Adalat, which is central to Shi'a Muslims. (The six articles do not make it explicit or emphasise it in such an important way, although Sunni Muslims do accept that Allah is just.) ✗ Sunni Muslims recognise angels in their central beliefs in the six articles. (Shi'a Muslims accept the existence of angels, but they are not part of the five roots.) ✗ Shi'a Muslims' central belief is that Ali, Muhammad's cousin and son-in-law, is the rightful leader chosen after Muhammad's death. The Imamate refers to the line of leadership they recognise. (Sunni Muslims do not accept this.)

Now try this

'Tawhid is the most important Muslim belief.'
Evaluate this statement. In your answer you should:
- refer to Muslim teaching
- give reasoned arguments to support this statement
- give reasoned arguments to support a different point of view
- reach a justified conclusion. **(12 marks plus 3 SPaG marks)**

See page 21 on Tawhid to help you answer this question.

The different understanding of who the Imamate is provides the key difference between the six articles and the five roots, and is one of the main dividing features between Sunni and Shi'a Islam.

The Oneness and nature of God

Islam is a **monotheistic** religion, which means Muslims believe in one god, Allah. Beliefs about Allah and what he is like are described in many religious texts, including the Muslim holy book, the Qur'an.

Meaning and impact of Tawhid

Tawhid is the Islamic word to describe the idea that Muslims only accept one god (monotheism).

Islam means 'submission to Allah', so Muslims believe they should submit to Allah in all things.

This is the most fundamental belief of Islam, as all other principles relate to it.

- It is part of the six articles of faith of Sunni Islam and the five roots of Usul ad-Din of Shi'a Islam.
- It is the central belief contained in the Shahadah, the first of the Five Pillars of Islam.

- Tawhid underpins all other key beliefs in Islam, for example about life after death and prophethood.

Qur'an Surah 112

Qur'an Surah 112, in four verses, summarises the idea of Tawhid and describes the unity of Allah.

Say, 'He is Allah, [who is] One,

There is only one god, who is Allah.

Allah has no start or end, being eternal.

Allah, the Eternal Refuge.

He neither begets nor is born,

Allah was not born and neither is anyone born from him.

Allah is unique – nothing is equal to him.

Nor is there to Him any equivalent.' (Surah 112)

The nature of God

1 Tawhid
The Oneness of God

Arabic for Allah

2 Omnipotence
Allah is more powerful than anything in existence. He created the world and is in control of everything.

3 Beneficence
Allah is caring and loves his creation.

5 Adalat (justice)
Allah is equitable and just. He created the world in a fair way and will judge humans in this way too.

4 Mercy
Allah forgives people for the wrong things they do.

Allah's relationship with the world

- **Immanence:** Allah is close to and involved within the world.
- **Transcendence:** Allah is above and beyond human understanding, so it can be difficult for Muslims to fully understand Allah.

These opposite ideas reflect the dual relationship Allah has with the world in being above and beyond it yet close to and involved in it.

Importance of the characteristics

Muslims believe that by knowing what Allah is like they can:
- ✓ understand him better
- ✓ follow the way he wants them to live their lives
- ✓ strengthen their relationship with Allah
- ✓ encourage Muslims to strive to be better as this is what they believe Allah wants.

Now try this

Explain **two** ways in which belief in Tawhid (the Oneness of God) impacts on Muslims today. **(4 marks)**

The most beautiful names belong to Allah: so call on him by them. (Surah 7:180)

Angels

Angels are spiritual beings created from elements of light. Muslims believe they give messages from Allah to the prophets and watch over humans.

There can be no images of Allah or Muhammad in Islam.

Angels are not thought to have free will or physical bodies, but can take on human shape when needed. Belief in angels is contained in the six articles of faith for Sunni Muslims.

[All] praise is [due] to Allah, Creator of the heavens and the earth, [who] made the angels messengers having wings, two or three or four. (Surah 35:1)

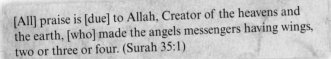

This painting shows how angels are described in Islamic texts.

Importance of the angels

Angel	Why are the angels important?	What do they teach Muslims today?
Jibril, or Gabriel as he is known in Christianity and Judaism, is an important angel, as it was through him that Allah revealed the Qur'an to Muhammad over 23 years. It is believed that Jibril also taught Muhammad how to pray. ... then We sent her our angel, and he appeared before her as a man in all respects. (Surah 19:17)	Without Jibril, the message of the Qur'an would not have been received.	To live around the teachings of the holy book, often reading it every day to understand how they should live their lives.
Izra'il is the Angel of Death and is responsible for signalling the coming of the Day of Judgement (when all Muslims will be judged by Allah) by blowing a trumpet. It is believed that he will return human souls to Allah. The angel of death will take you who has been entrusted with you. Then to your Lord you will be returned. (Surah 32:11)	Izra'il is important in helping Muslims to understand that they need to live their lives how Allah wants them to, following his rules, so that they may be rewarded and not punished, in the afterlife.	To live their lives in the knowledge that they will one day be judged by Allah on their actions on Earth.
Mika'il is often understood to be the Angel of Mercy or Sustenance, given the role of rewarding those who have led good lives. He is believed to bring rain and thunder to Earth. Whoever is an enemy to Jibril – for he brings down the (revelation) to thy heart by Allah's will, a confirmation of what went before, and guidance and glad tidings for those who believe, – Whoever is an enemy to Allah and His angels and messengers, to Jibril and Mikael, – Lo! Allah is an enemy to those who reject Faith. (Surah 2:97–98)	Muslims wish to be rewarded in the afterlife and not punished so the teaching of Mika'il reassures them that it is possible.	Reassurance that it is possible to be rewarded in the afterlife.

This question tests your recall of knowledge – you need to state **two** pieces of accurate information, each in a short sentence.

Identify **two** relevant teachings, then develop each one by giving more detail. Remember to link to a source of Muslim belief and teaching within your answer too.

Now try this

1 Give **two** reasons why angels are important in Islam. **(2 marks)**

2 Explain **two** Muslim teachings about angels.
   Refer to sacred writings or another source of Muslim belief and teaching in your answer. **(5 marks)**

al-Qadr and Akhirah

Muslims believe in **al-Qadr** (predestination) – that Allah has already decided everything that happens – and in **Akhirah** (life after death), which affects how Muslims choose to live.

> Sunni Muslims recognise predestination as one of the six articles of faith. Shi'a Muslims do not fully accept these ideas.

The Day of Judgement

There is a direct link between predestination and the Day of Judgement, as Muslims believe that once this day comes, it is too late to beg forgiveness for wrongdoing. Predestination teaches Muslims that everything is the will of Allah and, although Muslims may not understand it, the important thing is how they react to it. Reacting the right way will mean a reward on the Day of Judgement.

Implications of al-Qadr

1. Muslims will want to live their lives according to the beliefs of the Day of Judgement and al-Qadr to ensure they gain reward in the afterlife.

2. They will constantly try to follow the duties given to them by Allah (e.g. the Five Pillars).

3. They will try to help others, as they believe this is what the Qur'an and Muhammad teach them.

Akhirah

> [Mention, O Muhammad], the Day We will call forth every people with their record [of deeds]. Then whoever is given his record in his right hand – those will read their records, and injustice will not be done to them, [even] as much as a thread [inside the date seed]. (Surah 17:71)

After death, the angel of death will take a person's soul to *barzakh* (the stage between when a person dies and when they face judgement).	→ Allah will judge each individual on the way they lived their life. ↓ On the Day of Judgement, the body will be resurrected. →	Two angels will open the book that contains the record of what a person has done in their lifetime. →	If their name is recorded on the right-hand side of the book, they will be sent to heaven (paradise). If their name is recorded on the left-hand side of the book, they will be sent to hell.

Human accountability

Muslims believe that they have free will and that they must be willing to accept the consequences of their actions. Sahih al Bukhari 78:685 describes this.

Resurrection

Muslims believe that after death, all people will be raised from death to face Allah's judgement – this is believed to be a physical resurrection of the body.

Hell in the Qur'an

This Qur'anic quote describes **Jahannam** or hell as a place where unbelievers are punished and face dreadful torments such as fires of hell.

> And ward off the Fire which has been prepared for the disbelievers. (Surah 3:131)

The Qur'an describes **al-Jannah** (paradise) as a reward for believers. It is described as a garden full of flowers and birds.

How Akhirah affects Muslims today

1. It makes them more aware that Allah is always watching.

2. It makes them realise the importance of asking for forgiveness.

3. Every action they perform is a way of worshipping Allah.

4. They try to live life as good Muslims: read the Qur'an; perform the Five Pillars; go to the mosque; help others, etc.

For more about the Five Pillars, see page 27.

Now try this

Explain **two** ways in which beliefs about predestination influence Muslims today. **(4 marks)**

Risalah (prophethood)

Risalah is the Islamic word for prophethood or **messengers of Allah**. These messengers are the channel of communication that links Allah to humanity.

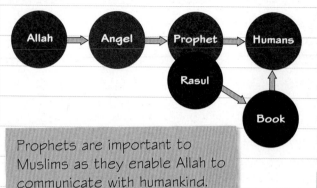

Prophets are important to Muslims as they enable Allah to communicate with humankind.

Prophets

Islam teaches that there have been many **prophets** who have acted as messengers of Allah, such as Isma'il, Muhammad and Adam. It is thought there have been as many as 124 000, but only 25 are named in the Qur'an. Prophets whose message has been written down are called **rasuls**.

Rasuls	Where their message has been written
Ibrahim	Sahifah
Musa	Tawrat
Dawud	Zabur
Isa	Injil

Adam

He was the first prophet (and human) to be created. His task was to look after the world (to be a **khalifah**), which teaches Muslims today that they, too, should look after and care for Allah's creation.

Muhammad

Muhammad is called by Muslims 'the Seal of the Prophets' as he was the last prophet and received the final and perfect message from Allah – the Qur'an. Muslims are taught from a young age that they should follow the example set by Muhammad – the Hadith is a document of his recorded sayings and used to guide Muslims so they can follow his example. It supplements the authority of the Qur'an.

Isa

Isa is more often associated with Christianity (Jesus), but is recognised in Islam as the messenger of Allah and who received the Injil (Gospel). Muslims do not accept his resurrection or that he was the Son of God.

Ibrahim

Ibrahim is mentioned many times in the Qur'an. It is believed that he tried to encourage the worship of Allah. The story of Ibrahim having his faith tested by Allah by being willing to sacrifice his son teaches Muslims to submit to Allah in their lives.

Prophets in the Qur'an

Isma'il

Isma'il is the son of Ibrahim and was associated with the construction of the Ka'aba in Makkah. He is praised for characteristics such as patience and kindness, showing Muslims that they too should develop these sorts of characteristics.

Musa

The Qur'an states that Musa was sent by Allah to the Pharaoh of Egypt and the Israelites for guidance and warning. His presence is also seen to confirm the message and authority of the prophets before him.

Dawud

Dawud is recognised by Muslims as being a lawgiver of Allah and the King of Israel, as well as a prophet. He is best known for defeating Goliath.

Say (O Muslims): 'We believe in Allah and that which is revealed unto us and that which was revealed unto Ibrahim, and Ismail, and Ishaque and Yaqoob, and the tribes and that which Musa and Christ received and that which the Prophets received from their Lord.' (Surah 2:136)

Now try this

1 Name **two** prophets in Islam. **(2 marks)**
2 Give **two** reasons why prophets are important in Islam. **(2 marks)**

Both of these questions test your recall of knowledge – you need to state **two** pieces of accurate information, each in a short sentence. The first question asks you to name just two examples. The second question asks you to focus on **why** prophets are important.

The holy books

The Qur'an is the most important holy book for Muslims. They accept four other holy books (**kutub**) as books of revelation. Muslims are commanded in the Qur'an to believe in the books revealed to Christians and Jews, which is why Muslims are often called 'People of the Book'.

The Qur'an

- The word 'Qur'an' means 'recitation', because Allah spoke it to Muhammad, as Muhammad was illiterate (unable to read or write).

- It is divided into 114 **surahs** (chapters) made up of **ayats** (verses).

- It is written in Arabic.

> It is not but a revelation revealed, taught to him by one intense in strength. (Surah 53:4–5)

Authority of the Qur'an

- It contains the true words of Allah, so is the direct revelation from Allah to humanity – unchanging and unchangeable. As it is the words of Allah, Muslims believe it cannot be criticised, as this would be disrespectful.

- To preserve Allah's words, the Qur'an is always read in Arabic. It cannot be truly studied in other languages, as its true meaning is only found in Arabic.

> No prophet or messenger will come after me and no new faith will emerge. (Prophet's last sermon)

How Muslims use the Qur'an

- Daily in worship – verses will be spoken
- In the Jummah service on a Friday
- In celebrations, festivals and rites of passage
- As a source of law for Islamic matters
- When guidance or support is needed.

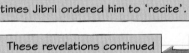

Muslims treat the Qur'an with great respect. When the Qur'an is being used, Muslims do not speak, eat or drink. When it is not being used, it is placed at the highest point in the room as a mark of respect.

Revelation

In 611 CE, Muhammad was meditating in a cave when Angel Jibril appeared to him. → Muhammad could not read but three times Jibril ordered him to 'recite'. → Recite in the name of your Lord... (Surah 96:1) ↓

Muhammad's friends and followers wrote down the chapters of the Qur'an for him. ← These revelations continued for the next 23 years. ← Jibril told Muhammad that he was to be the messenger of Allah.

---

1 ## The Torah (Tawrat)
Muslims believe Allah gave this holy book to Musa (Moses). Tawrat means 'instruction' and Muslims recognise that there are important laws contained within it.

2 ## The Psalms (Zabur)
The holy book of Dawud (David), which some Muslims today believe is still relevant.

Kutub

4 ## The Scrolls of Abraham (Sahifah)
An early scripture believed to have been revealed to Ibrahim and used by his sons Ishma'il and Ishac. The scrolls are thought to be lost.

There are many common messages between these books, reinforcing the messages given by Muhammad and the Qur'an – all are all identified as sources of authority, although the Qur'an is the only unchanged message from Allah.

3 ## The Gospel (Injil)
The Gospel of Isa (Jesus), believed to have been revealed by Allah, and contained in the books of Matthew, Mark, Luke and John.

Now try this

1 Explain **two** ways in which Muslims use holy books. **(4 marks)**

2 Explain **two** Muslim teachings about the Qur'an.
Refer to sacred writings or another source of Muslim belief and teaching in your answer. **(5 marks)**

The Imamate in Shi'a Islam

'Imam' means 'leader and 'imamate' means 'leadership'. In Shi'a Islam, **Imamate** refers to the twelve imams who succeeded Muhammad as the leaders of Islam after his death.

Imam

- **Shi'a Muslims** hold that imams have the same characteristics as prophets (though imams do not receive revelation). They believe Allah appoints the imams. Imams are seen as the best from the ummah, who have been selected to lead for their exceptional qualities.
- **Sunni Muslims** recognise the role of the imam differently – he simply leads prayers in the mosque. The Muslim community can appoint the imam, who can be from the Muslim congregation. Sunni Muslims do not view the role as being divinely appointed or requiring exceptional qualities as Shi'a Muslims do.

The divide between Sunni and Shi'a Muslims

After the death of Muhammad, it was unclear who should lead Islam.

- ✓ Those following Sunni Islam chose Abu Bakr – a close companion of Prophet Muhammad – to lead.
- ✓ Those following Shi'a Islam believed Prophet Muhammad's son-in-law and cousin, Ali, should lead – they understood that Muhammad had appointed him.

In the end, Abu Bakr was appointed, but this led to the first divide within Islam.

Role and significance of the Imamate

Role	Significance
• The twelve imams are the spiritual and political successors to Muhammad. • They are considered to be infallible human beings who rule justly over the community to maintain and interpret Islamic law and guide the community. They have a close relationship with Allah, who guides them. The imams, in turn, can guide Muslims – this stems from Shi'a Muslim belief that Allah would not leave humanity without access to divine guidance.	• It is one of the five roots of Usul ad-Din – the foundations and beliefs of Shi'a Islam. • The Prophet Muhammad gives the Imamate its teaching and leadership role. • The Imamate proves Allah's beneficence, as it allows all Muslims to receive further guidance after Muhammad's death. • Shi'a Muslims recognise the role and importance of the Imamate through the first caliph – Ali; this is detailed in the Shahadah.

At the end of the time of my ummah, the Mahdi will appear. (Hadith)

Shi'a Muslims believe the final imam – Al-Mahdi – disappeared hundreds of years ago and went into a hidden state but will reappear around the end of the world, before the Day of Judgement, to lead Muslims.

Now try this

Explain **two** Muslim teachings about the Imamate in Shi'a Islam. Refer to sacred writings or another source of Muslim belief and teaching in your answer. **(5 marks)**

You need to focus on the teachings from Shi'a Islam. Remember, leadership is one of the differences between Sunni and Shi'a Muslims.

The Qur'an and Imamate

We made them leaders guiding by Our command. And we inspired to them the doing of good deeds, establishment of prayer, and giving of Zakah; and they were worshippers of Us. (Surah 21:73)

Shi'a Muslims use this surah to show that Allah provides leadership through the imams.

I have left among you two weighty things, if you follow them you will never be misguided after me, the Book of Allah and my progeny, the people of my house. (Hadith)

This hadith reinforces the view that Allah did not abandon his people but left sources of authority through the Qur'an and imams.

The Five Pillars and the Ten Obligatory Acts

Sunni Muslims observe the Five Pillars of Islam. The Ten Obligatory Acts are important to Shi'a Muslims. Four of the Five Pillars of Islam are included in the Ten Obligatory Acts.

The Five Pillars of Islam

- They support Islam – they encourage the development of good character and a good attitude and behaviour

- They provide a framework – beliefs and actions that unite Muslims and give structure to their daily lives.

Carrying out the Five Pillars demonstrates that Sunni Muslims are putting their faith first rather than simply fitting religion into their lives.

For more information on each of the Five Pillars, see pages 28–33.

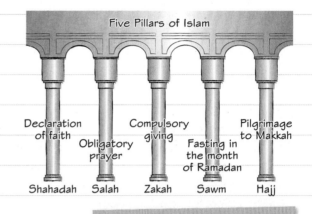

Five Pillars of Islam

Declaration of faith — Shahadah
Obligatory prayer — Salah
Compulsory giving — Zakah
Fasting in the month of Ramadan — Sawm
Pilgrimage to Makkah — Hajj

A visual representation of the Five Pillars of Islam.

The Ten Obligatory Acts

1 **Salah** – compulsory prayer five times a day. Shi'a Muslims combine some of the prayers and pray three times.

2 **Sawm** – fasting during daylight hours in the ninth Islamic month (Ramadan).

3 **Zakah** – donating 2.5 per cent of wealth to help the needy.

4 **Hajj** – pilgrimage to Makkah made by every Muslim once in their lifetime.

5 **Khums** – annual taxation was the historical obligation of Muslims in the army to pay one-fifth of the spoils of war. Today, this money is given to the descendants of Muhammad and Shi'a Muslims, but is also used to help the needy and Shi'a Islamic leaders.

6 **Jihad** – striving to overcome evil, e.g. defending an individual, holy war and personal struggles to resist daily temptations.

7 **Amr-bil-Maroof** – commandment from the Qur'an that instructs Shi'a Muslims on how they should act and behave.

8 **Nahi Anil Munkar** – forbidding what is evil – the need to resist temptation and not sin against Allah.

9 **Tawalla** – expressing love towards what is good, following the examples of the prophets.

10 **Tabarra** – moving away from evil, such as staying away from those who choose to turn away from Allah.

Nature and purpose of the Acts

- Guide Shi'a Muslims in how to live their lives

- Allow them to get closer to Allah in performing the actions he wants

- Help them achieve the reward of paradise after death by following the rules of Allah

- Help them continually focus actions in their lives towards Allah

- Unite all Shi'a Muslims and give meaning to their lives.

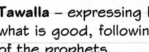

Now try this

1 Which **one** of the following is **not** one of the Five Pillars of Islam?
A Hajj ☐   B Shahadah ☐
C Zakah ☐   D khums ☐   **(1 mark)**

2 Give **two** ways in which the Five Pillars of Islam for Sunni Islam and the Ten Obligatory Acts for Shi'a Islam are similar.   **(2 marks)**

The Shahadah

The **Shahadah** is the first Pillar of Islam – the Muslim declaration of faith or statement of belief that is accepted by all Muslims, both Sunni and Shi'a. It is believed to uphold all other beliefs of Islam and shows acceptance of both Allah and Muhammad.

There is no God but Allah and Muhammad is his Messenger.

Nature of the Shahadah

The Shahadah is the basic statement of Islamic faith and Muslims consider that anyone who cannot recite this is not a Muslim. Muslims believe it demonstrates their loyalty to Allah, the Prophet Muhammad and the religion of Islam. Muslims recite this daily to remind them of the importance of these beliefs.

The Shahadah in the Qur'an

The patient, the true, the obedient, those who spend [in the way of Allah], and those who seek forgiveness before dawn. Allah witnesses that there is no deity except Him, and [so do] the angels and those of knowledge – [that He is] maintaining [creation] in justice. There is no deity except Him, the Exalted in Might, the Wise. (Surah 3:17–18)

The key belief in Allah demonstrates its importance for Muslims and is considered to be at the centre of the Islamic faith.

Differences

• For **Sunni Muslims**, the Shahadah is the first of the Five Pillars of Islam.

• **Shi'a Muslims** do not accept the Shahadah to be a separate pillar, nor do they include it in their Ten Obligatory Acts (where the four other pillars are recognised). Instead, Shi'a Muslims link it with their creed (adiqah). The version of the Shahadah used by Shi'a Muslims also has a third phrase added:

There is no god but God. Muhammad is the messenger of God, **and Ali is the protector of Allah.** (Shahadah)

Recited aloud in front of witnesses to profess the Muslim faith.

Whispered into the ears of newborn babies so it is the first thing they hear.

Role of the Shahadah today

Said before death to demonstrate a commitment to the religion of Islam.

Recited throughout the day to remind Muslims of the basic beliefs of Islam. It forms part of Salah as it is contained in the **adhan**, (call to prayer).

This answer gives two detailed explanations that are developed.

Worked example

Explain **two** ways in which Muslims demonstrate the importance of the Shahadah in their lives today.

(4 marks)

Muslims recite the Shahadah in front of witnesses, which shows its importance. This is because the Shahadah contains the key beliefs for being a committed Muslim – accepting the oneness of Allah, and Muhammad being the messenger in Islam.

The Shahadah is also important because it is whispered into the ears of newborn babies, so the first thing a baby hears is the basic beliefs of Islam. The hope is they will accept the Islamic faith for themselves when they are older.

Now try this

'The Shahadah is the most important pillar for Muslims.'

Evaluate this statement. In your answer you should:

• refer to Muslim teaching
• give reasoned arguments to support this statement

• give reasoned arguments to support a different point of view
• reach a justified conclusion.   **(12 marks)**

Salah I

Salah is the second of the Five Pillars of Islam. It is the compulsory prayer that takes place five times a day.

Nature of Salah

Salah takes place five times a day:

Dawn	Midday	Afternoon	Sunset	Night
Fajr	Dhuhr	Asr	Maghrib	Isha'a

Before prayer, Muslims perform wudu, which is a ritual cleansing. This is done to ensure they are spiritually and physically clean for Allah. It also gives them time to be in the correct frame of mind to be able to pray to Allah.

Muslims pray facing towards the Ka'aba, the sacred shrine or black cube-shaped building that is in the centre of the grand mosque in Makkah.

When praying, Muslims follow a set pattern of movements (rakahs).

bowing

standing   prostrating

How prayer is performed

- Muslim men are expected to attend the mosque to pray; women are not.
- Prayer can happen anywhere that is clean and if wudu has been performed.
- On a Friday, all Muslim men are expected to attend the Jummah service as part of Salah. Women may also attend.

Friday prayer is known as Jummah.

While performing Salah, Muslims recite prayers and verses from the Qur'an. These quotations are two examples of words that are recited:

> O Allah, how perfect You are and praise be to You. Blessed is Your name, and exalted is Your majesty. There is no god but You. … In the name of Allah, the Entirely Merciful, the Especially Merciful. [All] praise is [due] to Allah, Lord of the worlds – The Entirely Merciful, the Especially Merciful, Sovereign of the Day of Recompense. (Surah 1:1–4)

Regular communication with Allah is essential to developing a relationship with him.

Significance of prayer

Prayer is the second of the Five Pillars of Islam, so is considered a duty.

> Verily, I am God! There is none worthy of worship but I, so worship Me and offer prayer perfectly for My remembrance. (Surah 20:14)

Prayer was established by Muhammad and made compulsory – Islam teaches that Muslims will be judged after death.

> The first matter that the slave will be brought to account for on the Day of Judgement is the prayer. If it is sound, then the rest of his deeds will be sound. And if it is incomplete, then the rest of his deeds will be incomplete. (Hadith)

This shows the importance of prayer, as the actions of Muslims determine their afterlife.

Now try this

Explain **two** Muslim teachings about prayer.
Refer to sacred writings or another source of Muslim belief and teaching in your answer. **(5 marks)**

Identify **two** relevant teachings and then develop each one by giving more detail. Remember to link to a source of Muslim belief and teaching within your answer too – for example, a quote from the Qur'an or Hadith.

Salah II

Prayer in Islam can take different forms. Sunni and Shi'a Muslims hold different attitudes and interpretations of how prayer should be performed.

The Qur'an and prayer

> So exalt [Allah] with praise of your Lord and be of those who prostrate [to Him]. And worship your Lord until there comes to you the certainty (death). (Surah 15:98–99)

This quote highlights the importance of worshipping Allah. Prostrating, which is when a Muslim submits to Allah, can be seen in the rakahs.

> Recite, [O Muhammad], what has been revealed to you of the Book and establish prayer. Indeed, prayer prohibits immorality and wrongdoing, and the remembrance of Allah is greater. And Allah knows that which you do. (Surah 29:45)

This quote demonstrates the importance of prayer as regular communication with Allah and the significant role it has in the life of every Muslim.

Salah in the home, mosque and elsewhere

- Salah is the second of the Five Pillars of Islam. All Muslims are expected to pray five times a day.
- Muslims do not have to attend the mosque to complete each prayer – they can pray wherever they are as long as it is clean.
- Muslims attend the mosque for Friday prayer (Jummah).
- To allow for Muslims to complete Salah, prayer rooms have been established in schools, at hospitals, airports and other public places.

Key differences

Shi'a	Sunni
Combine five daily prayers into three	Five daily prayers
Raise hands three times at end of prayers	Move head from right to left
May rest their head while prostrating on a piece of wood	Touch foreheads directly to the floor when prostrating

Other differences are the wording of prayers.

Jummah in the mosque

✓ Jummah is the weekly communal Salah performed after midday on Friday.

✓ Muslim men (and women, if possible) are expected to attend Jummah. Women do not have to attend, as it is recognised that they have an important role looking after the house and children, but they would still be expected to pray at home.

✓ Men and women pray separately in the mosque, so as to stop all distractions.

✓ The imam leads the Jummah prayers and gives a sermon as part of the service.

Many Muslims feel prayer is of the greatest importance, as it is one of the Five Pillars of Islam, was commanded by Allah, established by Muhammad and features heavily in the Qur'an.

Many Muslims argue that prayer alone is not enough to be a full Muslim and that practices and actions are also important.

Some Sunni Muslims believe that anyone who doesn't pray five times a day is an 'unbeliever'.

As Shi'a Muslims combine five prayers into three, it could be that they do not see prayer as important as Sunni Muslims do, believing other aspects of Islam to hold more significance.

Different Muslim views about prayer

Now try this

1 Which **one** of the following is the Islamic name for Friday prayer?
   A Jummah ☐   **B** Salah ☐   **C** wudu ☐   **D** rakahs ☐   **(1 mark)**
2 Explain **two** contrasting ways in which Muslims perform Salah. **(4 marks)**

Make sure you identify **two** ways that are different and develop each one by giving further information or an example.

Sawm

Sawm (fasting) is the fourth Pillar of Islam. The main period of fasting is during **Ramadan** – the ninth month of the Islamic calendar, when all Muslims are required to not eat or drink during daylight hours, as well as to avoid evil thoughts and deeds.

Origins and role of Sawm

O ye who believe! Fasting is prescribed for you ... (Surah 2:183)

Muslims believe the Qur'an was first revealed to Muhammad during the month of Ramadan, which gives Sawm importance. Fasting is an act of worship of Allah and has a long history.

Significance of Sawm

Sawm is important to Muslims because it:

- ✓ is one of the Five Pillars and is compulsory for most healthy adult Muslims – it shows a Muslim is obeying God
- ✓ helps Muslims to learn self-discipline
- ✓ helps Muslims to appreciate what Allah has provided, develop sympathy with the poor and realise the importance of charity
- ✓ helps Muslims to remember the importance of the Qur'an, which was first revealed during Ramadan
- ✓ brings the Muslim community (ummah) together and strengthens their unity.

What is forbidden in daylight hours during Sawm?

No food or drink   No smoking   No sexual activity   No bad thoughts or deeds

Who is exempt from Sawm?

The elderly, young children, pregnant women, those travelling and Muslims who are physically or mentally unwell do not have to take part, as it could be considered harmful if they did. If a Muslim adult does not fast, they should do so at another time or make a donation to the poor.

Benefits of Sawm

👍 Muslims are able to sympathise with those in the world who experience poverty.

👍 Through increased devotion during Sawm, Muslims can reflect on Islam.

👍 Muslims will feel closer to Allah, as they give up food and drink for him.

👍 Muslims give more to charity during Sawm, so develop feelings of generosity.

👍 They develop ideas of self-control and discipline.

This quote in the Qur'an reflects the importance of the Night of Power, with Allah communicating to humanity through Muhammad.

The Night of Power

Sawm is performed to remember the 'Night of Power', when the Angel Jibril appeared to Muhammad and revealed the Qur'an to him from Allah. During Sawm, Muslims:

- recall Allah's gift of the Qur'an to humanity
- ask for forgiveness for things they have done wrong
- worship Allah.

Recite in the name of your Lord who created man from a clinging substance. Recite, and your Lord is the most Generous – Who taught by the pen –Taught man that which he knew not. (Surah 96:1–5)

Now try this

1 Give **two** reasons why some Muslims may not have to fast during Sawm. **(2 marks)**

2 Explain **two** reasons why Sawm is important to Muslims today.
   Refer to sacred writings or another source of Muslim belief and teaching in your answer. **(5 marks)**

Zakah and khums

Zakah, giving money to charity, is the third Pillar of Islam. Khums is a religious tax.

Zakah

Zakah is a type of worship or self-purification involving obligatory alms giving. It involves giving 2.5 per cent of one's wealth each year to benefit the poor. This duty is contained in the Qur'an and has a long history within Islam. Benefits of Zakah are to obey Allah, to show that everything a Muslim owns comes from Allah, and to support the idea of sharing and charitable actions.

Khums

In Shi'a Islam, khums is one of the Ten Obligatory Acts.

Khums is paying 20 per cent of one's surplus income – half to the ummah and half to the poor. This form of giving is mentioned in the Qur'an. Traditionally, the recipients of khums have been the descendants of Muhammad and those within the Shi'a Islamic faith.

The Qur'an and Zakah and khums

Zakah expenditures are only for the poor and for the needy and for those employed to collect [Zakah] and for bringing hearts together [for Islam] and for freeing captives [or slaves] and for those in debt and for the cause of Allah and for the [stranded] traveller. (Surah 9:60)

This talks about the purpose of Zakah. It recognises that it is commanded by Allah.

And know that anything you obtain of war booty – then indeed, for Allah is one fifth of it and for the Messenger and for [his] near relatives and the orphans, the needy, and the [stranded] traveler. (Surah 8:41)

This demonstrates the use of khums.

Importance of Zakah for Sunni Muslims

- It is one of the Five Pillars, so is a duty.
- Wealth is believed to be a gift from Allah that should be shared.
- Muslims believe it is what Allah wants them to do and they will be judged on their actions and the way they helped others after death.
- It is a sign of unity and supports the ummah.
- It helps a Muslim to grow spiritually and frees them from greed and selfishness.
- It helps those who need it most – some Zakah money is used by Islamic charities, such as Islamic Relief, to respond to disasters around the world.

Importance of khums for Shi'a Muslims

- It gives special recognition to Muhammad, his descendants and leaders within Shi'a Islam.
- It is used to help build Islamic schools or Islamic projects.
- It is used to help the poor or those who may be suffering.
- It is used to promote the religion of Islam through education.
- It is one of the Ten Obligatory Acts.

Shi'a Muslims also perform Zakah.

Sunni Muslims also recognise the historical importance of khums, but do not attribute the same significance to it.

Now try this

'The best way for Muslims to serve Allah is through giving Zakah.'
Evaluate this statement. In your answer you should:
- refer to Muslim teaching
- give reasoned arguments to support this statement
- give reasoned arguments to support a different point of view
- reach a justified conclusion.   **(12 marks)**

Hajj

Hajj, the fifth Pillar of Islam, is the annual Muslim pilgrimage that takes place in and around Makkah. All Muslims are required to make this journey once in their lifetime if they are physically fit and can afford to do so.

Nature

Hajj is a holy journey that Muslims are expected to make to Makkah, Saudi Arabia. It is held annually in the month of Dhul-Hijjah, lasts five days and over two million Muslims attend. Makkah is the holy city for Muslims as it is where Muhammad was born and lived, and where Muslims face when they pray.

Role

Hajj is intended to allow Muslims to get closer to Allah, as well as to follow the example of Muhammad, who began the ritual.

Significance

Hajj is important to Muslims as it is one of the Five Pillars. It reminds them of the importance of recognising that all Muslims are equal and equally part of the ummah. It is a struggle to complete Hajj, but Muslims believe it teaches them to be patient and gives them time to reflect on Allah and their faith.

Origins

Hajj is built around many events and people who hold importance in Islam. The rituals completed during Hajj were established by the Prophet Muhammad, who demonstrated the actions to his followers shortly before his death.

The Qur'an

Surah 2:124–127 talks about the story of Ibrahim who, it is believed, built the first **Ka'aba** (House of Allah) – the sacred shrine in Makkah. Surah 22:27–29 also talks of proclaiming the Hajj to followers.

How Hajj is performed

Place and actions performed		Significance
Arriving on Hajj	Muslims put on ihram (white seamless robes). This is also understood by Muslims to be a 'state of ihram', as it includes ideas of behaving appropriately and focusing only on Allah.	• Demonstrates unity, with all Muslims dressed identically. • Shows equality before Allah. • Strengthens the feeling of commitment between all Muslims in the ummah.
Makkah	• Muslims perform Tawaf, which is circling the Ka'aba seven times in an anticlockwise direction. This is also repeated at the end of Hajj. • Muslims also complete the sa'y – running between the hills of Safa and Marwa.	• Tawaf demonstrates the unity of all Muslims together in submission to Allah as they move in harmony around the Ka'aba. • Sa'y is done in remembrance of the story of Hagar searching for water in the desert.
Muzdalifah	Muslims camp here overnight.	Muslims need to ensure they rest, as Hajj is a difficult and tiring journey.
Arafat	The 'Stand' where Muslims: • praise Allah • read from the Qur'an • ask for forgiveness.	• The heat of standing in the sun reminds Muslims of the Day of Judgement. • This is a time for Muslims to reflect on what they have done wrong and ask Allah for forgiveness.
Mina	• Muslims collect and throw stones at pillars. • An animal is sacrificed, men's heads will be shaved and women cut off a lock of their hair.	• Symbolises rejecting the devil and evil. • The animal is sacrificed as part of the celebration of the festival of Id-ul-Adha, which remembers the sacrifice Ibrahim was willing to make of his son Ishma'el. • The hair is cut as a symbol of purity.

Now try this

This question requires you to state **two** pieces of accurate information, each in a short sentence.

1 Give **two** rituals that Muslims perform during Hajj. **(2 marks)**

2 Explain **two** ways that Muslims show commitment to Allah on Hajj. **(4 marks)**

Identify **two** ways and develop each one by giving further information or perhaps an example.

Jihad

Jihad means 'to struggle' and has its origins in the Qur'an. It describes the personal struggle of every Muslim to follow the teachings of Islam and obey Allah.

Greater and lesser jihad

Greater jihad	Lesser jihad
Inner struggle to be a better Muslim.	**Military struggle** to defend Islam.
The duty of every Muslim to live a good life, staying faithful to beliefs and obeying the commands of Islam by: • studying the Qur'an • doing good deeds • attending mosque regularly • resisting temptation, greed and envy.	It is carried out according to strict and clear-cut rules: • Can be non-violent, and in some cases violent. • Fought for a just cause. • Fought as a last resort. • Authorised and accepted by Muslim authority. • The minimum amount of suffering should be caused. • Ends when enemy surrenders. • Innocent civilians not attacked. • Aims to restore peace and freedom.

The Prophet returned from one of his battles, and thereupon told us, 'You have arrived with an excellent arrival, you have come from the Lesser Jihad to the Greater Jihad – the striving of a servant (of Allah) against his desires.' (Hadith)

Lesser jihad and the Qur'an

Fight in the cause of Allah those who fight you, but do not transgress limits; for Allah loveth not transgressors. (Surah 2:190)

Permission [to fight] has been given to those who are being fought, because they were wronged. And indeed, Allah is competent to give them victory. (Surah 22:39)

The Qur'an makes it clear that there are strict conditions when lesser jihad can be declared and therefore justified.

Divergent understandings of jihad

• Most Muslims agree that greater jihad is the most important as this is stressed in the Qur'an.

• Greater jihad is a personal battle, which many Muslims understand to be the true meaning of the term.

• Even though Muhammad was involved in military battles, he supported greater jihad as being more important.

• There may be occasions when the religion of Islam or the name of Allah is threatened and it would be appropriate to defend Islam, but Islam does have set conditions for this.

This answer gives two contrasting ways in which jihad is understood by Muslims. Each explanation given is accurate and shows the student's knowledge of this topic.

Worked example

Explain **two** contrasting understandings of jihad. **(4 marks)**

Greater jihad is the inner struggle to be a better Muslim. It involves every Muslim trying to stay committed to Islam and to get closer to Allah through obeying the commands of Islam, for example by following the Five Pillars of Islam.

Lesser jihad is the military struggle to defend Islam, fighting when commanded, which the Qur'an allows. This must always take place in defence, with the intention of bringing peace, and fought as a last resort.

Now try this

1 Which **one** of the following is the meaning of 'jihad'?

   A resurrection ☐   **B** festival ☐   **C** to struggle ☐   **D** charity ☐   **(1 mark)**

2 'Greater jihad is more important than lesser jihad.'

   Evaluate this statement. In your answer you should:
   • refer to Islamic teaching
   • give reasoned arguments to support this statement
   • give reasoned arguments to support a different point of view
   • reach a justified conclusion.   **(12 marks)**

Festivals and commemorations

Muslims celebrate or commemorate special days and events throughout the year. For example, **Id-ul-Fitr** celebrates the end of Ramadan. A commemoration, such as **Id-ul-Adha**, is a reminder of an important event that occurred in the past.

Why Muslims have celebrations and commemorations

1. To remember past events and important people within Islam.

2. To strengthen the ummah and unite Muslims together.

3. To share beliefs that they have in common.

4. To have a cycle of special days and events that are marked throughout the year.

Importance for Muslims in the UK today

Festivals and commemorations are important because they:

- give Muslims a sense of identity and belonging in a country where the main religious tradition is Christianity

- help Muslims to feel connected to the ummah – all Muslims worldwide

- allow Muslims to reflect on the traditions and history of Islam

- allow Muslims to celebrate and mark special days in the Islamic calendar.

Festival	Sunni	Shi'a
Id-ul-Adha End of Hajj *May Allah's blessings be with you today & always!* **ID-UL-ADHA**	• Known as the 'Festival of Sacrifice'. • Remembers Ibrahim's willingness to sacrifice his son when God asked him to. This story is found in Surah 37:100–111 and reminds Muslims of the test of faith faced by Ibrahim and how they should apply this to their own lives, as well as the mercy shown by Allah. • Signifies the end of Hajj. • Muslims remember their own willingness to sacrifice anything to God's wishes. They celebrate with the sacrifice of an animal, which is shared among family, friends and the poor. • Prayers, cards and presents are given.	
Id-ul-Fitr End of Ramadan *Id Mubarak*	• A time to celebrate and thank Allah for his help in getting through the month of fasting. • Begins when first new moon is seen. • The first Id is believed to have been celebrated by Muhammad, so it commemorates this event in Islamic history. • Homes are decorated. There will be special services and a celebratory meal is shared. Id Mubarak means 'blessed celebration' and is the traditional greeting used by Muslims.	
Ashura Tenth day of Muharran, the first month of the Islamic calendar	• A day of fasting and mourning to remember how Nuh (Noah) left the Ark and how Musa (Moses) and the Israelites were saved from the Egyptians. • People wear black and no music is allowed.	• As Sunni, but the event is also one of mourning to remember the martyrdom at Karbala in 680CE of Hussain, who was a grandson of Prophet Muhammad.

Now try this

This question tests your recall of knowledge – you need to state **two** pieces of accurate information, each in a short sentence.

1 Give **two** reasons why Muslims in the UK believe it is important to celebrate festivals. **(2 marks)**

2 Explain **two** ways in which Muslims celebrate the festival of Id-ul-Fitr. **(4 marks)**

Sexual relationships

Sexual relationships can be understood as **heterosexual**, where a person is sexually attracted to someone of the opposite sex, and **homosexual**, where a person is sexually attracted to someone of the same sex as them. Many Christians believe that sex is a gift from God that should only take place between a man and a woman who are married to each other.

Christian teachings on relationships

Traditionally, the Christian Church has supported heterosexual relationships.

> A man leaves his father and mother and is united to his wife, and they become one flesh. (Genesis 2:24)

> Men also abandoned natural relations with women and were inflamed with lust for one another. Men committed shameful acts with other men, and received in themselves the due penalty for their error. (Romans 1:27)

Traditional Church teachings meant that many Christians opposed homosexual relationships. Yet, as society has changed, so too have some Christian attitudes.

Christian attitudes to homosexuality

Some Christians follow traditional and Bible teachings against homosexuality. They believe:

1. God intended marriage to be between one man and one woman

2. same-sex partners cannot have children naturally, which is a purpose of marriage

3. homosexuality undermines the family unit.

Other Christians are more tolerant, believing:

1. homosexuality is natural

2. all humans were created in God's image

3. love between all people, including same-sex couples, should be celebrated

4. the Bible teaches us to respect everyone.

> Love your neighbour as yourself. (Matthew 22:39)

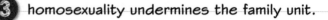

In the UK, homosexuality was illegal until 1967. In 2013, the law changed to allow people of the same sex to marry in the UK. Although the law allows this to happen in a church, it is up to the individual minister.

Sex before marriage

1. Saint Paul taught that sexual relationships before marriage (premarital sex) are wrong.

2. Some Christians take a vow of chastity not to have sex until after marriage.

3. Christians believe **procreation** (having children) is a key purpose of marriage, and that marriage provides stability and a family unit.

Sex outside marriage (adultery)

Christians teach that adultery is always wrong.

- It is forbidden in the Ten Commandments.

> You shall not commit adultery. (Exodus 20:14)

- The Bible teaches married couples should be faithful, as promised in the marriage vows.

> Marriage should be honoured by all, and the marriage bed kept pure, for God will judge the adulterer and all the sexually immoral. (Hebrews 13:4)

Non-religious attitudes

- Consenting adults should be allowed to share a sexual relationship, provided it does not harm anyone else, so sex outside of marriage is fine.
- Many non-religious believers accept the full range of human sexuality, including homosexuality.

Now try this

Give **two** religious beliefs about sex before marriage. **(2 marks)**

Sexual relationships

Muslims believe sexual relationships should only take place within marriage, as sex is an important bond between a couple and an opportunity to start a family.

Islamic teachings on relationships

Muslims support heterosexual relationships. Islam teaches that:

- sex is an act of worship – it is a gift given by Allah so people can procreate
- sexual relationships fulfil physical, emotional and spiritual needs and should only take place within marriage between a man and a woman.

> Meetings between unmarried couples are often chaperoned. Many Muslims take a vow of chastity until after marriage.

Islam does not tolerate homosexuality because of strict rules about sexual relationships only taking place between a husband and wife.

Different attitudes to homosexuality

Most Muslims follow Islamic teachings and traditional arguments against homosexuality.

1 The Qur'an says homosexuality is unnatural.

2 Homosexual relationships are seen to be wrong, as they do not produce children.

3 Homosexuality is seen as a threat to society, as it undermines the family unit.

4 Homosexuality is understood to be a choice and not a natural sexual orientation.

Yet some modern Muslims are more tolerant.

- They support Muslims who are homosexual, so their community does not exclude them.
- They may accept scientific evidence that suggests homosexuality is not a choice but a natural sexual orientation.

> This passage is against homosexuality, yet shows Allah is merciful if Muslims are sorry.

> And the two who commit [homosexual acts] among you, dishonour them both. But if they repent and correct themselves, leave them alone. Indeed, Allah is ever Accepting of repentance and Merciful. (Surah 4:16)

Sex outside marriage

Adultery is as a serious crime – some Muslim countries give the death penalty as punishment.

> The [unmarried] woman or [unmarried] man found guilty of sexual intercourse – lash each one of them with a hundred lashes, and do not be taken by pity for them in the religion of Allah… And let a group of the believers witness their punishment. (Surah 24:2)

Sex before marriage

Muslims believe they will be rewarded for staying chaste until after marriage.

> When a husband and wife share intimacy it is rewarded and a blessing from Allah; just as they would be punished if they had engaged in illicit sex. (Hadith)

Non-religious views

- Many humanists and atheists agree with Muslims that adultery is wrong, as it involves breaking trust and promises made.
- They may be more accepting of sex before marriage, seeing it as doing nothing wrong.

Now try this

'Homosexual relationships are wrong.'
Evaluate this statement. In your answer you:
- should give reasoned arguments in support of the statement
- should give reasoned arguments to support a different point of view
- should refer to religious arguments
- may refer to non-religious arguments
- should reach a justified conclusion.   **(12 marks plus 3 SPaG marks)**

Contraception

Contraception is the intentional prevention of pregnancy, and Christians hold differing views about whether or not it is acceptable.

Types of contraception

- ✓ **Natural** methods of contraception include the rhythm method, which is when a couple has sex when the woman is not fertile (ovulating).

- ✓ **Artificial** methods are human-made objects designed to prevent pregnancy. They include the condom and the birth control pill.

Christian teachings

Contraception is a challenging issue for Christians. There are no direct teachings in the Bible, since it is a more modern issue, but Christians rely on their Church teachings.

> As for you, be fruitful and increase in number; multiply on the earth and increase upon it. (Genesis 9:7)

Christians understand this to mean they have a responsibility to procreate.

Catholic beliefs about contraception

- Every sexual act should be open to the possibility of a child, so artificial methods of contraception should not be used.

- Contraception prevents one of the main purposes of sex – having children.

- Contraception could encourage promiscuity or casual sex, which could lead to sexually transmitted infections (STIs).

- Natural forms of contraception are acceptable as procreation is still possible.

- Pope Paul VI's *Humanae Vitae* (1968) affirms that contraception is not acceptable.

Protestant beliefs about contraception

Some Protestants agree with using contraception because:

- the main purpose of sex is procreation, but sex is also for pleasure as an expression of love between a husband and wife

- contraception is a sensible method of family planning

- using artificial methods of contraception does not go against God's teachings.

Christian responses to these beliefs differ. Catholics maintain that the use of contraception prevents procreation, which is a key purpose of sex. Some Protestants (e.g. Church of England) may agree with some of the views, although for religious rather than any other reasoning.

Non-religious responses

Atheists might argue that each person's situation should be taken into consideration. They believe people may use contraception if:

- they want to plan when to have a family

- they are not ready to have children

- a couple's lifestyle may not be compatible with having children

- pregnancy could be harmful to the mother

- they want to be safe from STIs

- the couple carry genetic disorders.

Humanists generally have no issue with the use of contraception. The British Humanist Association argues that if contraception 'results in every child being a wanted child, and in better, healthier lives for women, it must be a good thing'.

Now try this

Explain **two** contrasting beliefs in contemporary British society about the use of contraception within marriage.

In your answer you should refer to the main religious tradition of Great Britain and one or more other religious traditions. **(4 marks)**

One of the views you give **must** be Christian. The second viewpoint could be another contrasting Christian view, or a view from another religion.

Contraception

There are many different types of contraception, and Muslims hold differing views about whether or not they are acceptable.

Guidance from the Hadith Sahih al-Bukhari

Sahih al-Bukhari is a collection of books (**Hadith**) compiled by Imam Muhammad al-Bukhari and gives some guidance on contraception.

'What is your opinion about coitus interruptus?' The Prophet said, 'Do you really do that? It is better for you not to do it. No soul that which Allah has destined to exist, but will surely come into existence. (Sahih al-Bukhari 34:432)

We used to practise coitus interruptus during the lifetime of Allah's Apostle while the Quran was being Revealed. (Sahih al-Bukhari 62:136)

Muslims may hold different views about the use of contraception as there is no single approach to this issue. The first quote suggests Prophet Muhammad did not support the use of natural forms of contraception such as the withdrawal method. The second quote, however, appears to contradict this, saying that it was a common practice during the time of Muhammad. Many Muslims believe that in matters such as contraception, if Allah wills for a new life to be created, it should be his decision.

Differing opinions on contraception

Some Muslim authorities may accept the use of contraception for the following purposes:

- to preserve the life of the mother if her life would be under threat through having another pregnancy
- to protect the well-being of the current family unit if having another child would put too much strain on the family in terms of money or support
- to plan when to have a family by using non-permanent methods, because this still allows for procreation in the future.

Some may not accept contraception because:

- only natural methods are allowed – this is what many Muslims feel sources of authority promote
- there is no possibility of procreation – which is the purpose of a sexual relationship – if permanent methods are used
- some methods could be considered an early abortion and therefore infanticide
- having children is what Allah intended for humans and using contraception prevents this.

Muslim response to non-religious views

Why couples might use contraception in non-religious communities	The Muslim response
They can plan when to have a family	Some agree this is OK, others do not
Pregnancy could be harmful to the mother	OK if to preserve the life of the mother
Lifestyle not compatible with having children	OK if having another child would put a strain on the current family unit
To avoid sexually transmitted infections (STIs)	Shouldn't be an issue as Muslims do not believe in sex outside of marriage
To avoid genetic disorders being passed on	Most agree that it is OK in this case

You need to refer to **two** religious teachings from one or more religions. If you choose to answer this question from the Muslim perspective, you can use the teachings from the Hadith on this page.

Now try this

Explain **two** religious teachings about the use of contraception.

Refer to sacred writings or another source of religious belief and teaching in your answer.   **(5 marks)**

Marriage

The Christian purpose of marriage

1 To provide companionship, friendship and support between husband and wife.

2 To enjoy a sexual relationship within marriage and have children and raise a family.

3 To make a lifelong commitment to another person, establishing a permanent and stable relationship, thereby also providing stability to society through the teaching of good moral and social behaviour.

Marriage is an important bond between a man and a woman.

What the Bible says

The Bible states that marriage should be **monogamous** between a man and woman and **for life**.

> But at the beginning of creation God made them male and female. For this reason a man will leave his father and mother and be united to his wife, and the two will become one flesh. So they are no longer two, but one flesh. Therefore what God has joined together, let no one separate. (Mark 10:6–9)

Christian beliefs about marriage

- Most Christians believe marriage is a **sacrament** – a ceremony in which God is involved. Vows, such as being faithful, are made between the man and woman and also to God, showing the marriage is sacred and binding.

- Marriage is believed to be a **gift from God** – it is part of God's plan for men and women to live together as stated in the Bible.

- Marriage is a lifelong commitment to another person, providing stability to themselves and society through demonstrating good moral behaviour.

- Although marriage is important, some Christians believe that God doesn't want everyone to be married. Jesus himself wasn't married and some Christians believe they have a **vocation from God** (for example, being a monk or nun) where marriage is not a requirement.

Non-religious attitudes

Humanists do not use religion in their lives; instead they rely on their use of reason. They do not accept marriage as a religious institution blessed by God, but they do accept marriage in a secular sense as a couple making a **commitment** to each other.

It is possible to have a humanist wedding, although this is not accepted legally and a civil ceremony would also be required.

The marriage vows and their meaning

I, [name], take you, [name], to be my wife/husband, to have and to hold from this day forward;

← The couple gives their consent.

for better, for worse, for richer, for poorer,

← They recognise that marriage may have challenges and promise to support each other.

in sickness and in health, to love and to cherish,

← Marriage is intended to be a lifelong commitment.

till death us do part;

according to God's holy law.

← The promises the couple make are according to how God intended marriage to be.

In the presence of God I make this vow.

← Marriage is a sacrament – a ceremony in which God is involved.

Now try this

Give **two** religious beliefs about the purpose of marriage. **(2 marks)**

The couple may exchange wedding rings as a symbol of their never-ending love for each other.

Marriage

Purpose of marriage

 1 For a man and woman to have children.

2 To share love, companionship and sex, which is Allah's intention for humans.

3 To create a family and strengthen society.

> Marry those among you who are single. (Surah 24:32)

> Muslims believe that marriage is important so they can have children and pass on the Islamic faith to them.

Muslim beliefs

- Marriage in Islam is intended to be for life.
- Muslim women are expected to marry within the Islamic faith so children will be raised as Muslim.
- Muslim men can marry, for example, a Christian, as children will follow the faith of the father.
- Marriage is seen as a legal contract.
- Islam allows polygamy for men – Muslims men may have up to four wives. However, Muslim women may only have one husband.
- Islam encourages people to marry, following the example of Muhammad.
- Allah is believed to have created man and woman for each other.

Arranged marriage

Marriages in Islam are often arranged – the families of the bride and groom will introduce the couple.

Often from puberty boys and girls in Islam will be kept separate, so an arranged marriage is a good way of them meeting an appropriate partner.

The marriage, however, can only take place with the consent of both parties. If you forced someone to get married, Islam teaches that the marriage would be invalid.

The couple are able to have an engagement, although they may be chaperoned on their meetings together.

Non-religious views

> Being an **atheist**, I would have a **secular** marriage ceremony – I still believe that marriage is the best environment to raise children. I would happily cohabit though, too.

> Being a **humanist**, I too would have a secular marriage ceremony to show my commitment to my partner. I also would happily cohabit.

> You could answer from a Christian point of view too.

Worked example

Explain **two** religious beliefs about the importance of marriage. Refer to sacred writings or another source of religious belief and teaching in your answer. **(5 marks)**

Marriage is important to Muslims because it is seen as the joining of a couple who want to make a commitment to each other. The Qur'an instructs 'Marry those among you who are single' (Surah 24:32).

Marriage is also important to Muslims because they believe it provides a secure basis for family, so that children can be raised, taught about Islam and shown how to be good citizens.

Now try this

'The most important purpose of marriage is to have children.'
Evaluate this statement. In your answer you:

- should give reasoned arguments in support of this statement
- should give reasoned arguments to support a different point of view

- should refer to religious arguments
- may refer to non-religious arguments
- should reach a justified conclusion

(12 marks plus 3 SPaG marks)

Different relationships

Same-sex couples are now able to get married in Great Britain. **Cohabitation** is when a couple lives together without being married. Christianity holds differing views on these issues.

Traditional Christian attitudes

Christian teaching is traditionally against same-sex marriage. The Church teaches that marriage is intended for a man and woman so they can have a sexual relationship and start a family. As same-sex couples cannot do this naturally, they argue that same-sex marriage is not what God intended.

Denomination	Attitude to same-sex marriage
Catholic	• It does not support homosexuality, although recognises that some people are naturally homosexual. • It believes marriage can only be between a man and a woman, as same-sex couples cannot have children naturally. • Leading figures in the Catholic Church have sometimes actively campaigned against same-sex marriage.
Church of England	• It does not regard homosexuality as a sin but believes marriage should be between a man and a woman. • Ministers are prevented from carrying out same-sex marriages.

Changing Christian attitudes

Some Christians are changing their attitudes towards homosexuality and same-sex marriage. They focus on teachings about equality and argue that same-sex couples should be allowed to express this love for each other through the commitment of marriage.

Bible teachings

These quotes support traditional attitudes about marriage:

So God created mankind in his own image, in the image of God he created them; male and female he created them. God blessed them and said to them, 'Be fruitful and increase in number; fill the earth and subdue it.' (Genesis 1:27–28)

That is why a man leaves his father and mother and is united to his wife, and they become one flesh. (Genesis 2:24)

This quote can be used to support same-sex marriage:

Love your neighbour as yourself. (Matthew 22:39)

Cohabitation

Today, not everyone wishes to get married. Some couples prefer to **cohabit** – to live together without being married. Weddings can be very expensive, so many choose not to marry at all.

One Christian denomination that campaigns for marriage equality is the Quakers. They officiate at same-sex marriage ceremonies.

Denomination	Attitude to cohabitation
Catholic	• Does not accept cohabitation – sex should only happen in marriage. • Marriage provides stability and is the basis for family life. • Marriage involves sacred vows.
Church of England	Marriage is the ideal but it accepts cohabitation if it will lead to marriage.
Other Christians	• Accept some people do not want to get married. • Accept cohabitation.

Now try this

Which **one** of the following describes a couple living together in a committed relationship without being married?

A adultery ☐   **B** cohabitation ☐   **C** contraception ☐   **D** divorce ☐   **(1 mark)**

Different relationships

Same-sex couples are now able to get married in Great Britain. Islam holds very traditional and strict views on same-sex marriage and cohabitation.

Same-sex marriage

 Islam traditionally forbids same-sex relationships and does not recognise same-sex marriage.

 Muslims believe marriage is intended between a man and a woman to fulfil emotional, physical and spiritual needs and for the purpose of procreation.

③ Islam teaches that same-sex marriage is unnatural and against the will of Allah.

Today, some homosexual couples are challenging traditional views of same-sex marriage in Islam.

And the two who commit [homosexual acts] among you, dishonour them both. But if they repent and correct themselves, leave them alone. Indeed, Allah is ever Accepting of repentance and Merciful. (Surah 4:16)

This surah is against homosexuality, yet shows Allah is merciful if Muslims are sorry.

Worked example

'Same sex marriages should not be allowed.'
Evaluate this statement. In your answer you:
- should give reasoned arguments in support of this statement
- should give reasoned arguments to support a different point of view
- should refer to religious arguments
- may refer to non-religious arguments
- should reach a justified conclusion.

(12 marks plus 3 SPaG marks)

Muslims would agree with this statement. Many Muslims do not accept same-sex marriage, as they believe marriage should be between a man and a woman. This is because one of the purposes of marriage is for a couple to procreate, which a same-sex couple cannot do naturally. Also, many Muslims look to the Qur'an for teachings on issues such as this, and they believe the Qur'an teaches that same-sex relationships are not what Allah intended, so are wrong.

Cohabitation

- Muslims do not believe that cohabitation is acceptable and they would not cohabit.
- Muslims have very traditional views about members of the opposite sex meeting up prior to marriage – generally, the woman would be chaperoned (accompanied) by a member of her family.

The student has successfully given an Islamic view that supports the statement. They have given a good explanation, which is developed with a link to Islamic teachings. This addresses the criteria required by the first bullet point. Although same-sex marriage is legal in the UK, it is forbidden for same-sex couples to marry in a mosque.

The student now needs to continue the answer by giving alternative developed arguments that disagree with the statement. These could be from another religion (Christianity) or an alternative Muslim view. They could also include non-religious arguments.

Now try this

Give **two** religious beliefs about same-sex marriage. **(2 marks)**

Divorce and remarriage

Divorce is the legal termination of a marriage. Christians hold different views about divorce, and attitudes to divorce have changed significantly in recent times.

Reasons for divorce

A divorce in Great Britain can be given for 'irreconcilable differences':

- adultery
- desertion
- unreasonable behaviour
- two years of separation with consent
- five years of separation without consent.

Christians believe God intended marriage to be for life, so Christians should do everything possible to reconcile before considering divorce.

Catholic beliefs about divorce

Catholicism does not recognise divorce because marriage is for life.

- Jesus said divorce is wrong.
- Marriage is a sacrament and divorce would break the promises made with God.
- A legal separation may be accepted in some cases, for example where care of children is needed but the relationship has broken down beyond repair.
- An **annulment** can be issued where the marriage is regarded as never having taken place – this is done only for special reasons.

Bible teachings about divorce

Therefore what God has joined together, let no one separate. (Mark 10:9)

Jesus replied, 'Moses permitted you to divorce your wives because your hearts were hard. But it was not this way from the beginning. I tell you that anyone who divorces his wife, except for sexual immorality, and marries another woman commits adultery.' (Matthew 19:8–9)

The Bible teaches that marriage is for life. This is symbolised by the unbroken circle of the ring given in the marriage ceremony.

Protestant beliefs about divorce

- Divorce is not to be encouraged, but may sometimes be necessary.
- Divorce must be acceptable, as UK law allows it.
- People can make mistakes and God is ready to forgive sins.

Christian views on remarriage

- Catholics do not accept remarriage. If a divorced person remarries, the ceremony cannot be held in a Catholic church.
- Protestants allow remarriage, but it is up to the individual minister to decide whether a couple can remarry in church.

An annulment is a court statement that a marriage is now invalid.

Non-religious views

- **Humanists** believe that the breakdown of a marriage can cause problems within the family, but they accept that divorce can sometimes be necessary. They do not associate marriage with religion, so do not feel any promises to any sort of god are broken.
- **Atheists** may hold similar views. They may adopt an ethical standpoint similar to that of **situation ethics**, where they consider the best action in each individual situation.

Ethical arguments

- Sanctity of the marriage vows – Christians would argue that the vows made before God in marriage are sacred – to break them would be wrong in a religious and a moral sense.
- Many Christians recognise that an unhappy marriage is not best for husband, wife or children. They may use Jesus' teachings on compassion to argue that sometimes divorce may be best.

Now try this

Give **two** religious beliefs about remarriage.   **(2 marks)**

Divorce and remarriage

Muslim teachings on divorce

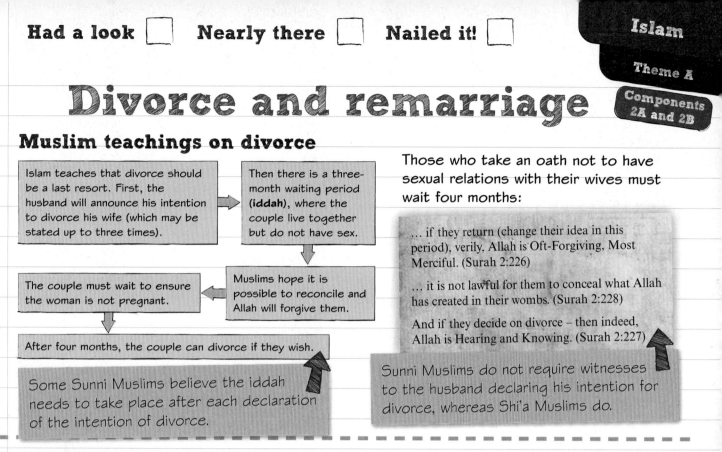

Islam teaches that divorce should be a last resort. First, the husband will announce his intention to divorce his wife (which may be stated up to three times).

Then there is a three-month waiting period (**iddah**), where the couple live together but do not have sex.

Muslims hope it is possible to reconcile and Allah will forgive them.

The couple must wait to ensure the woman is not pregnant.

After four months, the couple can divorce if they wish.

Some Sunni Muslims believe the iddah needs to take place after each declaration of the intention of divorce.

Those who take an oath not to have sexual relations with their wives must wait four months:

… if they return (change their idea in this period), verily, Allah is Oft-Forgiving, Most Merciful. (Surah 2:226)

… it is not lawful for them to conceal what Allah has created in their wombs. (Surah 2:228)

And if they decide on divorce – then indeed, Allah is Hearing and Knowing. (Surah 2:227)

Sunni Muslims do not require witnesses to the husband declaring his intention for divorce, whereas Shi'a Muslims do.

Muslim beliefs and attitudes

Although divorce is allowed by Allah, Muslims believe it is detestable – it is hated by Allah as it is disrespectful to him and the gift of marriage. Most Muslims would maintain that marriage is intended to be for life and is a contract, but if the marriage has broken down and reconciliation is not possible, then divorce may be the only answer. When a couple experience problems in their marriage they are expected to attempt to reconcile. The extended family, as well as the local community, may be involved in trying to resolve their issues.

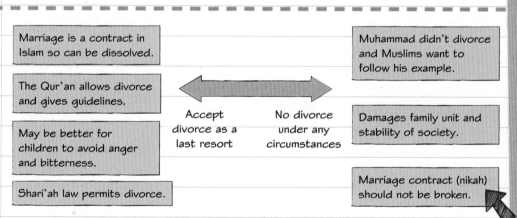

Marriage is a contract in Islam so can be dissolved.

The Qur'an allows divorce and gives guidelines.

May be better for children to avoid anger and bitterness.

Shari'ah law permits divorce.

Accept divorce as a last resort ⟷ No divorce under any circumstances

Muhammad didn't divorce and Muslims want to follow his example.

Damages family unit and stability of society.

Marriage contract (nikah) should not be broken.

Although a Muslim woman may, perhaps, have more reasons to seek a divorce – including desertion, cruelty and a lack of maintenance – it is far easier for Muslim men to obtain divorces. If a woman wishes to divorce, she usually needs the consent of her husband.

Remarriage

Muslims can remarry after divorce, and it is even encouraged, in order to provide the stability of family.

A man and woman can remarry the same partner twice, but if they get a third divorce, remarriage cannot take place between the same man and woman unless the woman has been married to another man in the meantime.

You can answer this question from one religious tradition or you can refer to more than one. Link the points you develop to teachings from holy books such as the Qur'an or Bible.

Now try this

Explain **two** religious teachings about divorce. Refer to sacred writings or another source of religious belief and teaching in your answer.

(5 marks)

Families

The family unit and family life are important to Christians. Each member within the family is taught to have specific roles, which they believe God expects them to fulfil.

1 **Nuclear family:** two parents (man/woman) and their children living together

2 **Blended family:** stepfamilies that have joined together through remarriage

5 **Family with same-sex parents:** two same-sex parents and child/children

Types of family

4 **Single-parent family:** one parent and child/children

3 **Extended family:** parents, children, grandparents, aunts, uncles and cousins

Most Christians prefer the traditional family unit of a nuclear family, as it reflects the idea of family in the Bible. Yet Christians are realistic about changes in society and believe a stable family is more important than the type.

Christian teachings about the importance of family and roles within the family

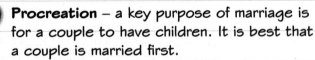

Parents

- Most Christians believe they have a responsibility to get married and have children if able, as this is what God intended.
- Parents have a responsibility to love, support and care for their children and keep them safe.
- Christian parents raise their children as Christians – getting them baptised or christened and introducing them to the Christian community, Church and religious teachings.

Parents do not embitter your children, or they will become discouraged. (Colossians 3:21)

Fathers do not exasperate your children; instead bring them up in the training and instruction of the Lord. (Ephesians 6:4)

FAMILY

Children

- The Bible teaches that children should honour, obey and respect their parents.
- Children are expected to care for their parents in their old age, just as their parents once cared for them.

Children are a heritage from the Lord, offspring a reward from him. (Psalm 127:3)

Children, obey your parents in the Lord. (Ephesians 6:1)

Church teachings

- The Church is seen as a family that Christians belong to wherever they are in the world.
- The Christian community can provide support for the family unit when it faces problems.

Importance of family today

- Family strengthens society, providing structure and support.
- Family is where people feel safest – with the people they love.

Purpose of the family

1 **Procreation** – a key purpose of marriage is for a couple to have children. It is best that a couple is married first.

2 **Stability and the protection of children** – family life provides a safe and nurturing environment.

3 **Educating children** – parents can help their children develop a Christian world view by:

- teaching them to pray
- taking them to church and/or sending them to a Church school or to Sunday School classes
- having their children baptised or confirmed.

These commandments that I give you today are to be on your hearts. Impress them on your children. (Deuteronomy 6:6–7)

Anyone who does not provide for their relatives, and especially for their own household, has denied the faith and is worse than an unbeliever. (1 Timothy 5:8)

Now try this

Which **one** of the following terms is used to describe a family of two parents (man and woman) living with their children?

A nuclear ☐   B extended ☐
C single-parent ☐   D blended ☐ **(1 mark)**

Families

For Muslims, family is at the heart of Islam and provides security and stability in society.

Teachings about the importance of family

- Muslims believe that Allah created family life in order to keep society together, so they see family as the foundation of the community. They also follow the example of Muhammad, who was married with a family.

- The family is the appropriate place to learn about love, kindness, mercy and compassion. Within a family, children can be raised within the Islamic faith and be part of the ummah – the Muslim community.

- Children are taught to respect and obey their parents and to care for family members when they are old.

> O mankind! We have created you from a male and a female, and made you into nations and tribes, that you may know one another. (Surah 49:13)
>
> Your Lord has commanded that you worship none but Him and that you be kind to your parents. If one of them or both of them reach old age with you, do not say to them a word of disrespect… and act humbly to them in mercy. (Surah 17:23–24)

These quotes show the importance of the family, as well as the importance of caring for your parents.

1 Procreation

A key purpose of marriage for Muslims is having children and starting a family.

The purpose of family in Islam

2 Stability and the protection of children

Muslims believe family life is the foundation of society and provides a secure, healthy and nurturing environment, both for parents and growing children. Parents have complementary roles: the father provides for and protects the family; the mother runs the home and cares for the children.

4 Caring for the elderly

Muslims believe the elderly in society and in the ummah deserve special respect and attention – they should be treated with dignity. They consider it a privilege and a duty to care for elderly family members. This is why Muslims often live in extended families.

3 Educating children

Muslims believe that within a family, children can be raised as good Muslims. Parents must teach their children right from wrong and care for them physically and emotionally, so that they grow into self-disciplined and independent adults. The mother teaches the children about Islam and the father takes them to the mosque. Children pray with their family and attend (Islamic school) to learn Arabic, study Islam and read the Qur'an.

Muslims often live in extended families.

Divergent Muslim responses

Traditional Muslim families are often extended, enabling them to care for both young and old. However, today some Muslims live in nuclear families because:

- issues such as **migration** make it impossible to keep everyone together

- Muslims in Western countries become used to the nuclear family as normal.

Many Muslims recognise other types of family, but prefer more traditional family structures.

Consider the purposes of family. What arguments can you use to agree or disagree with the statement?

Now try this

'The most important purpose of family is to educate children within a faith.' Evaluate this statement. In your answer you:

- should give reasoned arguments in support of this statement
- should give reasoned arguments to support a different point of view
- should refer to religious arguments
- may refer to non-religious arguments
- should reach a justified conclusion.

(12 marks plus 3 SPaG marks)

Contemporary issues

Some aspects of family life that once seemed to contradict traditional Christian teachings are now acceptable. Many women work, and men play a role in caring for children. Issues that may challenge Christians today are same-sex parenting, polygamy and gender equality.

Christian teachings on same-sex parents

> Children, obey your parents in the Lord. (Ephesians 6:1)
>
> Children, obey your parents in everything, for this pleases the Lord. (Colossians 3:20)

These Bible quotes do not state the gender of parents, so could apply to parents of the opposite sex or the same sex.

> Honour your father and your mother, so that you may live long in the land the Lord your God is giving you. (Exodus 20:12)
>
> Listen to your father, who gave you life, and do not despise your mother when she is old. (Proverbs 23:22)

Some Christians use Bible teaching which refer to the roles of mother and father to suggest that same-sex parenting is not what God intended.

Christian views on polygamy

Christians do not accept **polygamy** – the practice of having more than one husband or wife at the same time, which is against the law in the UK. Rather, Christians accept **monogamy** – married to one person at a time only.

Christians believe that marriage is a sacred union made before God, which God intends to be exclusive between one man and one woman.

> At the beginning of Creation God 'made them male and female'. For this reason a man will leave his father and mother and be united to his wife, and the two will become one flesh. So they are no longer two, but one flesh. Therefore what God has joined together, let no one separate. (Mark 10:6–9)

This quote shows the intention in Christianity for monogamy.

---

② Some parts of the Bible suggest that God made woman as a 'helpmate' for man. A literal interpretation could be that men are the head of the household with women looking after the home and children. Another interpretation is that men and women are intended to work together alongside each other equally.

> It is not good for the man to be alone; I will make a helper suitable for him. (Genesis 2:18)
>
> Then the Lord God made a woman from the rib he had taken out of the man, and he brought her to the man. (Genesis 2:22)

③ Many Christians today may feel that a traditional understanding of men as providers and women as carers is outdated.

Roles of men and women

④ Catholics accept men and women were created in the image of God but were given different roles: man was created physically different to work the land; while woman was designed to assist him. Yet, they are seen to have complementary roles.

⑤ Other Christians today may argue that men and women are equal and either can provide or take care of the home and children.

⑥ Many denominations in Christianity allow men and women to hold positions of authority. However, there still exists inequality in Christianity. For example, in the Catholic Church, women cannot be ordained as priests or elected pope.

 Men and women were both made in the image of God. God made humans to be different from all other creations.

Non-religious beliefs

Humanists and atheists are likely to accept more modern interpretations of the roles of men and women. They believe in the equality of men and women and support their roles as long as they are happy in them.

Now try this

Give **two** religious beliefs about the roles of men and women being equal.   **(2 marks)**

Contemporary issues

As society changes, Muslims may struggle to adapt to contemporary family issues, due to their respect for traditional Islamic teachings.

Same-sex parents

Family holds great importance in Islam – Muslims believe it is the foundation of stability in society. They support traditional views about a family being a man, his wife and their children.

> O mankind! We have created you from a male and a female, and made you into nations and tribes, that you may know one another. (Surah 49:13)

This quote supports the idea of a family being a man, his wife and their children.

Polygamy

Islam accepts polygamy, as the Qur'an says Muslim men are allowed to marry up to four wives, provided the husband can take care of all of them and each wife agrees to it.

> Then marry those that please you of [other] women, two or three or four. But if you fear that you will not be just, then [marry only] one… That is more suitable that you may not incline [to injustice]. (Surah 4:3)

However, Muslim women are only allowed to have one husband, as Muslims believe that it is crucial that Muslim children know who their father is.

Polygamy is against the law in the UK.

Roles of men and women

Men	Women
• Are seen as the 'protectors' of women • Must provide for their family • Must help to raise children as good Muslims.	• Are required to have children • Must help raise children as good Muslims • Are expected to look after the home • Can work and have a career if they wish.

> The righteous among the women of Quraish are those who are kind to their young ones and who look after their husband's property. (Sahih al-Bukhari 64:278)

Worship

- Men are expected to attend the mosque for the Jummah (Friday) service; women do not have to attend, as they have responsibilities at home.
- Men and women are separated in the mosque for prayer – men using the prayer hall, while women use a separate room.
- Only men can be imams and hold positions of authority in Islam.

Divergent Muslim beliefs

> O mankind! Be careful of your duty to your Lord Who created you from a single soul and from it created its mate and from them twain hath spread abroad a multitude of men and women. (Surah 4:1)
>
> All people are equal … as the teeth of a comb. (Hadith)

The first quote suggests men and women were created equally from one soul, while the second suggests equality between men and women.

> Men are in charge of women by … So righteous women are devoutly obedient … But those [wives] from whom you fear arrogance – [first] advise them; [then if they persist], forsake them in bed; and [finally], strike them. But if they obey you [once more], seek no means against them. Indeed, Allah is ever Exalted and Grand. (Surah 4:34)

The Qur'an, however, also contains quotes that suggest inequality.

Now try this

'The roles of men and women are not equal.'
Evaluate this statement. In your answer you:

- should give reasoned arguments in support of this statement
- should give reasoned arguments to support a different point of view
- should refer to religious arguments
- may refer to non-religious arguments
- should reach a justified conclusion.

(12 marks plus 3 SPaG marks)

Even within the religion of Islam, Muslims may hold different views on this statement. You can include Muslim views as well as views from other religions and non-religious arguments.

Gender prejudice and discrimination

While Christian teachings state that equality between males and females is very important, there have been examples where gender equality was not fully encouraged. This includes where men have traditionally been given higher status than women, for example in roles of authority within the Church.

Definitions

✓ **Gender prejudice** is when a person is judged to be superior or inferior, based on their gender.

✓ **Gender discrimination**, also known as sexism, is when a person is treated differently from another person as a direct result of their gender. This could be positive (in their favour) or negative (against them).

Libby Lane was made the Church of England's first female bishop in 2015.

Gender discrimination in the Church

Catholic Christians only allow men to hold the positions of bishop, priest, deacon and pope. They believe that these roles represent Jesus, who was male, and follow the teaching in the Catechism of the Catholic Church which states that only a baptised man can hold these positions.

Bible teachings

There is neither Jew nor Gentile, neither slave nor free, nor is there male and female, for you are all one in Christ Jesus (Galatians 3:28)

This verse states that all humans – male and female – are equal before God. Yet gender inequality still exists in the world.

Promoting gender equality

Many Christian organisations promote gender equality, including Christian Aid and Tearfund, which believe gender inequality goes against issues of human rights. They work in partnership with communities to try to tackle inequality. They use Christian teachings such as those of stewardship and all people being cared for to support their views.

Non-religious attitudes

Atheists and humanists are likely to share the view that men and women are equal, although for different reasons. They may argue that it is a matter of principle that all people are seen to be of equal value and worth. They may argue that everyone, of whatever gender, should be given the same opportunities.

Christians would respond to these views by arguing that it goes beyond simply being a matter of equality that men and women are the same, but that it is a teaching from God (as in Galatians 3).

Now try this

Which **one** of the following means for a person to be treated differently to another person because of their gender?

A gender prejudice ☐
B gender discrimination ☐
C gender equality ☐
D gender procreation ☐ **(1 mark)**

Gender prejudice and discrimination

Prejudice and discrimination

Gender prejudice (or **sexism**) is when a person is judged on their gender to be superior or inferior. It is an opinion or judgement being made, not an action.

Gender discrimination is when a person is treated differently from another as a direct result of their gender. It is an action rather than just an opinion.

Muslim attitudes

Muslims believe gender prejudice and discrimination are wrong because:

1 Islam teaches everyone was created by Allah and is therefore equal

2 Muslims believe men and women will be treated equally and judged in the same way by Allah after death

3 men and women are both expected to marry and they have the same rights in terms of religion and education.

However, although Muslims accept men and women are equal before Allah, they believe that men and women are physically and psychologically different and suited to different roles and responsibilities.

Teachings about gender prejudice and discrimination

For Muslim men and women – for believing men and women, for devout men and women, for true men and women, for men and women who are patient and constant, for men and women who humble themselves, for men and women who give in Charity, for men and women who fast (and deny themselves), for men and women who guard their chastity, and for men and women who engage much in Allah's praise – for them has Allah prepared forgiveness and great reward. (Surah 33:35)

This quote supports the idea of gender prejudice and discrimination being wrong because all people – male and female – have the same opportunities and abilities to be rewarded.

Malala Yousafzai stood up to the Taliban to achieve equality in education.

Inspirational Muslims, such as Nadiya Hussain, who won 'The Great British Bake Off' competition, have raised the importance of gender equality in promoting that all people can achieve.

Sisters in Islam works to empower women with a voice to oppose mistreatment and gender discrimination through challenging laws that appear to make women inferior, including: polygamy; child marriage; dress in Islam; and violence against women.

Gender equality in action

The Inclusive Mosque Initiative campaigns for more equality when praying in mosques.

Expectations about the traditional role of women in Islam may appear to reflect gender discrimination. In some Islamic countries, women:
- must wear the hijab (headscarf) or burqa (full dress covering)
- are not allowed to be educated
- are unable to vote, drive or go out unsupervised.

Now try this

Give **two** religious beliefs that show gender discrimination is wrong. **(2 marks)**

Christianity
Islam

Theme A

Components
2A and 2B

Had a look ☐   Nearly there ☐   Nailed it! ☐

Relationships and families: Contrasting beliefs

A requirement of one type of examination question is to explain two contrasting or similar religious beliefs about three possible topics – for Theme A, these topics are contraception, sexual relationships before marriage and homosexual relationships. The question may ask you to refer to the main religious tradition in Britain, which is Christianity, plus one or more religious traditions, or you may be required to give two contrasting beliefs from two religious traditions. This page helps you to compare and contrast these beliefs.

Christian beliefs about contraception

- **Catholics** believe artificial methods of contraception are wrong as they prevent the main purpose of sex, which is to have children.

- **Catholics** believe natural forms of contraception such as the rhythm method are more acceptable, as they still allow for procreation.

- Some **Protestants** agree with using contraception because sex is for pleasure as well as conception. Also, contraception is sensible for family planning.

- Some **Protestants** believe using artificial methods of contraception does not go against God's teachings.

Islamic beliefs about contraception

- Some Muslims accept the use of contraception if it is used to protect and preserve the life of the mother and current children.

- Some Muslims accept the use of non-permanent methods of contraception as sensible for family planning, if it means a couple can still have children in the future.

- Some Muslims will not accept artificial contraception as they believe only natural forms are allowed. This view is supported by Muslim sources of authority such as in the Hadith Sahih al-Bukhari.

- Some Muslims believe contraception is wrong because it goes against Allah's intention that married couples have children.

Beliefs about sexual relationships before marriage

Christians believe sex before marriage is wrong, as this was the teaching of St Paul (which is recorded in the Bible).

Some Christians take a vow of chastity before marriage, to show that they believe sexual relationships should be saved until after marriage.

Christianity

Some modern Christians may accept a sexual relationship as a form of commitment for a couple in a long-term relationship, provided that they intend to marry in the future.

Christianity teaches the purpose of marriage is to have children, and that sexual relationships before marriage do not provide a stable basis for bringing children into the world.

Muslims view sex before marriage as always wrong, as sex is a gift from Allah that should be saved for a committed married relationship.

Islam

Muslims believe the Qur'an teaches that they should save themselves for a sexual relationship until after marriage. Muslims will often take a vow not to have sex until after marriage.

Muslims believe Allah will reward them for not having a sexual relationship until after marriage, as they believe this is how Allah intended couples to live.

Christianity
Islam

Theme A

Components
2A and 2B

Relationships and families: Contrasting beliefs

This page helps you to compare and contrast Christian and Islamic beliefs about relationships and families.

Beliefs about homosexual relationships

Christian beliefs	Islamic beliefs
Many Christians oppose homosexual relationships because they believe they are not what God intended – the Bible teaches that marriage should be between one man and one woman.	In Islam, homosexual relationships are forbidden. Muslims believe that the purpose of a sexual relationship is to have children, and homosexual couples cannot do this naturally.
Many Christians believe that couples in homosexual relationships cannot have children naturally, and so this means it is not what God intended.	Muslims follow teachings from the Qur'an that emphasise that Allah rewards heterosexual relationships – this suggests homosexual relationships are wrong.
Some Christians believe homosexual relationships are acceptable as all humans were created in the image of God to be special and all forms of love should be celebrated.	Some Muslim countries and states believe homosexuality is always wrong and should receive the harshest punishments, which may include the death penalty.
Some Christians use teachings from the Bible about respecting everyone to show that all relationships are acceptable, including homosexual relationships.	Some modern Muslims offer support to homosexual Muslims, and may look to scientific evidence that suggests homosexuality is not a choice but is innate (something you are born with).

Worked example

Explain **two** contrasting beliefs in contemporary British society about sexual relationships before marriage.

In your answer you should refer to the main religious tradition of Great Britain and one or more other religious traditions.   **(4 marks)**

Some modern Christians may accept that if a couple are in a committed and long-term relationship, they can have a sexual relationship to show commitment, as long as they intend to marry in the future.

Muslims do not accept sexual relationships before marriage. Rather, they believe you should remain pure, as they believe sex is a gift from Allah that should be saved for a married couple.

This answer successfully gives a detailed view from Christianity and a detailed contrasting view from Islam. The information given is accurate and appropriate to the question asked.

Now try this

1 Explain **two** contrasting religious beliefs about homosexual relationships.

   In your answer you must refer to one or more religious traditions.   **(4 marks)**

2 Explain **two** contrasting beliefs in contemporary British society about married couples using contraception.

   In your answer you must refer to the main religious tradition of Great Britain and one or more other religious traditions.   **(4 marks)**

For contrasting beliefs, you can give **two different religions**, for example the main religion of Great Britain, which is Christianity, and then offer a contrasting belief from another religion, such as Islam. Alternatively, you can offer **two contrasting views from within Christianity** – so for example, a Catholic and a Protestant view.

Origins of the universe

Christian accounts of Creation are found in the Bible in Genesis 1 and 2. Christians believe that God created the universe, but they may interpret the biblical accounts of Creation in different ways. The main scientific explanation is the Big Bang theory.

The Christian Creation story

Day 1

And God said, 'Let there be light', and there was light. God saw that the light was good, and he separated the light from the darkness. God called the light 'day', and the darkness he called 'night'. (Genesis 1:3–5)

Day 2

So God made the vault and separated the water under the vault from the water above it. And it was so. God called the vault 'sky'. (Genesis 1:7–8)

Day 3

And God said, 'Let the water under the sky be gathered to one place, and let dry ground appear.' (Genesis 1:9)

Day 4

And God said, 'Let there be lights in the vault of the sky to separate the day from the night, and let them serve as signs to mark sacred times, and days and years, and let them be lights in the vault of the sky to give light on the earth.' (Genesis 1:14–15)

Day 7

God saw all that he had made, and it was very good. (Genesis 1:31)

Day 6

God made the wild animals according to their kinds …
Then God said, 'Let us make mankind in our image, in our likeness, so that they may rule over the fish in the sea and the birds in the sky, over the livestock and all the wild animals, and over all the creatures that move along the ground.' (Genesis 1:25 and 26)

Day 5

So God created the great creatures of the sea and every living thing with which the water teems and that moves about in it, according to their kinds, and every winged bird according to its kind. (Genesis 1:21)

The Big Bang theory

- The scientific Big Bang theory is the belief that an enormous explosion started the universe around 14 billion years ago. It suggests that all matter was concentrated into a great mass, which then began to expand to form the universe.

- Georges Lemaître is thought to be the first person to write about this idea, in 1927. He proposed the theory of the expansion of the universe, which was later called the Big Bang theory.

- The expansion that started with the Big Bang is thought to continue even today.

Christian responses to scientific explanations

Christians believe the story of Creation found in Genesis, the first book of the Bible. They believe the world is a gift from God, created over six days with the seventh day being a day of rest.

Fundamental Christians **reject scientific theories** of Creation, instead believing that the Creation story in the Bible is true in all detail. Where there is conflict between religion and science, they believe science is wrong.

Liberal Christians believe that there is **no conflict** between science and religion. They believe the Big Bang did cause the universe to exist and evolution is correct, but that the Big Bang and evolution are part of God's plan.

See page 4 for more on the differences between fundamental and liberal Christians.

Now try this

Which **one** of the following is the theory that an explosion started the world around 14 billion years ago?

A evolution ☐
B Creation ☐
C Big Bang ☐
D stewardship ☐   **(1 mark)**

Origins of the universe

The Islamic account of Creation is found in the Qur'an. The main scientific explanation for the origin of the universe is the Big Bang theory. Muslims respond to this theory in different ways.

The Qur'an

Allah is the Creator of all things, and He is, over all things, Disposer of affairs. (Surah 39:62)

This quote reinforces the belief that Allah is the creator of the universe and everything originates from him. This is important as it shows Allah as the one true God.

Indeed, your Lord is Allah, who created the heavens and earth in six days and then established Himself above the Throne. He covers the night with the day, [another night] chasing it rapidly; and [He created] the sun, the moon, and the stars, subjected by His command. Unquestionably, His is the creation and the command; blessed is Allah, Lord of the worlds. (Surah 7:54)

This quote gives further detail about the origin of the universe – establishing six periods of time and giving details of some of Allah's creations, including night and day, the sun, moon and stars.

Muslims beliefs about Creation

1. Muslims believe Allah created the universe and everything within it.

2. The Qur'an talks of the universe being created in six 'days'.

3. No information is given about the order in which things were created.

4. Angels hold an important role within Islam and are mentioned in the Qur'an as part of Allah's creation of the universe. Turn to page 22 for more on the importance of angels within Islam.

Different interpretations

- Some Muslims take a **literal** interpretation of the Muslim account of Creation. They accept what is said in the Qur'an as the literal truth – so anything that is not mentioned in the Qur'an did not happen. They believe Allah planned Creation and created everything in the universe.

- Some Muslims accept that Allah created the universe and everything within it, but also accept more modern interpretations of Creation such as the inclusion of science.

Muslim responses to scientific explanations

Most Muslims believe science does not affect their beliefs in Allah's creation of the universe because:

- the explanation of the Big Bang helps to fill in gaps for what is not explained in the Qur'an

- they believe scientific explanations give them a better understanding of Allah and his creation.

They believe the Qur'an has an account of the creation of the universe similar to that offered by science.

And the heaven We constructed with strength, and indeed, We are [its] expander. (Surah 51:47)

However, some Muslims may view the Big Bang theory as contradicting the Islamic Creation story, as it appears to question whether a loving God planned the creation of the universe. See page 54 for an explanation of the Big Bang theory.

Blessed is He in whose hand is dominion, and He is over all things competent – [He] who created death and life to test you [as to] which of you is best in deed – and He is the Exalted in Might, the Forgiving – [And] who created seven heavens in layers. You do not see in the creation of the Most Merciful any inconsistency. So return [your] vision [to the sky]; do you see any breaks? Then return [your] vision twice again. [Your] vision will return to you humbled while it is fatigued. And We have certainly beautified the nearest heaven with stars and have made [from] them what is thrown at the devils and have prepared for them the punishment of the Blaze. (Surah 67:1–5)

The Qur'an is the source for beliefs about the universe.

Now try this

1. Give **two** religious beliefs about scientific views of the origin of the universe.   **(2 marks)**

2. Explain **two** beliefs about the origins of the universe. Refer to sacred writings or another source of religious belief and teaching in your answer.   **(5 marks)**

The value of the world

Christians believe that God created the universe, so everything in it – including the Earth – is sacred. Christians believe they have a duty to protect the world as God's creation. The Bible teaches ideas of stewardship, dominion, responsibility, awe and wonder in relation to the Earth.

1 Stewardship

Christians believe God gave humans the responsibility of stewardship – of acting as 'caretakers' for the Earth, which is part of his sacred creation. Christians believe they must look after the world to protect it for future generations.

> I believe in one God, the Father, the almighty, maker of heaven and earth. (Apostles Creed)
>
> The earth is the Lord's, and everything in it, the world, and all who live in it. (Psalm 24:1)

2 Dominion

The Book of Genesis states that God made humans to be superior to everything else in his creation. He gave them dominion (power over) the Earth. This can be interpreted in two ways:

- God gave the world to humans, so they are in control of it and can do what they like with it.
- God gave the world to humans for them to use responsibly in line with God's will.

> Then God said, 'Let us make mankind in our image, in our likeness, so that they may rule over the fish in the sea and the birds in the sky, over the livestock and all the wild animals, and over all the creatures that move along the ground.' (Genesis 1:26)
>
> God blessed them and said to them, 'Be fruitful and increase in number; fill the earth and subdue it. Rule over the fish in the sea and the birds in the sky and over every living creature that moves on the ground.' (Genesis 1:28)

The phrase 'rule over' supports the idea of humanity having dominion (power or authority) over the Earth and suggests its superiority.

4 Awe and wonder

Christians believe God's creation of the world and universe is amazing – it inspires awe and wonder in them. This awe at God's creation reinforces the God-given responsibility they have to take care of it and maintain it as he intended. They view the Earth as a gift from God that they should value.

> When I consider your heavens, the work of your fingers, the moon and the stars, which you have set in place, what is mankind that you are mindful of them, human beings that you care for them? (Psalm 8:3–4)

Protecting God's world

3 Responsibility

Christians believe that ideas of stewardship and dominion contained in the Bible show that God intended humans to be responsible for caring for his creation. They accept that the world is valuable and should be looked after for future generations.

> Do to others as you would have them do to you. (Luke 6:31)
>
> The Lord God took the man and put him in the Garden of Eden to work it and take care of it. (Genesis 2:15)

This quote suggests that God created humanity to take care of his creation.

Worked example

Which **one** of the following describes the duty Christians have to care for the world for future generations?

A stewardship ☐   B dominion ☐
C awe ☐   D evolution ☐   **(1 mark)**

A stewardship

The student has correctly identified the answer from those given. Remember, for multiple-choice questions you are not required to explain the answer; you only need to identify the correct one.

Now try this

Give **two** religious beliefs about the duty of humans to protect the world.   **(2 marks)**

This question tests your recall of knowledge – you need to state **two** pieces of accurate information, each in a short sentence. These can be from the same religion or from different religions.

The value of the world

Muslims believe that the world is special because Allah created it. They feel they have a duty to care for Allah's creation, as it does not belong to them.

Awe and wonder

For Muslims, Allah's creation of the universe inspires awe and wonder in them.

Muslims accept teachings that Allah gave the world to humans as a gift, which is why they should protect it.

> And it is He who spread the earth and placed therein firmly set mountains and rivers; and from all of the fruits He made therein two mates; He causes the night to cover the day. Indeed in that are signs for a people who give thought. (Surah 13:3)

This quote shows Allah's power in creating the universe. Amazement at Allah's creation inspires Muslims to worship Allah and provides them with a sense of duty to care for his creation.

Responsibility

Muslims believe Allah has given the world to humanity as a gift, but that it ultimately belongs to Allah and they have a responsibility or duty to care for it.

> And to Him belongs whoever is in the heavens and earth. All are to Him devoutly obedient. (Surah 30:26)

Dominion

Muslims believe humans were made different to all other parts of Allah's creation, as they were given responsibilities and duties to care for the world and for each other. This is the idea of **dominion** – to have power over what Allah created for them. Muslims believe they have a responsibility to use this power over Allah's creation wisely and responsibly, meaning they should take care of it and not exploit this precious resource.

> It is He who has made you successors upon the earth. (Surah 35:39)

This quote reinforces the idea of Allah giving humanity dominion over the Earth.

Khalifah (stewardship)

- The Qur'an is clear that Allah is the creator of the world and humans are on Earth as trustees or vicegerents (representatives of Allah on Earth). This reinforces the view that the world does not belong to humans and they have a duty of stewardship to care for it.

- Muslims are understood to be **khalifahs**, which is the Arabic term for being a steward or deputy, who has a responsibility to care for the universe.

> The Earth is green and beautiful, and Allah has appointed you his stewards over it. The whole Earth has been created a place of worship, pure and clean. Whoever plants a tree and diligently looks after it until it matures and bears fruit is rewarded. If a Muslim plants a tree or sows a field and humans and beasts and birds eat from it, all of it is love on his part. (Hadith)

Identify **two** relevant beliefs, then develop each one by giving more detail. You can answer from one religious tradition or you can refer to more than one. Make sure you link the points you develop to teachings from holy books such as the Qur'an or Bible.

Now try this

Explain **two** religious beliefs about stewardship.
Refer to sacred writings or another source of religious belief and teaching in your answer.   **(5 marks)**

The natural world

Threats in the world

The world today is being damaged by pollution, global warming and humanity's excessive use of natural resources. Many animal species are threatened with extinction, while the world's fast-growing human population is becoming unsustainable.

Christian responses

Christians believe they should care for the world and not waste its resources because:

- the Bible teaches that humans were put on Earth with a duty to care for it
- Christians see the world as a sacred gift from God
- Christianity teaches that humans will be judged after death on how they treated the Earth
- God gave humans the responsibility of stewardship of the Earth – caring for it for future generations.

Actions to help the environment

✓ Do not buy food that damages the environment, for example palm oil, fish from depleted fish stocks.

✓ Use renewable power, not fossil fuels.

✓ Recycle, for example glass and cardboard.

✓ Keep pollution to a minimum.

✓ Pray for the strength to care for the environment.

✓ Support environmental campaigns such as fair trade.

✓ Use church collections for environmental projects.

✓ Support environmental charities such as Christian Aid.

Use of animals for food

Christians tend to agree that it is acceptable to eat animals and use their produce for food, as the Bible says God gave animals to humans for this purpose and he also gave humans dominion over animals.

> Every moving thing that lives shall be food for you. And as I gave you the green plants, I give you everything. (Genesis 9:3)

Animal experimentation

Animal experimentation is when medicines, chemical products and make-up are tested on animals to determine if they are safe for use. Christians consider ideas of stewardship and dominion when considering this issue. See page 56 more information on stewardship and dominion.

> Every human act of irresponsibility towards creatures is an abomination. (Christian Declaration on Nature – Assisi, 1986, an interfaith meeting to discuss ways of saving the natural world)

Christians are expected to make their own judgements in relation to Christian teachings.

> Are not two sparrows sold for a penny? Yet not one of them will fall to the ground outside your Father's care. (Matthew 10:29)

Arguments in support of animal experimentation:

- May be acceptable if used to save human life or further human knowledge for advances in medical treatment, as the Bible states humans are superior to animals.
- Animals used in experiments should be treated humanely (suffering kept to a minimum) as they are part of God's creation and humans have a duty to care for them.

Arguments against animal experimentation:

- Cosmetic testing is not supported, as cosmetics are not essential to life.
- Animals should not be used in experiments if there is an appropriate alternative.

This suggests all animals are important, as they are part of God's creation and he cares for them.

Now try this

Explain **two** contrasting religious beliefs about the use of animal experimentation.
In your answer, you must refer to one or more religious traditions.

(4 marks)

The natural world

The world is being damaged by humans through pollution, deforestation and use of fossil fuels.

Eat and drink from the provision of Allah, and do not commit abuse on the earth, spreading corruption. (Surah 2:60)

Muslim responses

✓ Allah created the world and humans are its trustees.

✓ Muslims have been given a duty by Allah to be khalifahs – stewards who care for the world.

✓ After death, Muslims will be called to answer for any ill-treatment of the planet.

✓ Allah created the world with love and Muslims should show respect by treating it in the same way.

How Muslims can care for the environment

✓ Reduce use of fossil fuels (coal, oil, gas).

✓ Use renewable energy.

✓ Do not waste the Earth's resources.

✓ Reduce pollution, for example by walking.

✓ Use environmentally friendly products.

✓ Help with local environmental projects.

✓ Support environmental organisations.

✓ Recycle.

✓ Pray to Allah for the strength to care for the environment.

Use of animals for food

• Allah created animals and gave them to humanity, so Muslims can eat meat.

It is Allah who made for you the grazing animals upon which you ride and some of them you eat. (Surah 40:79)

• Animals exist for the benefit of humans, but should be treated with respect and kindness.

• Meat should be killed according to **halal** rules, to cause the animals as little pain as possible.

• Some Muslims may choose to be vegetarian, believing that animals should not be eaten.

Animal experimentation

Muslims may support animal experimentation:

• when it can be used to save human lives or further human knowledge, because humanity is at the top of Allah's creation

• if the animal does not suffer unnecessarily, because Muslims have a duty to care for Allah's creation.

Some Muslims may be against animal experimentation because it can be painful, unnecessary and cruel, and Allah gave humanity the duty of being khalifahs.

And there is no creature on [or within] the earth or bird that flies with its wings except [that they are] communities like you. (Surah 6:38)

This shows that animals are important in Islam, as Allah created them.

It is Allah who made for you the grazing animals upon which you ride, and some of them you eat. And for you therein are [other] benefits and that you may realise upon them a need... (Surah 40:79–80)

This suggests that Allah created animals for Muslims to use as they are advantageous to humans.

Now try this

'Animal experimentation is acceptable.'

Evaluate this statement. In your answer you:

• should give reasoned arguments in support of this statement

• should give reasoned arguments to support a different point of view

• should refer to religious arguments

• may refer to non-religious arguments

• should reach a justified conclusion.

(12 marks plus 3 SPaG marks)

Origins of human life

Christians believe a key teaching in the Bible is that God created humans, although there are differing interpretations of this account. Christians have different responses to scientific explanations such as evolution and survival of the fittest.

The creation of Adam and Eve

> So God created mankind in his own image, in the image of God he created them; male and female he created them. (Genesis 1:27)

God made humans in his image – that is, they have his characteristics, including a soul. Christians believes this is what makes humans different from animals.

These quotes suggest God made Adam from the dust of the ground and breathed life into him. They show the role and responsibility God gave Adam, as well as how God made Eve out of Adam's rib to provide company and help for him.

> Then the Lord God formed a man from the dust of the ground and breathed into his nostrils the breath of life, and the man became a living being. (Genesis 2:7)
>
> The Lord God took the man and put him in the Garden of Eden to work it and take care of it. (Genesis 2:15)
>
> The Lord God said, 'It is not good for the man to be alone. I will make a helper suitable for him.' (Genesis 2:18)
>
> So the Lord God caused the man to fall into a deep sleep; and while he was sleeping, he took one of the man's ribs and then closed up the place with flesh. Then the Lord God made a woman from the rib he had taken out of the man, and he brought her to the man. The man said, 'This is now bone of my bones and flesh of my flesh; she shall be called "woman", for she was taken out of man.' (Genesis 2:21-23)

Christian interpretations of the origin of humans

Fundamentalist/Literalist Christians	Liberal or non-Literalist Christians
• Believe that the Bible, as the word of God, is literally true • Reject any scientific discoveries that contradict the Bible (for example, evolution) • Believe the biblical account of human origins shows the specialness of humanity	• Believe God created the universe and humans, but it did not happen exactly as the Bible says – the Bible account is more symbolic • Claim that God did make humans and made them the high point of his creation

The theory of evolution

- Based on Charles Darwin's theories that human life developed (**evolved**) through gradual changes over millions of years.

- 'Survival of the fittest': individuals within a species who are better adapted to the environment ('fitter') survive to pass on their genes to the next generation.

- Over time species evolve so only those individuals with the characteristics or features that are strongest survive.

Christian responses to evolution

 Some Christians feel the theory of evolution conflicts with the belief in God creating the universe. The theory could be used as evidence that God does not exist, as it suggests species evolved to their current forms by chance.

 Other Christians see no conflict between religion and science, viewing evolution as part of God's plan.

'Special Agenda IV Diocesan Synod' is a document that attempts to bring together ideas of evolution and traditional Christian teachings on Creation, to show they can work together.

Now try this

Give **two** religious responses to the theory of evolution. **(2 marks)**

Origins of human life

The Qur'an states that human life began when Allah created Adam from clay. Within Islam, there are different responses to scientific explanations about the origins of humans.

Creation of humans

> What is [the matter] with you that you do not attribute to Allah [due] grandeur while He has created you in stages? Do you not consider how Allah has created seven heavens in layers and made the moon therein a [reflected] light and made the sun a burning lamp? (Surah 71:13–16)

The Qur'an states that Allah planned and designed humans in stages and has a set purpose for them.

> Have those who disbelieved not considered that the heavens and the earth were a joined entity, and We separated them and made from water every living thing? Then will they not believe? (Surah 21:30)

This reinforces the view that Allah is the origin of human life.

Creation of Adam and Hawa (Eve)

Adam and Hawa appear in the Qur'an as the first man and woman.

Adam and Hawa

- Adam is believed to be the first Muslim and prophet in Islam. The Qur'an mentions Adam in many chapters, but no explicit detail is given about his creation, other than that he was created from dust or clay.

> Indeed, the example of Isa to Allah is like that of Adam. He created him from dust; then He said to him, 'Be', and he was. (Surah 3:59)

> Who perfected everything which He created and began the creation of man from clay. (Surah 32:7)

- Hawa is mentioned in the Qur'an as the wife of Adam, but little detail is given about her.

> And We said, 'O Adam, dwell, you and your wife, in Paradise.' (Surah 2:35)

The theory of evolution

In *On the Origin of the Species* (1859), Charles Darwin argued that:

- ✓ human life developed gradually (evolved) over millions of years, from simple to complicated life forms
- ✓ human characteristics or features that were strongest survived, while weaker ones died out and disappeared – natural selection
- ✓ 'survival of the fittest' means the species best suited to the environment survives.

Muslim responses to the theory of evolution

The majority of Muslims and other religious people, as well as non-religious people, in today's world hold that science offers more believable explanations for the origin of the world than religion. Therefore, it is important for religious believers such as Muslims to try to adapt their beliefs to be able to accept what both religion and science tell them.

Now try this

'It is possible to accept both evolution and religious beliefs about the origin of humans.'
Evaluate this statement. In your answer you:

- should give reasoned arguments in support of this statement
- should give reasoned arguments to support a different point of view
- should refer to religious arguments
- may refer to non-religious arguments
- should reach a justified conclusion.

(12 marks plus 3 SPaG marks)

Sanctity and quality of life

Christians view human life as holy because it is a gift from God – this is known as **sanctity of life**. Christians also believe that life must have a certain level of happiness and comfort – this is known as **quality of life**.

Why human life is holy

Passages in the Bible show that life is sacred.

> … your bodies are temples of the Holy Spirit…
> (1 Corinthians 6:19)
>
> You shall not murder. (Exodus 20:13)

Image of God

> So God created mankind in his own image, in the image of God he created them; male and female he created them.
> (Genesis 1:27)

The Bible teaches Christians that God made them 'in his image'. This refers not to how they look, but to the idea that humans are different from the rest of Creation – God breathed life into them in a special way.

Importance of sanctity of life today

The sanctity of life teaching is important to Christians today because:

* it will determine their **beliefs about issues** such as abortion and euthanasia
* they will **value human life** and this will impact on the way they live
* it will guide them when making **moral decisions** and determine how they treat others.

Human life is sacred.

Quality of life

If a person has a poor quality of life, they may feel more inclined to want their life to end.

> But who are you, a human being, to talk back to God? Shall what is formed say to the one who formed it, 'Why did you make me like this?' (Romans 9:20)

This suggests that God made all life with a given purpose, suggesting that all life – even when difficult – has quality.

Christian views on quality of life

Christians may argue that all life is valuable, and that a person's quality of life should not impact on this. They might point out that Christianity teaches that:

* suffering, pain and a poor quality of life do not stop life being valuable
* each person can face his or her struggles in life with the support of God
* all life is a gift from God – regardless of its quality – so all life is worthy of respect and protection.

Ethical arguments

When considering ideas about the sanctity and quality of life and applying them to the issue of abortion and euthanasia, there is a dilemma.

* Christians believe all life is sacred because God created it, so ethically it would be considered 'morally right' to do everything possible to preserve human life, therefore suggesting that abortion and euthanasia is always wrong.
* In contrast, the quality of life argument suggests that if a person (or potential person in the case of abortion) has a poor quality of life, it would be more compassionate to end this life. For example, if a foetus has the potential to be severely disabled, even though Christians accept all life is sacred, it may be ethically right to support an abortion in this situation.

Now try this

Explain **two** religious beliefs about the sanctity of life.
Refer to sacred writings or another source of religious belief and teaching in your answer.

(5 marks)

Sanctity and quality of life

Components 2A and 2B

Muslims believe that life is holy – a sacred gift from Allah.

Muslim views on sanctity of life

Sanctity of life is the belief that life is holy and special.

Muslims believe:

1. life is special and holy as all life is created by Allah

2. they should respect all life and not harm any living thing

3. that, as all life is holy, every human life is worth the same value as any other

4. that, as Allah is the creator of life, only he can take it away.

See page 65 for more information on abortion and euthanasia.

Because of that, We decreed upon the Children of Israel that whoever kills a soul unless for a soul or for corruption [done] in the land – it is as if he had slain mankind entirely. And whoever saves one – it is as if he had saved mankind entirely. And our messengers had certainly come to them with clear proofs. Then indeed many of them, [even] after that, throughout the land, were transgressors. (Surah 5:32)

This suggests that it is wrong to take a life away as it is holy. Preserving life and recognising that it is special benefits the whole of mankind.

O you who have believed, do not consume one another's wealth unjustly but only [in lawful] business by mutual consent. And do not kill yourselves [or one another]. Indeed, Allah is to you ever Merciful. (Surah 4:29)

Muslims will have views on issues such as abortion, euthanasia and murder that agree with their view that life is special and holy.

- -

Muslim views on quality of life

Muslims recognise that the quality of a person's life is important. However, they do not accept the ending of life under any circumstances. They believe:

1. life is sacred, as Allah created it

2. Allah chooses how long each life lasts – only he decides when a life can end

3. suffering is a test from Allah – a poorer quality of life is something to be faced up to, not given up on. Allah does not give a person more than they can cope with, so a poorer quality of life is not a reason to end life.

And do not kill the soul which Allah has forbidden, except by right. And whoever is killed unjustly – We have given his heir authority, but let him not exceed limits in [the matter of] taking life. Indeed, he has been supported [by the law]. (Surah 17:33)

And when their term has come, they will not remain behind an hour, nor will they precede [it]. (Surah 16:61)

And it is not [possible] for one to die except by permission of Allah at a decree determined. (Surah 3:145)

These quotes teach Muslims that taking life (by suicide or euthanasia) is always wrong. They state that Allah sets a certain time for each life, so life should not be ended prematurely – only Allah can determine when it is the right time for a person to die.

- -

Now try this

Use the bullet points as a checklist to help you cover all aspects this question requires. You can include both Christian and Muslim arguments or just focus on one religion in your answer. You can also refer to non-religious arguments.

'Quality of life is more important than sanctity of life.'
Evaluate this statement. In your answer you:

- should give reasoned arguments in support of this statement
- should give reasoned arguments to support a different point of view
- should refer to religious arguments
- may refer to non-religious arguments
- should reach a justified conclusion.

(12 marks plus 3 SPaG marks)

Abortion and euthanasia

Christians may hold different views about **abortion** and **euthanasia**.

Abortion

Abortion is the deliberate termination (ending) of a human pregnancy so that a child is not born. Currently in the UK, it is legal to have an abortion up to 24 weeks of pregnancy with the consent of two doctors.

Pope Paul VI in 1968 issued the *Humanae Vitae*, which said abortion was wrong:

> … all direct abortion, even for therapeutic reasons, are to be absolutely excluded as lawful means of regulating the number of children. (*Humanae Vitae*)

However, in November 2016 Pope Francis declared that priests can forgive abortions.

Euthanasia

There are three types of euthanasia:

1. **voluntary euthanasia** – where a person's life is ended deliberately and painlessly at their request

2. **assisted suicide** – where a person is given the means to end their own life

3. **non-voluntary euthanasia** – ending a person's life when they are unable to ask, but there is good reason for thinking it is what they would want. For example, if a person is on life support and there is no medical chance of recovery.

Arguments against abortion and euthanasia	Arguments for abortion and euthanasia
Life is a sacred gift from God.	Jesus taught compassion towards others.
Life is believed to begin at conception.	We cannot be sure life begins at conception.
All life has value, despite illness or disability, and is part of God's plan.	In cases of rape or incest, abortion may be the kindest action.
God has a plan for every human.	A dying person should be able to choose.
Abortion and euthanasia are murder; the Bible tells us 'You shall not kill'.	Abortion is best if the mother's life is at risk. Abortion is the mother's right to choose. Euthanasia allows a person to die a gentle, pain-free death with dignity.
Examples in the Bible show that suffering may have a purpose: 'Shall we accept good from God, and not trouble?' (Job 2:10).	Insisting on suffering to continue when there is an alternative could be said to be cruel.
Hospices provide palliative care – relieving the symptoms of a condition a person is dying from – so euthanasia is not needed.	Euthanasia can save medical costs and relieve the burden of a suffering relative on the family and society generally.

Christians may differ in their responses to non-religious arguments, following the arguments above.

Some may argue using principles of **situation ethics** – each situation should be judged individually.

Christians believe all life is sacred. If the mother's life were at risk by having the child, some Christians would argue that her life takes prominence, as she is already alive. Other Christians may argue that abortion is always wrong and it is up to God to decide.

Now try this

Explain **two** religious beliefs about euthanasia being wrong.
Refer to sacred writings or another source of religious belief and teaching in your answer. **(5 marks)**

Abortion and euthanasia

Many Muslims do not agree with abortion, using the sanctity of life argument as evidence for their views. Muslims view euthanasia (assisted dying) as always wrong. They do accept turning off life support because Muslims do not see this as euthanasia.

Muslim responses to abortion

The issue of abortion divides Muslims.

- Some Muslims believe abortion is acceptable if the life of the mother is at risk, or in the case of rape, because it upholds the sanctity of the mother's life.

- Some Muslims believe that by allowing abortion, it offers a 'slippery slope' to allowing other actions (such as euthanasia).

- Some Muslims follow traditional teachings such as those on the sanctity of life, maintaining that life is holy as it was created by Allah and should never be taken away, even if a person is very ill.

Euthanasia

Indeed we belong to Allah, and indeed to Him we will return. (Surah 2:156)

The Qur'an teaches the sanctity of life, which is the idea that life has value and is holy as it was created by Allah.

Ensoulment

… every one of you is collected in the womb of his mother for the first forty days, and then he becomes a clot for another forty days, and then a piece of flesh for forty days. Then Allah sends an angel to write four words: He writes his deeds, time of his death, means of his livelihood, and whether he will be wretched or blessed (in religion). Then the soul is breathed into his body.' (Sahih al-Bukhari 55:549)

This passage describes the point 120 days after conception when the soul enters the body – this is called ensoulment. Sunni Muslims forbid abortion before and after this time.

Non-religious views

- The rights of the mother outweigh those of the child, as it is not a person until birth.

- Abortion is a personal decision – it is the woman's right to decide what is best.

- The kindest thing might be to let a person end their life, if it is what they want, especially if they have a terminal illness.

- Abortion and euthanasia are wrong, but not for religions reasons.

- Life is special, but abortion and euthanasia need to be there as options.

Muslim responses

- The Qur'an teaches 'do not kill your children for fear of poverty' (Surah 17:32).

- An unplanned pregnancy and worry about providing for a child are not acceptable reasons for abortion.

- Suffering is a part of life – it is not a person's decision to end their life; only Allah can decide this. Euthanasia is suicide.

- Alternatives to euthanasia include hospices.

Now try this

One of the views you give **must** be Christian. The second viewpoint could be a contrasting Christian view, or a view from another religion.

Explain **two** contrasting beliefs in contemporary British society about euthanasia.

In your answer, you should refer to the main religious tradition of Great Britain and one or more other religious traditions.

(4 marks)

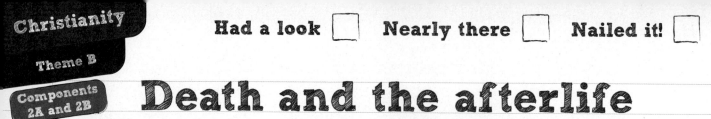

Death and the afterlife

Most Christians believe in the afterlife, accepting the existence of heaven and hell.

Christian beliefs about life after death

- The Bible and the Gospels talk of the death and resurrection of Jesus.

- Jesus taught Christians that there is an afterlife: 'My Father's house has many rooms; if that were not so, would I have told you that I am going there to prepare a place for you?' (John 14:2)

- Jesus taught that God sent him to Earth so that humanity may have eternal life in heaven.

And God raised us up with Christ and seated us with him in the heavenly realms in Christ Jesus. (Ephesians 2:6)

For God so loved the world, that he gave his one and only Son, that whoever believes in him shall not perish but have eternal life. (John 3:16)

I am the resurrection and the life. The one who believes in me will live, even though they die. (John 11:25)

Christians believe that Jesus' resurrection (that he rose again from death) shows there is life after death.

Non-religious arguments for life after death

Some non-religious people have reasons for believing in life after death.

Reason	Belief	Christian response
Remembered lives	People may believe they have flashback memories of previous lives, suggesting that death is not the end.	Christians believe that life after death is in heaven (or hell), so memories of previous lives are mistaken.
Paranormal events	Paranormal events are unexplained events with a spiritual cause, e.g. ghosts, which some people consider to be evidence of life after death.	Christians do not accept these as evidence of life after death as nothing in the Bible supports ideas of souls coming back to Earth after death.
Logic	Some may think it is logical there is an afterlife, to give life meaning.	Christians might respond that it is more than logic, as evidence is given in the Bible.
Reward	It makes sense to many people that there should be reward after death for living a good life on Earth – but this would not be with God.	Christians agree that good deeds may be rewarded in heaven, but that it is only through having faith in Jesus that they are reconciled with God. See page 8 on salvation.
Comfort	The idea of life after death can give people hope and make them less afraid of death.	Christians agree, but also believe they will be reunited with God in heaven.
Meeting loved ones who have passed on	Meeting loved ones who have died is a key reason people believe in the afterlife.	Views of heaven differ, but most Christians believe that they will be reunited with loved ones in heaven.

Impact on the value of human life

1. As a result of believing in an afterlife, Christians recognise life to have a purpose – to live as God intended so they can be rewarded after death.

2. Christians will want to make the most of their life on Earth, and try to live life as God intended, as they know this contributes to the quality of their afterlife.

3. Belief in the afterlife helps Christians cope with death – Christian teachings show them that death is not the end and that they will be comforted by their loved ones in the afterlife.

Now try this

Give **two** reasons why religious believers accept there is an afterlife.

(2 marks)

Death and the afterlife

Muslims believe in Akirah (life after death), accepting the existence of paradise and hell.

Muslim teachings

1 Allah has full control over life and death.

2 The world will end when Allah chooses and at this time people will face judgement.

3 Good deeds and bad deeds will be judged.

4 People will either be sent to al-Jannah as a reward for a good life or Jahannam for a bad life.

Barzakh is viewed as the barrier between the physical and spiritual worlds – it is where the soul waits after death before resurrection on Judgement Day.

The Qur'an, death and afterlife

And to every soul will be paid in full (the fruit) of its Deeds; and Allah knoweth best all that they do. (Surah 39:70)

This teaches that Allah is aware of every action and thought of humans.

… those who have believed and worked righteous deeds shall be made happy … those who have rejected faith and falsely denies our Signs … shall be brought forth to Punishment. (Surah 30:15–16)

This identifies the reward for those who deserve it and recognises that those who don't will be punished after death.

Impact on beliefs about the value of human life

It affects how I live. I am aware that Allah is watching me, so I try to make the most of my life.

I want to accept Allah's gift of life and achieve much before I die, as it will determine my afterlife.

The Qur'an teaches that life is a test and is precious, and death is the gateway to eternal life. I need to be prepared for being judged on the Day of Judgement.

Believing in Akhirah gives my life meaning and purpose, as I will live my life with the afterlife in mind.

2 Paranormal, e.g. ghosts and spirits
Muslims do not accept ideas of the paranormal.

3 Logically death cannot be the end
Muslims agree that having a reward or punishment after death and a belief in the afterlife gives life meaning and purpose.

Muslim responses to non-religious arguments for life after death

1 Memories of previous lives
Muslims recognise the afterlife, but Islam does not teach that people have had past lives.

4 Reward for living a good life
Muslims agree that those who have lived a good life deserve to be rewarded after death.

6 Meeting loved ones who have passed on
Meeting loved ones again is not of primary importance in Islam.

5 Makes people less afraid of death
Ideas of the afterlife give Muslims comfort.

Now try this

'Everyone should believe in the afterlife.'
Evaluate this statement. In your answer you:
- should give reasoned arguments in support of this statement
- should give reasoned arguments to support a different point of view
- should refer to religious arguments
- may refer to non-religious arguments
- should reach a justified conclusion.

(12 marks plus 3 SPaG marks)

Christianity
Islam

Theme B

Components
2A and 2B

Had a look ☐   Nearly there ☐   Nailed it! ☐

Religion and life: Contrasting beliefs

A requirement of one type of examination question is to explain two contrasting or similar religious beliefs about three possible topics – for Theme B these topics are abortion, euthanasia and animal experimentation. The question may ask you to refer to the main religious tradition in Britain, which is Christianity, plus one or more religious traditions, or you may be required to give two contrasting beliefs from two religious traditions. This page helps you to compare and contrast these beliefs.

Christian beliefs about abortion

- Some Christians do not support abortion because they believe life is sacred. The Bible teaches, 'Thou shalt not kill', which is a commandment from God.
- Some Christians believe life begins at conception and that all life has value and a purpose because it is God's gift.
- Other Christians may believe that in circumstances such as when the mother's life is at risk or in cases of rape, abortion may be 'the lesser of two evils' and therefore acceptable.
- Some Christians use the teachings of Jesus about compassion to argue that sometimes abortion may be the kindest action.

Islamic beliefs about abortion

- Many Muslims do not accept abortion as they believe in the sanctity of life – that all life is sacred as Allah created it.
- Many Muslims believe that life begins at ensoulment (when the soul enters the body 120 days after conception), so abortion prior to this time may be acceptable.
- Many Muslims believe that an unplanned pregnancy, worry about providing for a child or pregnancy as a result of adultery are not acceptable reasons for abortion.
- Some Muslims believe that if the life of the mother is at risk, abortion may be acceptable.

Beliefs about euthanasia

Many Christians are against euthanasia, as they believe all life is sacred (sanctity of life).

Some Christians argue that because hospices provide palliative care, euthanasia is not needed.

Christianity

Some Christians may view euthanasia as a kind action that allows a person to die a pain-free and dignified death, which shows compassion and care.

Christians believe euthanasia is against the Commandment 'Thou shalt not kill'.

Muslims believe that euthanasia is always wrong, as all life is sacred because Allah created it.

Muslims believe suffering is a test from Allah that should be endured; euthanasia should not be used as a way to avoid suffering.

Islam

Muslims believe that a hospice can offer palliative care to allow a person to die with dignity.

The Qur'an teaches that only Allah can decide when a life should end – a person does not have the right to end their own life, and doing so will not help them get to paradise after death.

Had a look ☐ Nearly there ☐ Nailed it! ☐

Christianity
Islam

Theme B

Components
2A and 2B

Religion and life: Contrasting beliefs

This page helps you to compare and contrast Christian and Islamic beliefs about **abortion**, **euthanasia** and **animal experimentation**.

Beliefs about animal experimentation

Christian beliefs	Islamic beliefs
Some Christian teachings suggest ideas of dominion (humans have power over animals), which means humans can do with them what they like, including experiment on them.	Muslims believe animals are important, as Allah created them, so they should not be used in animal experimentation.
The Bible teaches that only humans were made in the image of God, and many Christians believe this means humans can use animals in experiments if it contributes to saving human lives.	Some Muslims may support animal experimentation if it helps to save human lives, as Muslim teachings state that humans are at the top of Allah's creation.
Christians believe that unnecessary testing on animals is wrong – so they may not support cosmetic testing, which is for vanity and not medical purposes.	Many Muslims believe some animal testing – for example, cosmetic testing – is unnecessary, as it is not intended to help save lives, so would not support it.
Christians point to Bible teachings of stewardship, which suggest that humans have a duty from God to care for animals as part of God's creation.	Islam teaches that Muslims have the duties of being khalifahs (stewards). This means they should take care of Allah's creation, which includes animals.

Worked example

Explain **two** contrasting beliefs in contemporary British society about euthanasia.

In your answer, you should refer to the main religious tradition of Great Britain and one or more other religious traditions.

(4 marks)

Christians believe euthanasia is wrong, as they accept the sanctity of life argument that says all life is sacred as God created it.

Some Muslims may point to the existence of hospices, which are used to provide palliative care, to argue that this means people who are ill and dying can be made comfortable, so euthanasia is not needed in society today.

One of the views you give **must** be Christian. The second viewpoint could be another contrasting Christian view, or a view from another religion.

This student's answer gives a belief from Christianity and a belief from Islam. Although both argue that euthanasia is wrong, they give contrasting reasons to support their views.

Now try this

Make sure you identify **two** ways that are different and develop each one by giving further information or perhaps an example. Apply your knowledge using the information above to give contrasting views about why religious believers may support or be against the issue.

1 Explain **two** contrasting religious beliefs about abortion.
   In your answer you must refer to one or more religious traditions. **(4 marks)**

2 Explain **two** contrasting beliefs in contemporary British society about animals being used for medical experimentation.
   In your answer, you should refer to the main religious tradition of Great Britain and one or more other religious traditions. **(4 marks)**

The existence of God

The **Design** and **First Cause** arguments seek to show the existence of God.

The Design argument

William Paley (1743–1805) put forward a version of the Design argument:

- Imagine walking across a park and finding a stone – it belongs there, as it is natural and needs no further explanation.
- Now imagine finding a watch – in contrast to the stone it is clearly designed: it is complex, with many parts that work together for a set purpose.
- The watch is like the universe – they are both complex and require a designer to explain their existence.
- We can conclude that the universe is designed and therefore needs a designer – God.

Strengths of the argument:
– There is evidence of design in the world – plants and animals.
– Scientific theories of evolution could be part of the process.
Weaknesses of the argument:
– Evolution could happen without God – it could be due to chance.
– It can't be proved that God is the designer.
– Why did God design evil and suffering?

The First Cause argument

Thomas Aquinas (1225–74) put forward a version of the First Cause (cosmological) argument.

He argued that everything in the cosmos has a cause. You can track back through a chain of causes, but that chain cannot be infinite; there must have been a first cause – a **necessary being**. This is God, who does not rely on anything else for existence – he needs no explanation or cause.

Strengths of the argument:
– Evidence of cause and effect can be seen everywhere.
– God could have caused the Big Bang.
– Scientists agree that there is a first cause of the universe.
Weaknesses of the argument:
– It is impossible to prove God caused the universe.
– Why does God cause 'bad' things like earthquakes?
– What caused God?

The nature of God

Some Christians believe these arguments show that God is:

- omnipotent – all powerful, as he designed the world to suit human life
- omnipresent – all present, as he is found throughout his creation
- omnibenevolent – as he cared for his creation and took time to plan it
- unknowable in some ways – transcendent and too great for humans to understand.

For since the creation of the world God's invisible qualities – his eternal power and divine nature – have been clearly seen, being understood from what has been made ... (Romans 1:20)

This Bible passage suggests humans can never fully understand God, which supports the Design and First Cause arguments.

Now try this

1 Give **two** weaknesses of the Design argument for God's existence. **(2 marks)**

2 Give **two** characteristics of God shown by the First Cause argument. **(2 marks)**

The existence of God

The **Design** and **First Cause** arguments seek to show the existence of Allah.

The Design argument

| Design is the result of intelligent thought. | → | The universe shows evidence of being designed (e.g. gravity, ozone layer). | → | This suggests that a being with intelligence designed the universe. | → | The universe is too complex to have happened by chance or be designed by any being other than Allah. | → | Therefore, Allah exists. |

Existence of Allah

Muslims believe that the Design argument shows that Allah is omnipotent – all powerful. The fact that he was able to design the universe shows his power. Muslims also believe that Allah took time and care to plan and design the world to suit humans. This shows that he cares for his creation and is benevolent and omniscient.

The Qur'an and the Design argument

> Indeed, in the creation of the heavens and earth, and the alternation of the night and the day, and the [great] ships which sail through the sea with that which benefits people, and what Allah has sent down from the heavens of rain, giving life thereby to the earth after its lifelessness and dispersing therein every [kind of] moving creature, and [His] directing of the winds and the clouds controlled between the heaven and the earth are signs for a people who use reason. (Surah 2:164)

Muslims believe that the Qur'an offers good **philosophical proof** to suggest that Allah exists, and evidence that he designed the world can be seen all around.

The First Cause (cosmological) argument

| Nothing happens by itself. | → | Everything that happens must be **caused** by something else. | → | The universe cannot have caused itself. | → | A **powerful** cause was necessary to cause the universe. | → | This cause has to be Allah. | → | Therefore, Allah exists. |

The First Cause argument and its use in Islam

The argument was first put forward in the 12th century in 'the kalam', written by Abu Hamid Al-Ghazali in his book *Kitab al-Iqtisad fi'l I'tiqad*. Al-Ghazali argued:

| Whatever begins to exist has a cause. | → | The universe began to exist. | → | Therefore, the universe has a cause. |

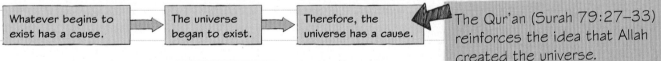 The Qur'an (Surah 79:27–33) reinforces the idea that Allah created the universe.

The nature of God

Muslims believe that the Design and First Cause arguments:

- ✓ show Allah's omnipotence in being able to create the universe
- ✓ show Allah's omniscience in being able to see everything he created.
- ✓ show Allah caused the universe to exist.
- ✓ show Allah is benevolent and cares for his creation.
- ✓ reinforce the teachings in the Qur'an about the creation of the universe.
- ✓ support the beliefs held about what Allah is like.

Now try this

'The Design argument successfully proves the existence of God.'
Evaluate this statement. In your answer you:
- should give reasoned arguments in support of this statement
- should give reasoned arguments to support a different point of view
- should refer to religious arguments
- may refer to non-religious arguments
- should reach a justified conclusion.
(12 marks plus 3 SPaG marks)

Miracles

Miracles are amazing events that science cannot explain. Christians may use the argument that miracles prove God's existence, believing there is no other explanation.

Importance of miracles to Christians

Christians believe that miracles:

- prove the existence of God as a greater being who is involved with and acting in the world
- show God cares for his creation
- show he wants to be involved in the world
- provide people with the comfort that God is close.

> 'Unless you people see signs and wonders,' Jesus told him, 'you will never believe.' (John 4:48)

Christians believe that, although they have faith in God, signs in the world that confirm his presence help to strengthen their faith.

Jesus walking on water

Examples of miracles

1 **Healing miracles** – there are reports of healing miracles happening in religious places, such as holy cities in Israel.

2 **The miracles of Jesus** – in the Bible, Jesus performs many miracles, such as walking on water, turning water into wine and feeding a large crowd of people. These are often called 'nature miracles'. Jesus also healed people and brought people back from the dead.

3 **Resurrection of Jesus** – it is considered a miracle that Jesus was crucified on the cross and then three days later came back to life.

4 **Modern-day miracles** – there are examples of events in today's world that many would consider 'miraculous'. For example, people surviving a fall 10,000 metres from a plane, or surviving hours alone in a cold sea, or recovering unexpectedly from an 'incurable' illness.

Strengths and weaknesses of the arguments from miracles

Strengths	Weaknesses
👍 People are amazed by what has happened and cannot explain it any other way (e.g. by science). This reflects the nature of God – who cannot be explained either.	👎 There could be other scientific explanations that require no mention of God.
👍 Miracles are evidence of a personal God acting within the world.	👎 It could be a misinterpretation of a natural event.
👍 Miracles are proof of God's existence and his love for the world. The power of God is shown through scientific laws being broken.	👎 A person could be mistaken, for example the 'miracle' could be the result of a medical cause, hallucinating or taking drugs.
	👎 Two people could experience a miracle and yet interpret it differently, so there is uncertainty and no proof it was real.

Now try this

1 Which **one** of the following is described as an amazing event that the laws of science and nature cannot explain?

   A divine ☐   **B** miracle ☐   C revelation ☐   D design ☐   **(1 mark)**

2 Give **two** reasons why miracles prove the existence of God.   **(2 marks)**

> State **two** strengths – each in an individual sentence.

Miracles

For Muslims, miracles prove Allah exists and is all powerful within the world.

Importance of miracles for Muslims

Miracles are important because:

- they suggest a greater being, such as Allah, who is involved and acting within the world
- the Qur'an makes it clear Allah can perform miracles if he wishes
- people often question the existence of Allah when people suffer. Therefore, when miracles happen that can be attributed to him, it gives comfort and belief in a loving Allah.

Why miracles might lead to belief in the existence of Allah

1 Amazement by what has happened – there is no other way to explain it except through Allah.

2 Evidence that Allah is active within the world – they show Allah cares for creation and wants humanity to know he is there.

3 Proof of the existence of Allah because they show his love for the world.

4 Demonstrate the power of Allah in that he can act within the world.

Examples of miracles

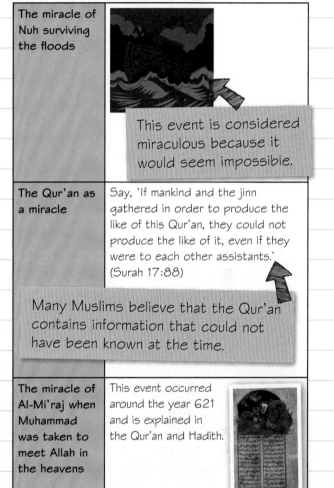

The miracle of Nuh surviving the floods	This event is considered miraculous because it would seem impossible.
The Qur'an as a miracle	Say, 'If mankind and the jinn gathered in order to produce the like of this Qur'an, they could not produce the like of it, even if they were to each other assistants.' (Surah 17:88)
	Many Muslims believe that the Qur'an contains information that could not have been known at the time.
The miracle of Al-Mi'raj when Muhammad was taken to meet Allah in the heavens	This event occurred around the year 621 and is explained in the Qur'an and Hadith.

Strengths and weaknesses of the arguments from miracles

Strengths	Weaknesses
👍 For Muslims, miracles 'prove' the existence of Allah – they cannot explain these events without reference to Allah.	👎 Miracles can be explained scientifically – they are simply everyday events misinterpreted as miracles.
👍 Miracles are seen to strengthen and confirm faith in Allah.	👎 Different interpretations of events cause doubt as to their truth – they do not 'prove' that Allah exists.
👍 There are examples of miracles in the Qur'an, which itself is a miracle as Islam's main holy book.	👎 A person could be mistaken, for example the 'miracle' could be the result of a medical cause, hallucinating or taking drugs.
👍 Miracles confirm Allah's nature – that he cares for and wants to interact with his creation.	

Now try this

Non-religious people may raise these kinds of problems with miracles.

'Miracles provide good evidence for belief in God.'
Evaluate this statement. In your answer you:

- should give reasoned arguments in support of this statement
- should give reasoned arguments to support a different point of view
- should refer to religious arguments
- may refer to non-religious arguments
- should reach a justified conclusion.

(12 marks plus 3 SPaG marks)

Evil and suffering

Christians may question how a loving and righteous God would allow people to do evil things and why people need to suffer.

Types of evil and suffering

1 **Moral evil/suffering** – actions carried out by humans who cause suffering, e.g. murder, rape, war and theft.

2 **Natural evil/suffering** – things that cause suffering but have nothing to do with humans, e.g. famine, disease and natural disasters.

The problem of evil and suffering

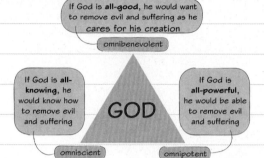

If God is **all-good**, he would want to remove evil and suffering as he cares for his creation
omnibenevolent

If God is **all-knowing**, he would know how to remove evil and suffering
omniscient

GOD

If God is **all-powerful**, he would be able to remove evil and suffering
omnipotent

What the Bible says about evil and suffering

- The Bible says God is benevolent and cares for his creation. Christians believe that God would want to help his creation if it were suffering.

- Christians believe God sent Jesus to Earth to overcome evil and die for the sins of humanity on the cross.

- Some Christians accept that evil came into the world through the devil, for example when the devil tempted Adam and Eve in the Garden of Eden.

See page 2 for more on what the Bible says about evil and suffering and Christian responses to it.

God is our refuge and our strength. (Psalm 46:1)

The Lord is compassionate and gracious, slow to anger, abounding in love. He will not always accuse, nor will he harbour his anger forever. (Psalm 103:8–9)

Teach me knowledge and good judgement, for I trust your commands. Before I was afflicted I went astray, but now I obey your word. (Psalm 119:66–67)

---

1 **Faith in God's plan**

Christians believe that while they may not understand why they suffer, they need to trust in God as he has a plan for everyone.

- The Book of Psalms states that the purpose of evil and suffering is to give people the opportunity to follow Jesus' example and live as God intended.

- The example of Job in the Bible describes how much pain Job suffered, including losing his family, yet he never lost his faith in God's plan for him.

- The philosopher John Hicks said that suffering can make a person stronger and help them appreciate the good things in their life – this may be God's purpose for us when we suffer.

2 **Free will**

God gave people free will and Christians recognise that humans sometimes choose to turn away from God. This explains acts of moral evil.

Christian responses to evil and suffering

5 **Forgiveness**

Many Christians follow the example of Jesus, who forgave those who crucified him with the words 'Father, forgive them for they know not what they do.' (Luke 23:34)

4 **Charity**

The suffering in their own lives and the world around them inspires many Christians to help others through charitable giving.

3 **Prayer**

Christians may pray to God, to ask him to give them the strength to cope with their problems. They can also pray for help and forgiveness of those who have done 'evil' acts.

Now try this

1 Give **two** religious beliefs about evil and suffering.   **(2 marks)**

2 Explain **two** contrasting religious beliefs about evil and suffering.

  Refer to sacred writings or another source of religious belief and teaching in your answer.   **(5 marks)**

Evil and suffering

Evil and suffering may create problems for Muslims who believe in Allah as compassionate.

Allah as compassionate

> In the name of Allah, the Entirely Merciful, the Especially Merciful. [All] praise is [due] to Allah, Lord of the worlds – The Entirely Merciful, the Especially Merciful, Sovereign of the Day of Recompense. It is You we worship and You we ask for help. (Surah 1:1–5)

This quote from the Qur'an suggests Allah is merciful and forgiving. Yet this view of Allah seems to be in conflict with the fact that there is evil and suffering in the world. It can lead some to question their faith, and others may reject religion altogether.

Suffering and evil

If there is suffering and evil in the world, then this raises questions for Muslims as to the compassionate nature of Allah.

- If Allah is omnibenevolent (all good) and cares for his creation, he would want to remove evil and suffering.
- If Allah is omniscient (all knowing), he would know how to remove evil and suffering.
- If Allah is omnipotent (all powerful), he would be able to remove evil and suffering.

Some Muslims may find this causes them to question their faith in Allah existing at all.

- If Allah exists, why doesn't he stop the evil?
- If Allah exists, surely there would be no evil?

What the Qur'an says about coping with suffering

> O you who have believed, seek help through patience and prayer. Indeed, Allah is with the patient. (Surah 2:153)

You need to distinguish between two types of evil: **natural evil** – disasters such as earthquakes, and **moral evil** – caused by people, e.g. murder.

> Surely we shall test you with something of fear and hunger, and loss of wealth and loves and crops ... but give glad tidings to the steadfast who say when misfortune strikes: we are Allah's and to Him we are returning. (Surah 2:155–156)

Muslims believe they should accept suffering if it is the will of Allah (Inshallah).

Muslim responses to the problem of evil and suffering

1 **Life is a test** – Most Muslims accept that there must be a purpose to suffering even if they do not understand it.

2 **Prayer** – Prayer helps Muslims to deal with the pain they are suffering and provides comfort from Allah.

3 **Charity** – Muslims believe that charity work is a practical way of helping those who are suffering to cope with what they are going through. Many Muslims may feel this has the most impact, as it will directly benefit those in need.

A Zakah box where charity money is collected.

Now try this

'Evil and suffering challenge the existence of God.'
Evaluate this statement. In your answer you:

- should give reasoned arguments in support of this statement
- should give reasoned arguments to support a different point of view
- should refer to religious arguments
- may refer to non-religious arguments
- should reach a justified conclusion.

(12 marks plus 3 SPaG marks)

Arguments against the existence of God

When considering the creation of the universe and humans, science can sometimes conflict with traditional Christian teachings. Theories such as the **Big Bang** and **evolution** offer answers to these questions without mentioning God, and in this way challenge the existence of God.

Big Bang theory

- Scientists think that an enormous explosion started the universe around 14 billion years ago.
- Scientists argue that everything within the universe – planets, stars, matter – is the result of the cooling and gathering of matter as a result of the Big Bang. Turn to page 54 for more on the Big Bang theory and Christian responses to it.

Theory of evolution

- Charles Darwin's theory that human life developed from gradual changes over millions of years.
- Survival of the fittest – individuals within a species who are better adapted to the environment (fitter) survive to pass on their genes to the next generation.
- Over time, individuals with the strongest characteristics or features survive. Turn to page 60 for more on the theory of evolution and Christian responses to it.

Challenge of science to Christianity

Scientific theories offer alternative explanations to the creation of the universe to those offered in the Bible.

They undermine the existence of God because:

- they are based on the scientific method, which is considered to be accurate and reliable
- they are more modern interpretations than the Christian account of Creation – so many people believe them to be more relevant.

In the beginning, God created the heavens and the earth. Now the earth was formless and empty, darkness was over the surface of the deep, and the Spirit of God was hovering over the waters. (Genesis 1:1–2)

Then the Lord God formed a man from the dust of the ground and breathed into his nostrils the breath of life, and the man became a living being. (Genesis 2:7)

Bible passages about the creation of the universe and the origins of humanity.

Some Christians reject all scientific discoveries, including the Big Bang and evolution, believing the Creation account in the Bible to be true in all its detail. Where there is conflict between religion and science, they claim science is wrong as the Bible is the word of God. They hold that scientific arguments do not 'prove' that God does not exist.

Christian response to challenges from science

Other Christians see no conflict between science and religion. They believe that God used the Big Bang and evolution to create the universe and humans, and that they were part of God's plan. They hold that science and religion together explain the universe and that God does exist.

Now try this

You may also want to consider the arguments against God's existence offered by evil and suffering. Turn to page 74 for more on evil and suffering.

1 Which **one** of the following is a scientific theory that appears to challenge the existence of God?

   A design ☐   **B** Big Bang ☐   **C** visions ☐   **D** miracles ☐   (1 mark)

2 'Arguments based on science offer the best evidence that God does not exist.'
   Evaluate this statement. In your answer you:
   - should give reasoned arguments in support of this statement
   - should give reasoned arguments to support a different point of view
   - should refer to religious arguments
   - may refer to non-religious arguments
   - should reach a justified conclusion.

   (12 marks plus 3 SPaG marks)

Arguments against the existence of God

1 The Big Bang theory and theory of evolution offer alternative explanations for the origins of the universe and humanity without any reference to Allah, whom Muslims believe created the universe and everything in it.

The challenge of science to Islam

2 Scientific theories that explain the creation of the universe and the origins of humanity are based on scientific evidence, which is observable, repeatable and therefore considered reliable.

3 Scientific theories are more modern than teachings found in the Qur'an, so some people may consider them more relevant and reliable.

Muslim responses to scientific explanations

Most Muslims believe science does not affect their beliefs in Allah's creation of the universe because:

- the Big Bang theory helps explain what is not in the Qur'an
- scientific explanations give a better understanding of Allah and his creation.

Some Muslims view the Big Bang theory as contradicting the Islamic creation story of a loving God who planned the universe.

They believe the Qur'an has an account of the creation of the universe similar to that offered by science:

> And the heaven We constructed with strength, and indeed, We are [its] expander. (Surah 51:47)

> Have those who disbelieved not considered that the heavens and the earth were a joined entity, and We separated them and made from water every living thing? Then will they not believe? (Surah 21:30)

This reinforces the view that Allah is the origin of human life.

Worked example

To complete this answer the student needs to add more reasons to agree and disagree, and then provide a justified conclusion.

'Scientific explanations for the creation of the universe are not compatible with religious explanations.'
Evaluate this statement. In your answer you:

- should give reasoned arguments in support of this statement
- should give reasoned arguments to support a different point of view
- should refer to religious arguments
- may refer to non-religious arguments
- should reach a justified conclusion.

(12 marks plus 3 SPaG marks)

Some Muslims may agree with this statement, as the Big Bang theory offers an explanation for how the universe began without needing any reference to Allah. They may argue that the written account in Surah 51:47 tells them Allah created the universe and they may not accept any challenge or alternative explanation.

In contrast, some Muslims will interpret Surah 51:47 differently, arguing that the reference to 'its expander' suggests that the Big Bang theory can be explained as Allah creating the universe. They believe that the explanation provided by the Big Bang fills in gaps in the explanation in the Qur'an and helps Muslims to gain a fuller understanding.

Now try this

Explain **two** religious responses to scientific arguments against the existence of God.
Refer to sacred writings or another source of religious belief and teaching in your answer. **(5 marks)**

Special revelation: Visions

Revelation in general means when the truth of something is revealed. In Christianity, it is the way in which God reveals his presence to humanity. **Special revelation** is understood as a direct form of revelation to individuals or groups, and one type of special revelation is **visions**.

Nature and importance of visions

Christian visions may involve the appearance of angels, saints or messengers; although some people believe they have seen God.

Visions generally pass on a message from God, helping people to understand him.

Visions are an important form of religious experience. Christians believe visions demonstrate some of God's characteristics, such as his omnipotence, omnibenevolence, immanence (found in everything) and omniscience.

Why might visions lead to belief in God?

1. People may believe that God is contacting them and passing on a message.

2. People may think that it connects them to God and helps them to get closer to him.

3. The visions will help Christians to understand God better and develop a relationship with him.

Biblical and non-biblical examples of visions

Saul/St Paul Saul, a persecutor of Christians, was on the road to Damascus when he saw a bright light and he heard the voice of Jesus. Saul was struck blind and could not see for three days. This experience convinced him of the truth of God and Christianity. When his vision returned, he became a Christian and changed his name to Paul.	 Saul discovered God after he was struck blind on the road to Damascus.
St Bernadette Bernadette was a child living in Lourdes, France, who, in 1858, was believed to have seen numerous visions of the Virgin Mary. During one of these, Mary asked her to drink from a spring, but as there was no spring visible, Bernadette dug in the mud to look for one. Many people thought she had gone mad, but soon afterwards a spring appeared on the spot. The spring is still there today and many Catholics believe it has healing properties.	 St Bernadette had a vision of the Virgin Mary.

Non-religious arguments

Non-religious people might suggest that visions are not 'proof' of God's existence because they may:

1. not believe that visions are 'real'

2. offer alternative explanations for visions, such as people experiencing hallucinations or having dreams

3. only believe things that can be verified (confirmed) scientifically.

Christian responses to non-religious arguments

Christians believe visions provide real evidence of God. Examples such as the healing miracles at Lourdes, which have resulted from the vision received by Bernadette Soubirous, provide this. They claim that religious believers would not be under the influence of stimulants and even though they may face persecution because of visions, they maintain them, claiming they have nothing to gain through lying. It is through visions that Christians claim they can 'know' God.

Now try this

Explain **two** contrasting beliefs in contemporary British society about visions.
In your answer you must refer to one or more religious traditions.

(4 marks)

Special revelation: Visions

Revelation is when a truth is revealed. **Special revelation** is a direct form of revelation to individuals or groups. **Visions** are one type of special revelation for Muslims.

Nature of visions in Islam

Many people associated with Islam, including prophets and **imams**, have undergone religious experiences where they have received a vision. Often angels or messengers appear and pass on messages from Allah, proving to Muslims that Allah is real.

Importance of visions in Islam

People often only believe things that they can see, so experiencing a vision may be considered to be better evidence than other types of experiences. Visions are important because they help to strengthen faith for believers or lead people to believe in the existence of Allah because they feel that:

- ✓ Allah is contacting them
- ✓ they can get closer to Allah
- ✓ they can understand Allah better.

Examples of visions

1 Musa's vision of Allah

And when Musa arrived at Our appointed time and his Lord spoke to him, he said, 'My Lord, show me (Yourself) that I may look at You.' (God) said, 'You will not see Me, but look at the mountain; if it should remain in place, then you will see Me.' But when his Lord appeared to the mountain, He rendered it level, and Musa fell unconscious. And when he awoke, he said, 'Exalted are You! I have repented to You, and I am the first of the believers.' (Surah 7:143)

These two visions are not direct visions of Allah, but Muslims believe that Allah is transcendent and, therefore, too great to be seen directly.

2 The vision of Mary

And mention, [O Muhammad], in the Book [the story of] Maryam, when she withdrew from her family to a place toward the east. And she took, in seclusion from them, a screen. Then We sent to her Our Angel, and he represented himself to her as a well-proportioned man. She said, 'Indeed, I seek refuge in the Most Merciful from you, [so leave me], if you should be fearing of Allah.' He said, 'I am only the messenger of your Lord to give you [news of] a pure boy.' She said, 'How can I have a boy while no man has touched me and I have not been unchaste?' (Surah 19:16–20)

Divergent understandings of visions

Different Muslims may place a different level of emphasis on visions as proof of the existence of Allah.

Some Sunni Muslims may accept visions and use them as proof of the existence of Allah to strengthen faith. However, other Muslims, including some Shi'a Muslims, believe that visions are not needed, as faith means to put trust in Allah and therefore proof is not required. Some Muslims, such as those in the **Sufi** tradition, are more spiritual and accept ideas of mysticism, meaning they may place more emphasis on visions within their faith.

Muslim responses to non-religious arguments

Visions are not real. They are hallucinations or dreams. I would only believe in them if they were verified scientifically.

Non-religious view

Visions do happen and they are evidence of the existence of Allah.

Muslim view

Now try this

Explain **two** religious beliefs about visions.
Refer to sacred writings or another source of religious belief and teaching in your answer. **(5 marks)**

Remember, you can answer this question from one religious tradition or you can refer to more than one. Make sure you link the points you develop to teachings from holy books such as the Qur'an or Bible.

General revelation

Revelation is communication from God – it could be a message or revealing something about his nature. As well as special revelation, Christians also accept **general revelation**.

General revelation through nature

Christians believe God's divine nature is revealed through the order, intricacy and wonder of his creation – the complexity of the physical universe shows his power, knowledge and love.

> The heavens declare the glory of God; the skies proclaim the work of his hands. (Psalm 19:1)

General revelation through nature provides the basis of the Design argument, which attempts to prove God's existence. Remind yourself of the Design argument on page 70.

General revelation through scripture

- Many Christians view the Bible as the literal word of God.

- Stories such as the account of Creation show God's power and love for his creation.

- Rules such as the Ten Commandments show how God wishes people to live.

- Stories of prophets (for example, Noah, Abraham) show how God communicates with people.

Revelation through Jesus

- Christians see Jesus as a form of revelation, as the incarnation (human form) of God.

- Stories and teachings from the life of Jesus are found in the Bible.

> In the past God spoke to our ancestors through the prophets at many times and in various ways, but in these last days he has spoken to us by his Son. (Hebrews 1:1–2)

Non-religious arguments

Some people, including atheists and humanists, may argue that religious experiences aren't real at all.

1 Lack of evidence

- There is not enough evidence to suggest religious experiences actually happen and 'prove' that God exists.

- Individual experiences are always subjective, giving opportunity for criticism and challenge of how it is interpreted.

- Any experience could be claimed to be 'religious'.

2 Use of stimulants

Those who undergo a religious experience may be under the influence of drugs or alcohol, so their experiences cannot be trusted. Stimulants change how a person interprets things around them.

3 Wish fulfilment

Some people may be so desperate for a message from God that they interpret normal events as religious experiences.

> **Arguments why religious experiences are not proof that God exists**

4 Hallucinations

Mental health issues or illness may cause a person to hallucinate and interpret normal events as religious experiences.

Christians might respond to non-religious arguments by saying:

- religious experiences are real and believers have no reason to lie or make them up

- many Christians have had personal revelation of God – how can they all be wrong?

- many religions are based on religious experiences, making revelation significant

- most religious believers are unlikely to take stimulants, so this does not explain their experiences.

Now try this

'Revelation proves the existence of God.'
Evaluate this statement. In your answer you:

- should give reasoned arguments in support of this statement
- should give reasoned arguments to support a different point of view
- should refer to religious arguments
- may refer to non-religious arguments
- should reach a justified conclusion.

(12 marks plus 3 SPaG marks)

General revelation

Direct and indirect revelation

Revelation is the way in which God reveals his presence.

- ✓ **Direct revelation** is revelation that comes directly from God.
- ✓ **Indirect revelation** is general revelation, available to everyone. This could take the form of revelation through nature, scripture or messages received by the prophets in Islam.

General revelation through scripture

The Qur'an is:

- a form of **special revelation**, as it was revealed directly to Muhammad
- also **general revelation**, as its messages from Allah are open to everybody.

> If I should err, I would only err against myself. But if I am guided, it is by what my Lord reveals to me. Indeed, He is Hearing and near. (Surah 34:50)

General revelation through nature

Muslims believe Allah reveals himself through the natural world. Nature is perfect, therefore Allah must be its creator as he, too, is perfect. The way in which the world works together – for example, through the laws of science – shows Allah must have designed the world, as only he would be able to do this.

Revelation through messengers

- Muslims believe that Allah chose to reveal himself through prophets – messengers who were specially chosen. These include Adam, Ibrahim, Isma'il, Musa, Dawud, Isa and Muhammad, who is the 'Seal of the Prophets' as the final messenger.
- Muslims believe these messengers reveal aspects of Allah, as they share his teachings with the world. This means Muslims look to sources of authority such as the Qur'an to understand what Allah is like.

Different ideas about Allah

One issue is the contradictory ideas about Allah that revelation shows. For example, Allah is:

- transcendent (beyond human understanding)
- immanent (found in everything)
- personal (humans can relate to him)
- impersonal (difficult to relate to).

All Muslims recognise revelation to some extent, as Allah revealed the Qur'an to Muhammad.

- Sufi Muslims (a smaller branch of Islam) place great importance on personal experiences through special revelation.

Muslim responses to revelation

> As a Muslim, I would argue that religious experiences do happen and there is evidence in the Qur'an.

> As a Muslim, I believe Allah reveals himself to us in order to confirm belief and provide understanding of who he is.

> As a Muslim, I believe that if Allah wants to communicate with us, he is able to do so through religious experiences.

Non-religious responses

Arguments against revelation might include:

- There is a lack of evidence.
- People might have been under the influence of drink or drugs.
- People may have been ill and hallucinating.
- People may be looking intentionally for experiences that give meaning to their lives.

Now try this

Explain **two** religious beliefs about general revelation.
Refer to sacred writings or another source of religious belief and teaching in your answer.   **(5 marks)**

Christianity
Islam

Theme C

Components
2A and 2B

Had a look ☐   Nearly there ☐   Nailed it! ☐

The existence of God and revelation: Contrasting beliefs

A requirement of one type of examination question is to explain two contrasting or similar religious beliefs about three possible topics – for Theme C, these topics are visions, miracles and nature as general revelation. The question may ask you to refer to the main religious tradition in Britain, which is Christianity, plus one or more religious traditions, or you may be required to give two contrasting beliefs from two religious traditions. This page helps you to compare and contrast these beliefs.

Christian beliefs about visions

- Some Christians emphasise visions, as they believe they are direct communication from God. They include important messages such as those received by St Paul or Abraham.

- Some Christians believe visions connect them to God and help them to get closer to him, so they can understand him better.

- Many Christians believe visions are important in helping humans understand God's nature – omnipotent, omniscient and omnibenevolent.

Non-religious views about visions:
- They may claim visions are not real, and only accept things that can be proven scientifically.
- They may explain visions as hallucinations, the effect of taking drugs, or dreams.

Islamic beliefs about visions

- There have been many examples of visions in Islam, including those experienced by Muhammad, so many Muslims believe they are important.

- Visions may strengthen the faith of some Muslims by helping them to understand Allah better – they may feel that the vision means Allah wants to connect with them, so they can be closer to him.

- Some Muslims do not place great emphasis on visions, as they do not need proof of Allah's existence – so while they accept that visions happen, sources of religious authority such as the Qur'an are more important to them.

Beliefs about miracles

Many Christians accept the importance of miracles as proving the existence of God – they believe miracles show that God is involved and acts within the world.

Christians may believe that miracles show that God is benevolent and cares for his creation.

Miracles are important to Muslims because they confirm their faith in Allah who is involved and acts within the world.

The Qur'an teaches that Allah is able to perform miracles in the world.

Christianity

Islam

Miracles may reassure some Christians that God is present and acting within the world.

Muslims believe that miracles give comfort and belief in a loving and caring God.

Non-religious views about miracles:
- There are scientific explanations for supposed miracles that require no mention of God.
- People who interpret something as a religious miracle may be misinterpreting a natural event.
- There is much uncertainty surrounding miracles, and they could be the result of hallucinations or drugs.

Components
2A and 2B

The existence of God and revelation: Contrasting beliefs

This page helps you to compare and contrast Christian and Islamic beliefs about visions, miracles and nature as general revelation.

Beliefs about nature as general revelation

Christian beliefs	Islamic beliefs	Non-religious beliefs
Christians believe God can be revealed through nature, as he is creator of the universe.	Muslims believe Allah created the world, so by looking at his creation they can understand him better.	Non-religious believers do not accept any sort of God and therefore do not believe the world is the result of a divine creator.
Christians believe that the complexity of the physical universe shows God's power, knowledge and love.	Muslims believe nature is perfect therefore Allah must be its creator, as only Allah is perfect.	Non-religious believers may use scientific theories such as the Big Bang and evolution to explain where the world came from.
General revelation through nature provides the basis of the Design argument, which attempts to prove God's existence.	Muslims use evidence such as the laws of science to show the power of Allah.	

Worked example

Explain **two** contrasting beliefs in contemporary British society about miracles as proof of God's existence.
In your answer you should refer to the main religious tradition of Great Britain and non-religious beliefs.

(4 marks)

Christians believe that miracles are proof of God's existence – they reveal God's power through his ability to defy the laws of nature.

Non-religious believers would not accept miracles as proof of God's existence – they would look for a scientific explanation of what has occurred.

Read the question carefully to ensure you know what you are being asked. Here you are being asked to contrast Christianity as the main religious tradition of Great Britain with non-religious beliefs.

This answer gives the first belief from Christianity and it is then contrasted successfully with a non-religious view about miracles.

Now try this

1 Explain **two** contrasting beliefs in contemporary British society about nature as a form of general revelation.
  In your answer you should refer to the main religious tradition of Great Britain and non-religious beliefs. **(4 marks)**

2 Explain **two** contrasting beliefs in contemporary British society about visions being evidence of God.
  In your answer you should refer to the main religious tradition of Great Britain and non-religious beliefs.

(4 marks)

Both questions require you to consider the explanations offered by Christians as well as non-religious believers. Make sure you identify **two** ways that are different and develop each one by giving further information or perhaps an example.

Peace and justice, forgiveness and reconciliation

Importance of peace and justice

- Peace (the absence of war or conflict) and justice (fair treatment or behaviour) are central beliefs in Christianity.
- Christians believe all members of the Church are part of a community: seeing everyone as equal shows justice; being united shows ideas of peace.

- There are many examples of peace and justice being promoted within the Bible.
- Christians also want to follow the example of Jesus, who taught ideas of peace and justice.

I have told you these things, so that in me you may have peace. (John 16:33)

... love your enemies and pray for those who persecute you. (Matthew 5:44)

The Christian Church uses Jesus' teachings to show that Christians should strive for peace.

Justice in Christianity

 God is seen to be just and people should act in the same way.

2 Jesus taught that everyone should be treated fairly and that we should aim to treat people as we would like to be treated.

Do to others as you would have them do to you. (Luke 6:31)

3 Christian churches teach the importance of justice.

4 God will judge people after death and will forgive those who are truly sorry for their sins.

 The Bible teaches that God wants people to act justly:

And what does the Lord require of you? To act justly and to love mercy and to walk humbly with your God. (Micah 6:8)

Christian teachings about forgiveness and reconciliation

- Jesus taught about forgiveness through the Lord's Prayer and through his actions.
- Jesus forgave those who crucified him before he died.

Forgiveness and reconciliation

- Forgiveness is being able to move on from what has happened and attain peace through working together. Christians believe they should follow the example of Jesus, who taught the importance of forgiveness.
- Reconciliation is the idea of making up after conflict. According to Christianity, when people talk through their issues and reconcile, peace can be achieved.

For if you forgive other people when they sin against you, your heavenly Father will also forgive you. But if you do not forgive others their sins, your Father will not forgive your sins. (Matthew 6:14–15)

But while he was still a long way off, his father saw him and was filled with compassion for him; he ran to his son, threw his arms around him and kissed him. (Luke 15:20)

The Parable of the Prodigal Son is based on ideas of forgiveness and reconciliation. The son, even though he had wasted his inheritance, was shown compassion and forgiven by his father.

Now try this

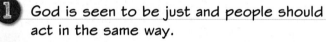

Explain **two** religious beliefs about peace.
Refer to sacred writings or another source of religious belief and teaching in your answer. **(5 marks)**

Peace and justice, forgiveness and reconciliation

'Islam' is derived from the root of the word 'salaam', which is often understood to mean peace. Justice is also a key idea within Islam – both the Qur'an and law of Allah require fair treatment.

Islam as a religion of peace

- Islam is a religion that has been misrepresented and associated with terrorism when, in reality, it is a religion of peace.
- Muslims believe Allah created and wants a peaceful world.
- There are many examples of peace being shown within Islam, demonstrating its importance. For example, Muslims greet each other with the words 'As-salamu alaykum' (peace be with you).

- The Qur'an is seen to promote messages of peace and Muslims promote peace and unity through being part of the ummah.

> And the servants of the Most Merciful are those who walk upon the earth easily, and when the ignorant address them [harshly], they say [words of] peace. (Surah 25:63)

Muslim teachings about peace

- Allah created the world with the intention that peace would be part of his creation.
- Muslims believe in the personal struggle for peace, or the greater jihad.
- All Muslims belong to the ummah, which is based on ideas of living together peacefully.
- Standing up for justice in the world is one way of achieving peace.
- However, in some cases, it may be necessary to go to war to secure peace.

The importance of justice

- Justice is a key idea in the Qur'an.
- Shari'ah law has strict rules about acting fairly.
- The Five Pillars support ideas of justice (for example, Zakah – sharing wealth makes society fairer).
- Muslims believe that justice is important to what Allah intended for the world.
- Muslims will be judged in the afterlife on how they treated others, so they should always act fairly and in a just way.

Importance of justice, forgiveness and reconciliation

Justice

Muslims believe there is a direct link between the ideas of **justice** and peace. If justice and fairness can be attained, peace will follow. The ummah demonstrates ideas of equality and justice, as all Muslims are of equal worth and value and support each other.

> And not equal are the good deed and the bad. Repel [evil] by that [deed] which is better; and thereupon the one whom between you and him is enmity [will become] as though he was a devoted friend. (Surah 41:34)

Forgiveness

Muslims believe that **forgiveness** is important to peace. Everyone makes mistakes and deserves a second chance. Allah is merciful and Muslims should follow his example and try to forgive others when they do wrong.

Reconciliation

Reconciliation is the idea of making up after conflict. According to Muslims, this is needed in order to live in an ordered and peaceful world as Allah intends.

Justice, forgiveness and reconciliation are important in overcoming conflict and bringing peace.

> O you who have believed, indeed, among your wives and your children are enemies to you, so beware of them. But if you pardon and overlook and forgive – then indeed, Allah is Forgiving and Merciful. (Surah 64:14)

Muslims believe they should be forgiving, like Allah.

Now try this

Which **one** of the following best describes the idea of accepting someone's apology and no longer blaming them?

A forgiveness ☐   B justice ☐
C reconciliation ☐   D peace ☐   (1 mark)

Violence and terrorism

Violence is behaviour, including physical force, intended to hurt, damage or potentially kill. There are many examples of violence in society today, including violent protests. Terrorism is the use of violence and intimidation to create fear. Christianity teaches that people should work for peace, so it is against terrorism.

Christian beliefs about violence

1. The Bible provides guidelines on how Christians can work for peace, reconciliation and justice, which they should follow.

2. Christians believe it is their duty to work for peace, as this is what God intended.

3. Christians follow the example of Jesus, who gave many teachings about peace and set the example of peace rather than violence.

Some Christians are **pacifists**, so do not accept any form of violence.

Teachings on violence

Blessed are the peacemakers, for they will be called children of God. (Matthew 5:9)

When Jesus' followers saw what was going to happen, they said, 'Lord, should we strike with our swords?' And one of them struck the servant of the high priest, cutting off his right ear. But Jesus answered, 'No more of this!' And he touched the man's ear and healed him. (Luke 22:49–51)

Terrorism

Terrorism is the use of violence to create fear. Often the victims are innocent. Many of those involved in terrorist attacks do not consider what they are doing is wrong, as they feel it has a higher purpose.

Terrorism has a long history within the world:

1. The roots can be traced back to the 1st century, with disputes between groups and where assassinations took place.

2. The first use of the term 'terrorism' is seen during the French Revolution.

3. Today, acts of terrorism have become more frequent, with particular countries or groups of people attacked.

Flowers at the scene of a terrorist attack in Westminster, London, on 22 March 2017, in which four people died and 50 people were injured.

Christian beliefs about terrorism

Christians do not support the use of terrorism.

- They see all human life as created by God and special, so it is wrong to take life.

- Christianity has many teachings on peace and living together in harmony.

- Violence goes against the teachings of Jesus, who taught ideas of peace.

Non-religious attitudes

- Many non-religious people, such as atheists and humanists, may claim that religion itself is at the root of conflict in the world and it is religion that causes terrorism. They may argue that without religion, there would be no terrorism.

- Non-religious people may not agree with the use of violence but may argue that sometimes violence is required in order to bring peace to the world.

Now try this

Explain **two** religious beliefs about why the use of violence is wrong.

Refer to sacred writings or another source of religious belief and teaching in your answer.   **(5 marks)**

Violence and terrorism

Islam is understood as a religion of peace, yet some Muslims believe that sometimes violence needs to be used in order to achieve peace. A small minority of Muslims use some teachings within the religion to justify terrorist acts.

Muslim beliefs towards the use of violence

1. Every Muslim is part of the ummah and deserves equality and respect.

2. Muslims believe Allah is merciful and forgiving, and they should follow his example.

3. Islam is understood as a religion of peace. Muslims believe peaceful methods should be used to end conflict, not violence.

4. Muslims recognise that in some cases violence and war may be necessary to secure peace – this should, however, be used as a last resort and all peaceful methods tried first.

Islamic teachings

These quotes reflect ideas of peace in Islam.

> And if they incline to peace, then incline to it [also] and rely upon Allah. (Surah 8:61)
>
> And the servants of the Most Merciful are those who walk upon the earth easily, and when the ignorant address them [harshly], they say [words of] peace. (Surah 25:63)
>
> O mankind, indeed We have created you from male and female and made you peoples and tribes that you may know one another. Indeed, the most noble of you in the sight of Allah is the most righteous of you. (Surah 49:13)
>
> Fight in the way of Allah those who fight you but do not transgress. Indeed, Allah does not like transgressors. (Surah 2:190)

Muslims believe that Allah commands that they should fight back when necessary, but remain just. This is a form of situation ethics, where sometimes conflict is needed to bring peace.

Terrorism within Islam

- Iraq, Afghanistan, Nigeria, Pakistan and Syria have the highest number of incidents and fatalities caused by Islamic terrorism.

- Islamic terrorist groups include: ISIS, Boko Haram, the Taliban and Al-Qaeda.

- One of the most high-profile attacks in the USA was the 9/11 attack by Al-Qaeda in 2001.

- There have been terrorist attacks linked to Islamic terrorist groups in the UK, including on the London transport system (2007), and at both Manchester Arena and Westminster (2017).

Different interpretations

A small minority of Muslims use passages from the Qur'an to justify terrorist acts.

> And when the sacred months have passed, then kill the polytheists wherever you find them and capture them and besiege them and sit in wait for them at every place of ambush. But if they should repent, establish prayer, and give Zakah, let them [go] on their way. Indeed, Allah is Forgiving and Merciful. (Surah 9:5)

Some Muslims use the first part of this quote to justify acts of terrorism. Yet most Muslims concentrate on the second part, arguing for peaceful methods to achieve harmony.

Remember, the vast majority of Muslims promote peace and reject terrorism absolutely.

Now try this

'Terrorism is the biggest threat in the world today.'
Evaluate this claim. In your answer you:

- should give reasoned arguments in support of this statement
- should give reasoned arguments to support a different point of view
- should refer to religious arguments
- may refer to non-religious arguments
- should reach a justified conclusion.

(12 marks plus 3 SPaG marks)

87

War and Just War theory

War is a state of armed conflict between different countries or groups. A 'just war' is one Christians believe is fought for the right reasons, in the right way.

Causes of war

1 Greed – for resources or control.

2 Self-defence – if attacked.

3 Retaliation – to launch a counterattack or seek revenge.

4 Economic/natural resources – to gain water, land, oil, valuable resources, etc.

5 Fear – to act first before someone attacks.

6 National pride – to fight to protect identity.

7 Fighting against injustice and aggression.

8 Protecting people – to stand up for others.

Christian teachings

At times in the Bible, God tells the Jewish people to attack those who oppose them.

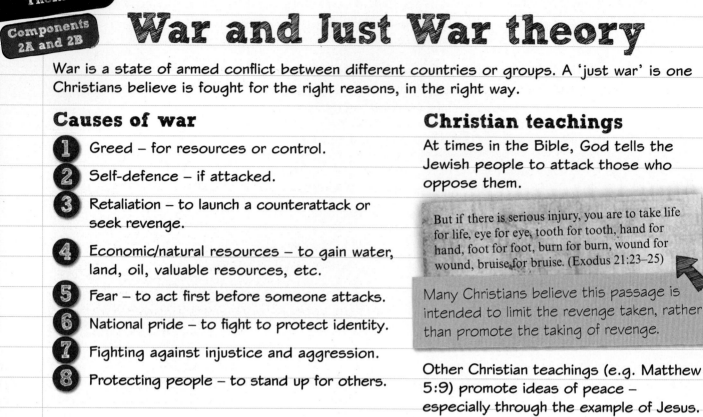

But if there is serious injury, you are to take life for life, eye for eye, tooth for tooth, hand for hand, foot for foot, burn for burn, wound for wound, bruise for bruise. (Exodus 21:23–25)

Many Christians believe this passage is intended to limit the revenge taken, rather than promote the taking of revenge.

Other Christian teachings (e.g. Matthew 5:9) promote ideas of peace – especially through the example of Jesus.

Criteria for a just war

Some religious believers think war is permitted when:

☑ there is reasonable chance of success

☑ its aim is to bring peace

☑ it is used only after other non-violent methods have failed

☑ no innocent civilians will be killed

☑ the cause of the war is just, e.g. resisting aggression or injustice

☑ the methods used are fair.

Just War theory

The Just War theory is a largely Christian doctrine employed by those in authority, providing guidance to help decide whether or not war is right and just. It applies to states, not individuals, and provides a framework for discussions of possible wars. It does not justify wars but prevents them by showing that going to war, except in certain limited circumstances, is wrong, so encourages other ways of resolving conflict.

The idea of a just war was first formulated by St Augustine. Centuries later, Thomas Aquinas formulated this into a set of criteria.

Christian teachings

- The Just War Doctrine of the Catholic Church is found in the 1992 Catechism of the Catholic Church. Many Christian Churches have accepted this doctrine.

- There appears to be some Bible support for the Just War theory.

- Many Christians believe it is right to have armed forces to protect a country.

- Sometimes it can be argued that violence is necessary. For example, if a country is invaded, the people of that country should be allowed to defend themselves.

Divergent Christian views

Christians disagree on whether war is ever justified. Some accept the Just War theory, yet others feel that both sides in war may claim their cause is just and, instead, use teachings relating to peace.

Now try this

Explain **two** religious beliefs about war.
Refer to sacred writings or another source of religious belief and teaching in your answer.

(5 marks)

War and Just War theory

Islam holds differing views on whether war is acceptable. A 'just war' is one fought for the right reasons, in the right way, which is therefore seen as justified. The Just War theory is a set of principles to decide whether a war is right, and therefore just.

Muslim teachings on war

Islam is a religion that supports peace and non-violence, as reflected in the Qur'an.

> O You who believe! Enter absolutely into peace (Islam). Do not follow in the footsteps of Satan. He is an outright enemy to you. (Surah 2:208)

> The believers are but brothers, so make settlement between your brothers. And fear Allah that you may receive mercy. (Surah 49:10)

Yet some passages in the Qur'an suggest war is permitted in certain circumstances, when all other peaceful methods have failed.

> Fight in the way of Allah those who fight you but do not transgress. Indeed. Allah does not like transgressors. (Surah 2:190)

A **transgressor** is someone who goes against the laws or rules, for example someone who fights when it is not justified or allowed.

Just War theory in Islam

- Has the support of the community and not one person
- Is an act of defence
- Is declared by a religious leader
- Will not harm the environment
- Does not aim to win new land or power
- Will not threaten lives
- Is a last resort
- Is not an act to convert people to Islam

Conditions of a just war – the lesser jihad

Is a just war possible?

Yes	No
Depending on the circumstances (situation ethics), it might be reasonable.	No circumstances would necessitate war.
Fighting might be the only way to achieve peace.	Other ways can achieve better results.
Weapons programmed to damage set targets rather than affect innocent lives.	There's always the risk of causing suffering.
Qur'an suggests fighting to defend Islam is acceptable.	Should a religious leader declare a just war, it may be too influenced by their faith

Divergent responses to the Just War theory

- Some Muslims recognise that war is necessary and sometimes required as a last resort – the Just War theory permits this.

- Sunni and Shi'a Muslims may conflict over the exact interpretation of the Just War theory. Shi'a Muslims recognise jihad as one of the Ten Obligatory Acts, whereas Sunni Muslims do not place the same emphasis on it.

- Some may traditionally accept that Islam allows war in self-defence and to protect the innocent and oppressed, for example, as seen in the Hijrah when Muhammad and his followers were persecuted or the Battle of Badr.

- Other Muslims may believe that war is never the right choice, believing that peace and reconciliation are at the heart of Islam.

Tanks at war

> And what is [the matter] with you that you fight not in the cause of Allah and [for] the oppressed among men, women, and children who say, 'Our Lord, take us out of this city of oppressive people and appoint for us from Yourself a protector and appoint for us from Yourself a helper?' (Surah 4:75)

This quote from the Qur'an refers to the people of Makkah, who were persecuted for embracing Islam. This illustrates one reason why it may be justified to fight – to protect the religion of Islam.

Now try this

Give **two** conditions of Just War theory.

(2 marks)

Holy war

A **holy war** is one where religious believers think God is 'on their side' and they are therefore fighting because it is the right thing to do.

Bible teachings

> Whoever does not take up their cross and follow me is not worthy of me. Whoever finds their life will lose it, and whoever loses their life for my sake will find it. (Matthew 10:38–39)
>
> ... love your enemies and pray for those who persecute you. (Matthew 5:44)
>
> For all who draw the sword will die by the sword. (Matthew 26:52)

Nature of a holy war

In the 11th, 12th and 13th centuries, Christians went on crusades to 'free' the holy places in Palestine. These were considered to be holy wars, as they were believed to be what God wanted.

Christian responses to holy war

- ✓ Some passages from the Bible seem to suggest that war may sometimes be the right action. 'The Lord said to Moses, "Take vengeance on the Midianites for the Israelites."' (Numbers 31:1–2). However, as these were Old Testament teachings, Christians today would not support the view that war is justified to defend God, believing it is better to find a peaceful solution to conflict.
- ✓ The Bible has a general message of peace, and Jesus was given the title 'Prince of Peace'. 'Blessed are the peacemakers, for they will be called children of God.' (Matthew 5:9) This recognises the importance of peace and that holy war is therefore wrong.
- ✓ Some Christians (e.g. Quakers) may be pacifist – they do not support war at all.

Non-religious attitudes

- As non-religious people do not accept God, they would almost certainly oppose holy wars.
- Most would also oppose war in general, except in exceptional circumstances, but religion would never be a justifiable reason for war.

See pages 88 and 92 for attitudes on war generally.

Christians would generally agree that wars should not be fought in God's name and violence should only be used as a very last resort, if at all.

Worked example

'Holy war can never be justified.' Evaluate this statement. In your answer you:
- should give reasoned arguments in support of this statement
- should give reasoned arguments to support a different point of view
- should refer to religious arguments
- may refer to non-religious arguments
- should reach a justified conclusion.

(12 marks plus 3 SPaG marks)

Some Christians may disagree with this statement, as they accept that war, especially holy war, may sometimes be necessary. There are examples in history of Christians taking part in holy wars such as the Crusades in defence of Christianity. There are also passages in the Bible, such as Numbers 31:1–2, which suggest that God authorises war in circumstances that need it. Christians may use this to show that holy war can be justified.

To continue, this answer could add further arguments to this paragraph. An alternative view then needs to be given – this could be from Christianity or another religion such as Islam, or could include non-religious arguments. The answer then needs to finish with a justified conclusion, based on the arguments used.

Now try this

Give **two** religious beliefs about holy war.   **(2 marks)**

Holy war

Holy war, or **Harb al-Muqadis**, is the name for war fought in the name of Allah because of religious differences. Certain conditions must be fulfilled before a holy war can be fought.

Harb al-Muqadis in Islam

Harb al-Muqadis is only justifiable in cases where the intention is to defend the religion of Islam. This can involve:

- protecting the freedom of Muslims to practise their faith

- strengthening the religion of Islam if it is being threatened

- protecting Muslims against an attack.

Muhammad and his followers were involved in holy wars, such as the Battle of Badr and the Conquest of Makkah.

Then when the sacred months have passed, then kill the polytheists wherever you find them and capture them and besiege them and sit in wait for them at every place of ambush. But if they should repent, establish prayer, and give Zakah, let them [go] on their way. Indeed, Allah is Forgiving and Merciful. (Surah 9:5)

'Polytheism' means worshipping more than one God. This is considered to be against Allah and wrong.

And if they incline to peace, then incline to it [also] and rely upon Allah. (Surah 8:61)

The first quote suggests the agreement of using violence when necessary, but gives allowance if the opposition repents. This suggests peace and forgiveness are important. The second quote supports ideas of working towards peace. These quotes may appear to be in conflict and this can also be applied to lesser jihad, with diversity over its understanding and justification for war.

Teachings about holy war

It must:

- ☑ be for reasons of defence
- ☑ be declared by a religious leader
- ☑ be a last resort
- ☑ avoid harming innocent civilians
- ☑ not be fought to gain land
- ☑ be fought to bring about an end goal
- ☑ not harm innocent people
- ☑ not cause women to be abused or raped
- ☑ treat enemies fairly, including enemy soldiers
- ☑ be stopped as soon as the enemy asks
- ☑ not target property.

Worked example

Explain **two** religious beliefs about holy war. Refer to sacred writings or another source of religious belief and teaching in your answer.

(5 marks)

Muslims believe holy war is justified in cases where it is seen as necessary to defend Islam. In the Qur'an, Surah 9:5 suggests that it is acceptable to use violence in such circumstances, such as when others are going against Allah by worshipping many gods.

Muslims also believe there are certain conditions for holy war. These include war being a last resort and the need to avoid harming innocent civilians. This is because the Qur'an teaches that Allah created all life, and life is therefore sacred.

This answer gives **two** religious beliefs and links them to teachings from the Qur'an. Each belief is fully developed.

Now try this

Which **one** of the following is used to describe a war being fought in the name of God?

A pacifism ☐   **B** conscientious objector ☐
C holy war ☐   **D** nuclear war ☐   **(1 mark)**

Pacifism

Pacifism is the belief that war and violence cannot be justified under any circumstance.

Christian views

- Some Christians refuse to take part in war and may join peace rallies.

- Some Christians may not accept pacifism, believing that sometimes fighting is the only way to bring about peace.

For more on Christian belief on when war is justified, see page 88.

History of pacifism

1. Many Christians see Jesus as a pacifist; many of his teachings were about peace: 'Blessed are the peacemakers' (Matthew 5:9).

2. Some British pacifists (**conscientious objectors**) refused to fight in the two world wars.

3. Martin Luther King Jr was a pacifist who refused to use violence in his fights against injustice.

Christian teachings on pacifism

You shall not murder. (Exodus 20:13)

You have heard that it was said, 'Love your neighbour and hate your enemy.' But I tell you, love your enemies and pray for those who persecute you. (Matthew 5:43–44)

'Put your sword back in its place,' Jesus said to him, 'for all who draw the sword will die by the sword.' (Matthew 26:52)

But I tell you, do not resist an evil person. If anyone slaps you on the right cheek, turn to them the other cheek also. (Matthew 5:39)

So God created mankind in his own image. (Genesis 1:27)

The Ten Commandments forbid killing, supporting the idea of pacifism.

Jesus taught that people should love their enemies.

This recognises the need for peace and not using violence in the world.

Passive resistance

Passive resistance is non-violent opposition to authority, especially a refusal to cooperate with legal requirements to fight. Some Christians agree with this.

Peace I leave with you; my peace I give you. (John 14:27)

Reverend Martin Luther King Jr led peaceful protests against racist laws in the USA in the 1950s and 1960s.

The Quakers

The **Quakers** (Religious Society of Friends) are a Christian denomination opposed to violence.

- They believe that God is in every person, and oppose anything that harms people.

- They believe they should act in the world against injustice – peacefully. Many Quakers may be conscientious objectors.

- In the past, some Quakers refused to defend themselves from attack.

Now try this

'Everyone should be a pacifist.'

Evaluate this statement. In your answer you:

- should give reasoned arguments in support of this statement

- should give reasoned arguments to support a different point of view

- should refer to religious arguments

- may refer to non-religious arguments

- should reach a justified conclusion.

(12 marks plus 3 SPaG marks)

Religion as a cause of conflict

Religion as a cause of conflict

- In the UK in recent years, there have been a number of terrorist attacks carried out by minority Islamic terror groups. The vast majority of Muslims condemn such attacks as cruel and inhumane.

- However, some people have come to negatively label and stereotype all Muslims as supporting terrorist attacks on non-Muslims. This kind of discrimination – known as **Islamophobia** – is based on ignorance of Islamic beliefs and teachings and is very damaging.

Buses in London carry Islamic messages of peace and respect as part of a 2017 national campaign.

Unprovoked attacks on Muslim civilians in the UK increased five-fold after the June 2017 terrorist attack on London Bridge, for which the radical Islamic terror group ISIS claimed responsibility.

Muslim beliefs and teachings

Islam teaches that war and violence can be used in certain circumstances to defend Islam.

And when the sacred months have passed, then kill the polytheists wherever you find them and capture them and besiege them and sit in wait for them at every place of ambush. But if they should repent, establish prayer, and give Zakah, let them [go] on their way. Indeed, Allah is Forgiving and Merciful. (Surah 9:5)

Islam, however, is a religion of peace:

And the servants of the Most Merciful are those who walk upon the earth easily, and when the ignorant address them [harshly], they say [words of] peace. (Surah 25:63)

Muslims believe that although religion can cause disagreements and highlight differences, all peaceful methods should be tried to resolve these.

Muslim responses to WMD

The Qur'an was recorded long before WMD came into existence, but lessons from the Qur'an can still be applied.

1 Use of WMD is not supported because they are impossible to regulate under Islamic conditions of war because of the extensive damage they would cause.

2 Innocent life should not be threatened.

Non-religious attitudes and utilitarianism

It is difficult to find any justification for the use of weapons that cause so much damage and threaten innocent life to such a great extent.

Non-religious view

WMD may be justified if peace is achieved in the long term and if they act as a deterrent.

Utilitarian view

WMD are too great a threat to life and the creation of Allah.

Muslim view

Now try this

'The use of WMD cannot be justified.'
Evaluate this statement. In your answer you:

- should give reasoned arguments in support of this statement
- should give reasoned arguments to support a different point of view

Remember that a key argument will be that WMD are so destructive that their use cannot be justified except perhaps as a deterrent.

- should refer to religious arguments
- may refer to non-religious arguments
- should reach a justified conclusion.

(12 marks plus 3 SPaG marks)

Religion and peacemaking

Peace is the absence of war or conflict. It is an important idea in Christianity, and Christians believe people need to follow the example of Jesus the peacemaker. Christians also believe they have a duty to help those affected by war.

Working for peace

- There are many Bible teachings about peace.

> But I tell you, love your enemies and pray for those who persecute you. (Matthew 5:44)
>
> I have told you these things, so that in me you may have peace. (John 16:33)

- Jesus promoted peace through his teachings: 'Blessed are the peacemakers' (Matthew 5:9); 'Love your neighbour as yourself' (Mark 12:31).
- Christians believe God intended humans to live in peace and harmony – in the Old Testament it is promised that there will be no war in the perfect Kingdom of God.

Work of Christian individuals for peace

1 Betty Williams (born 1943)

- She is a Christian who co-founded Community of Peace People, an organisation in Northern Ireland that promotes peace.
- She organised peace petitions and peace marches to raise awareness of the work of the organisation.
- She was awarded a Nobel Peace Prize in 1976.

2 Martin Luther King Jr (1929–68)

- He was a US Baptist minister and civil rights activist.
- He used peaceful methods (marches, boycotts, sit-ins) to challenge racism and promote peace and equality.
- He worked to bring about changes in the law to recognise all people as equal before God.
- He received a Nobel Peace Prize in 1964.

Difficulties faced by victims of war

1 They may be forced to leave their homes with very few belongings – some may become refugees in another country.

2 The death of family members and loved ones means many children may be left as orphans.

3 The loss of their source of income means they cannot provide for themselves and their families.

4 They may be traumatised by what they have seen and experienced in war.

Christian Aid

- A Christian charity that delivers urgent aid in emergencies experiencing war and conflict.
- It delivers humanitarian assistance to people in need.
- It speaks out against conflict in areas such as Israel or Colombia to push for peace.
- It works after conflict has ended to rebuild lives and bring communities together.

Christian actions and teachings

Christians may help victims of war by:

- donating money or goods to charity, to be used to provide food and shelter
- doing volunteer work to raise awareness of the difficulties facing victims of war
- taking in and helping to house refugees
- working with them to rebuild their lives.

Christians believe it is their duty to help others.

> So in everything, do to others what you would have them do to you. (Matthew 7:12)

Now try this

Give **two** ways in which religious believers try to help victims of war.
(2 marks)

This question simply requires you to state **two** different pieces of information.

Religion and peacemaking

Muslims recognise the need to work for peace in today's world. When war breaks out, it can affect people in different ways. Muslims believe they should try to help those suffering.

Why do Muslims work for peace?

- ✓ To follow the teachings of Islam, which promote peace and working together rather than conflict.
- ✓ The Qur'an contains many quotes relating to ideas of peace. Muslims believe they should apply these through supporting charity and helping others.
- ✓ To live as Allah intended and to work to try to bring justice to the world.
- ✓ To help care for others in the world, which is a duty outlined by Muhammad to humans.
- ✓ To support and strengthen the ummah.

These passages teach Muslims to strive for justice, forgiveness and peace.

And not equal are the good deed and the bad. Repel [evil] by that [deed] which is better; and thereupon the one whom between you and him is enmity [will become] as though he was a devoted friend. (Surah 41:34)

The servants of the Most Merciful are those who walk upon the earth easily, and when the ignorant address them [harshly], they say [words of] peace. (Surah 25:63)

Work of Muslim individuals for peace

Malala Yousafzai (born 1997) is a Pakistani Muslim who overcame an assassination attempt by the Taliban. Yousafzai campaigns for universal access to education and is a passionate supporter of human rights and the right of all children to education. She received Pakistan's first National Youth Peace Prize in 2011 and a Nobel Peace Prize in 2014.

Muhammad Ali (1942–2016) was a Muslim and professional boxer whose refusal to fight in the Vietnam War cost him his professional boxing licence. He undertook charity work to bring peace and equality between people. He also supported gender, racial and economic equality and religious tolerance, putting forward Muslim principles and teachings of peace.

Muslim teachings

None of you truly believes until he wishes for his brother what he wishes for himself. (Hadith 13)

[true] righteousness is [in] one who believes in Allah … and gives wealth, in spite of love for it, to relatives, orphans, the needy, the traveller, those who ask [for help], and for freeing slaves; [and who] establishes prayer and gives Zakah; … and [those who] are patient in poverty and hardship and during battle. (Surah 2:177)

Muslim charities

Islamic Relief

It works to help those affected by war in countries where there are difficulties in getting aid to where it is most needed. It focuses on short-term and long-term projects, to bring relief in emergencies and after war and conflict, and to help rebuild communities.
Other Muslim charities that help victims of war include the Red Crescent Movement.

Now try this

'Everyone should work for peace.'
Evaluate this statement. In your answer you:
- should give reasoned arguments in support of this statement
- should give reasoned arguments to support a different point of view
- should refer to religious arguments
- may refer to non-religious arguments
- should reach a justified conclusion.

(12 marks plus 3 SPaG marks)

Religion, peace and conflict: Contrasting beliefs

A requirement of one type of examination question is to explain two contrasting or similar religious beliefs about three possible topics – for Theme D, these topics are violence, weapons of mass destruction (WMD) and pacifism. The question may ask you to refer to the main religious tradition in Britain, which is Christianity, sometimes to compare religious to non-religious beliefs and sometimes to give two contrasting beliefs from two religious traditions. This page helps you to compare and contrast these beliefs.

Christian beliefs about violence

- Christians believe they should work for peace, reconciliation and justice.
- Many Christians may be pacifists and believe that the use of violence is always wrong.
- Christians will follow the example and teachings of Jesus, who showed the importance of peace rather than violence.
- Many Christians believe it is their duty from God to work to end violence in the world.
- However, sometimes Christians believe that the only way to bring about peace is to use violence – but only as a last resort.

Islamic beliefs about violence

- Muslims believe they have a duty to work to reconcile groups who are in conflict using peaceful methods.
- Islam is understood as a religion of peace and non-violence.
- Muslims believe Allah is merciful so they should try to be forgiving towards others.
- Some Muslims believe, however, that sometimes violence is needed in order to bring about peace in the world.

Beliefs about WMD

Christians believe the problems of WMD (high loss of life and damage to the environment) outweigh any potential benefits, so their use can never be justified.

Muslims apply Islamic teachings to this issue, arguing that the use of WMD can never be justified, due to the tremendous damage and loss of life they inflict.

Christianity

Islam

Christianity contains many teachings about peace, which suggests violence is wrong, so they would not support the use of WMD.

Muslims uphold that life is sacred, as it is Allah's creation, and since WMD threaten life, they will not support their use.

Had a look ☐   Nearly there ☐   Nailed it! ☐

Christianity
Islam

Theme D

Components
2A and 2B

Religion, peace and conflict: Contrasting beliefs

This page helps you to compare and contrast Christian and Islamic beliefs about violence, weapons of mass destruction (WMD) and pacifism.

Beliefs about pacifism

Christian beliefs	Islamic beliefs
Many Christians may take a pacifist approach, believing that violence is never the answer to solving conflict.	Islam is not a pacifist religion and many Muslims recognise that sometimes war and fighting are needed in order to bring about peace.
Christians may refer to one of the Ten Commandments – 'You shall not kill' – to support the idea that pacifism is the right approach.	There are some teachings that appear to be in line with pacifist ideas, and many Muslims promote ideas of peace.
There have been many famous Christian pacifists who refused to use violence, including Martin Luther King Jr.	Islam teaches the importance of working together for reconciliation and trying to achieve peace.
There are many teachings from Jesus in the Bible showing that peace should be achieved through pacifism rather than the use of violence.	'Islam' can be taken to mean 'peace' and 'submission to Allah', so many Muslims adopt a peaceful stance towards resolving conflict in the world
	Muslims who have refused to use violence and campaigned for peace include Muhammad Ali and Malala Yousafzai.

Worked example

Explain **two** similar religious beliefs about the use of weapons of mass destruction.
In your answer you must refer to one or more religious traditions.

(4 marks)

Christians and Muslims both believe that the use of weapons of mass destruction is wrong, as they cause tremendous destruction and huge loss of life. Both religions believe all life is sacred, as it is God's creation.

Christians and Muslims also both believe that peace is more important than war and that this is what they should try to achieve. Both religions have key teachings on peace: for example, Christianity promotes Jesus' teachings on peace and non-violence, and Muslims understand that Allah created the world with the intention that peace would be part of his creation.

> Read the question carefully to ensure you know what you are being asked. You must make sure the beliefs you offer to answer this question are **similar**.

> This answer successfully gives **two** detailed beliefs about why weapons of mass destruction are wrong. It shows that the student understands what each religion believes and the reason why these beliefs are held.

> Each question requires you to give a detailed explanation. Make sure you compare **two** religious beliefs that are **different** – these could be from the same religion or from different religious traditions, e.g. Christianity and Islam.

Now try this

1 Explain **two** contrasting beliefs in contemporary British society about pacifism.
In your answer, you must refer to one or more religious traditions.   **(4 marks)**

2 Explain **two** contrasting beliefs in contemporary British society about why the use of violence is wrong.
In your answer, you must refer to one or more religious traditions.   **(4 marks)**

Good and evil intentions and actions

Evil is understood to be morally wrong and to cause suffering. Christianity has clear teachings about good and evil – ultimately, that good actions will be rewarded and bad actions punished.

1 Good intentions

A good intention is doing something for the right reasons. For example, a Christian helping an elderly person across the road because they believe all humans are special and God gave them a duty to care for others may be considered a good intention behind an action.

2 Good actions

Christians believe that God wants them to perform good actions and live their lives according to his rules. They believe that God will reward them in the afterlife by sending them to heaven. Good actions for Christians may include helping others, doing charity work and caring for God's creation.

> Do not be overcome by evil but overcome evil with good. (Romans 12:21)

Good and evil

4 Evil actions

Christians believe that if a person is evil within their life, does wrong and hurts others, God will punish them in the afterlife by sending them to hell. Bad actions for Christians may include not following the rules of God (for example, the Ten Commandments), not helping others, abusing the world.

3 Evil intentions

An evil intention would be to do something for the wrong reasons. For example, a Christian helping an elderly person across the road because they want to be perceived as a good person and be rewarded for it may be considered the wrong intention.

> To those who by persistence in doing good seek for glory, honour and immortality, he will give eternal life. But for those who are self-seeking and who reject the truth and follow evil, there will be wrath and anger. (Romans 2:7–8)

Sometimes intentions and actions are not straightforward. Someone may perform a good action but for the wrong reasons. Similarly, someone may have the right intentions but inadvertently perform a bad action. Also, these ideas are all **relative** – they are subjective – and what is 'good' to one person may be considered 'bad' to another.

Can it ever be good to cause suffering?

Christians would argue that it is wrong to cause suffering. However, they do recognise that good can come from suffering.

> We must go through many hardships to enter the kingdom of God. (Acts 14:22)

Christians recognise that suffering can:

- teach people to be stronger – for example, a loved one dying helps people cope with the idea of death
- help Christians develop characteristics such as compassion and empathy for others, bringing people together and uniting them for a common aim. For example, when a natural disaster happens, it can cause people to apply the teaching 'love your neighbour as yourself' (Matthew 22:39).

Remember to support and explain the arguments you use in your answer by giving examples.

Now try this

'There is never a good reason to carry out a bad action.'

Evaluate this statement. In your answer you:

- should give reasoned arguments in support of this statement
- should give reasoned arguments to support a different point of view
- should refer to religious arguments
- may refer to non-religious arguments
- should reach a justified conclusion.

(12 marks plus 3 SPaG marks)

There are 3 SPaG marks available on this paper – you will be assessed for this skill on each of the 12-mark questions. You will be awarded for your best SPaG performance across these questions, so remember to check your answer carefully.

Good and evil intentions and actions

Good and evil intentions

- Muslims are taught that their intentions should be sincere. For example, any actions should be for the right reason, that is, for Allah.
- Muslims believe that after death they will be judged on both their actions and intentions in this life. So they believe their intentions are as important as their actions.

> I heard the Messenger of Allaah, sallallaahu alayhi wa sallam, saying, 'Verily actions are by intentions, and for every person is what he intended.' (Hadith)

Good actions

Helping and caring and leading a good life

↓

Reward is an afterlife in al-Jannah

Muslims believe that Allah is always watching them and they will be judged on their actions after death. For this reason, they will try to live their lives helping others.

Evil actions

Carrying out evil acts such as committing crimes

↓

Punishment is an afterlife in Jahannam – a place where unbelievers face terrible torments

> Indeed, Allah is ever Knowing and Wise. He admits whom He wills into His mercy; but the wrongdoers – He has prepared for them a painful punishment. (Surah 76:30–31)

This teaches Muslims that those who do wrong will receive a punishment from Allah in the afterlife.

Muslim responses to suffering

1. Suffering is part of Allah's plan.
2. Suffering is a test of faith and character.
3. Suffering is a reminder of sin and the revelation of Allah.
4. Some suffering is due to human action.
5. Good can come from suffering.

Worked example

Explain **two** religious beliefs about suffering. Refer to sacred writings or another source of religious belief and teaching in your answer. **(5 marks)**

Muslims believe that suffering is part of Allah's plan for humanity. They believe that it is a test of their faith to determine whether they deserve to go to paradise or to hell in the afterlife.

Christians believe suffering can help humans to develop compassion and caring for others. This is important as they can put teachings such as 'Love thy neighbour as thyself', from Matthew 22:39, into action. Christians believe this is how God wants them to behave towards others.

This student uses one belief from Islam and one from Christianity, linked to a Bible teaching.

Now try this

Explain **two** religious beliefs about good and evil intentions. Refer to sacred writings or another source of religious belief and teaching in your answer. **(5 marks)**

Remember, you can answer this question from one or more religious traditions. Make sure you link the points to teachings from holy books such as the Qur'an or Bible.

Reasons for crime

A crime is an action someone commits against the laws of the state, for example murder or theft. A crime is a type of sin – an action against God's will.

Crime and sin

Christianity teaches us that sin is part of human nature – the very first people, Adam and Eve, disobeyed God in the Garden of Eden and ate fruit from the forbidden tree – so everyone has the potential to commit crime.

> ... for all have sinned and fall short of the glory of God ... (Romans 3:23)
>
> Anyone who does not do what is right is not God's child. (1 John 3:10)

Crimes are sins that are not only disobeying God's wishes, but are also illegal.

Christianity and the law

- Most Christians believe they have a duty to follow the laws of the country in which they live, as they believe God has put those forms of authority in place.

> Let everyone be subject to the governing authorities, for there is no authority except that which God has established. (Romans 13:1)

- Many Christians believe God commands people follow their country's laws unless they are unjust (for example, racist), in which case they should be challenged.

Reasons for crime

① **Poverty and upbringing:** Some people commit crimes as a result of the circumstances into which they were born, for example to parents who are criminals. Christians believe that people should be educated about why crime is wrong.

② **Mental illness and addiction:** Some people who suffer from mental illnesses may not be fully in control of their actions, and so may commit crimes. Others may be addicted to substances such as drugs or alcohol and turn to crime to pay for these. Christians believe that people suffering from mental illness or addiction should be helped to overcome these challenges.

③ **Greed and hate:** Some people turn to crime as a result of hating and targeting certain groups. Christians believe that they should be taught why their actions are wrong.

④ **Opposition to an unjust law:** Some people may break laws they believe are wrong. For example, Martin Luther King Jr believed US laws making it legal for black people to be treated differently to white people were wrong.

Christian beliefs and teachings

- Christians believe God gave humanity the duty of caring for others: 'love your neighbour as yourself' (Mark 12:31).
- The Bible teaches that killing and stealing are wrong, e.g. in the Ten Commandments.
- Jesus taught us to forgive the sins of others in the same way that God forgives our sins.

Christianity and punishment

Most Christians believe crime requires fair punishment to achieve justice so the victim gains retribution and the criminal can reform.

- When Amos saw people exploiting the poor he said, 'let justice roll on like a river' (Isaiah 5:24).
- Isaiah called on people to behave justly towards others (Isaiah 58:6–7).
- Jesus was angry at the Temple courtyard being turned into a trader's marketplace (Matthew 21:12–13).

Now try this

Which **one** of the following is not a reason for crime?

A greed ☐   B poverty ☐

C equality ☐   D opposition to an an unjust law ☐

(1 mark)

Read the question carefully – this asks you to identify an answer that is **not** a reason for crime.

Reasons for crime

Muslims believe that those who break the law should be punished. Yet Islam also teaches about the importance of forgiveness.

Reasons for crime

1 Poverty and upbringing:

- A person may be influenced to commit crime by their family background and upbringing.
- Muslims believe they should support the poor, for example by Zakah, where money is collected to help the poor, and Sawm, where Muslims fast to sympathise with the poor.

> Zakah expenditures are only for the poor and for the needy... (Surah 9:60)

2 Greed and hatred:

- Muslims recognise that some crimes are the result of hatred or jealously between groups.
- Islam teaches the importance of peace and living alongside each other in harmony.
- Muslims believe education can help different groups to understand each other better.

3 Mental illness and addiction

- Muslims believe support needs to be given to individuals with mental illness and addiction, to help them avoid crime and cope with life.

4 Opposition to an unjust law

- Some laws in society may be considered to be wrong, for example discriminatory laws. Muslims have campaigned for laws to be changed; for example, Malcolm X campaigned for racial equality.
- Many Muslims believe that change should be brought about through peaceful means.

Muslim teachings

- ✓ Allah orders justice.
- ✓ Crime is a distraction from Allah. Muslims must follow Allah's rules.

> Intoxicants, gambling... are but defilement from the work of Satan, so avoid it that you may be successful. (Surah 5:90)

- ✓ The ummah is important. There is a duty to look after and help those affected by crime.
- ✓ Muhammad taught the importance of living a good life and not committing crimes.
- ✓ Islam teaches that Allah made all humans equal and they deserve to be treated fairly.

Divergent opinion

In the UK, law is made by parliament and crimes are judged in courts of law. In many Islamic countries, the law is derived from the Qur'an and the courts refer to Shari'ah law, which is based on the teachings of the Qur'an.

Shari'ah law was established when society was very different from today. For example, the punishment for theft in Shari'ah law is by amputation of the hand. Western law and society would say this is totally inappropriate. This can lead to differences of opinion.

Punishment

Muslims believe punishment is needed to:

- prevent further crimes, to build a peaceful society as Allah intended
- give offenders the chance to reflect and change
- enable the victim to gain retribution.

Some Muslims and Christians believe situation ethics should be applied. For example, if a crime has been committed because of poverty, this should be taken into account when deciding on punishment.

Now try this

Explain **two** religious beliefs about the importance of punishment.
Refer to sacred writings or another source of religious belief and teaching in your answer.   **(5 marks)**

Types of crime

There are many different types of crime in society, including hate crimes, theft and murder. Christians hold a variety of views about suitable punishments for these crimes. Possible punishments could include prison, fines and community service.

Christian attitudes to different types of crime

Type of crime and explanation	Christian attitudes
Hate crime: a crime motivated by racial, sexual, religious or other prejudice against an individual or group in society. Often involves the use of violence or aggressive behaviour. For example, assaulting/killing someone who is homosexual, or putting graffiti on someone's home.	• Christians are concerned about hate crimes – not only those directed at Christians but at other religions or for reasons other than religion. • Christians look to teachings from the Bible that suggest everyone is equal and deserves equal respect and dignity. So God created mankind in his own image, in the image of God he created them; male and female he created them. (Genesis 1:27) Love your neighbour as yourself. (Matthew 22:39) Do to others as you would have them do to you. (Luke 6:31) • Teachings from Jesus such as the Parable of the Good Samaritan (Luke 10:25–37) show Christians how they should behave towards each other.
Theft: the action or crime of stealing or taking things that do not belong to you. For example, stealing a person's wallet or purse.	• Christians believe stealing is wrong, as it is against the Ten Commandments. You shall not steal. (Exodus 20:15) • Christians, however, do recognise that there may be different reasons why people steal. If, for example, a person steals due to extreme hardship or poverty, Christians recognise that in addition to their punishment in law, the person needs support with their financial situation and to realise that what they have done is wrong.
Murder: the unlawful premeditated killing of one human being by another. For example, to shoot a person dead intentionally.	• Christianity teaches that murder is wrong and against the Ten Commandments. You shall not murder. (Exodus 20:13) • Jesus reinforced this teaching in the New Testament. You have heard that it was said to the people long ago, 'You shall not murder, and anyone who murders will be subject to judgement.' (Matthew 5:21) • Christianity teaches murder is wrong, as human life is sacred as God created it. • Some Christians may support the use of the death penalty for serious crimes such as murder.

Now try this

Explain **two** religious beliefs about the crime of murder. Refer to scripture or sacred writings in your answer.

(5 marks)

You can use teachings from the table above to support your answer. You only need to include **one** reference in your answer in addition to **two** developed points. You can reference scripture or writings by paraphrasing or by direct quotation.

Types of crime

Crimes committed today include hate crimes, theft and murder. Muslims have strict teachings on appropriate punishments for these crimes. They also strongly believe that if crimes are committed, those criminals will have to answer to Allah for their actions on the Day of Judgement.

Hate crimes

Hate crimes against Muslims have increased in the UK in recent years, due to a rise in 'Islamophobia' (an intense dislike or fear of Islam). Hate crimes often include violence.

This anti-Muslim graffiti is a type of Islamophobia.

Hate crime is motivated by racial, sexual, religious or other prejudice against an individual or group in society.

Muslim attitudes to hate crimes

Islam teaches that hate crimes are wrong, as the Qur'an states that Allah created all humans and so human life is sacred.

> And of His signs is the creation of the heavens and the earth and the diversity of your languages and your colours. Indeed in that are signs for those of knowledge. (Surah 30:22)

> O mankind, indeed We have created you from male and female and made you peoples and tribes that you may know one another. Indeed, the most noble of you in the sight of Allah is the most righteous of you. Indeed, Allah is Knowing and Acquainted. (Surah 49:13)

Theft

Theft is when a person steals or takes things that do not belong to them, for example a car.

Many Muslims apply Shari'ah law to theft, as there are clear guidelines on punishment.

Shari'ah law is only applied in Islamic countries such as Saudi Arabia; in the UK, citizens must follow UK laws.

Muslim attitudes to theft

Islam teaches that theft is wrong. In Islamic countries where Shari'ah law is applied, there are strict punishments for this type of crime.

> [As for] the thief, the male and the female, amputate their hands in recompense for what they committed as a deterrent [punishment] from Allah. And Allah is Exalted in Might and Wise. (Surah 5:38)

> The Prophet said, 'The hand should be cut off for stealing something that is worth a quarter of a dinar or more.' (Sahih al-Bukhari 81:780)

Murder

Murder is the act of deliberately taking the life of another person. Islam, again, has strict rulings for this crime.

Many Muslims consider the death penalty a suitable punishment for murder.

Muslim attitudes to murder

- In Islam, murder is such a serious crime that the most serious punishment – the death penalty – can be used if the laws of the country allow it. (Current UK law does not.)

> And do not kill the soul which Allah has forbidden [to be killed] except by [legal] right. This has He instructed you that you may use reason. (Surah 6:151)

- Islam teaches that all life is sacred, as Allah created it, so should never be deliberately taken.

Now try this

'Murder is the worst type of crime.'
Evaluate this statement. In your answer you:
- should give reasoned arguments in support of this statement
- should give reasoned arguments to support a different point of view

You could mention other types of crimes and say why murder might be seen as a worse crime.

- should refer to religious arguments
- may refer to non-religious arguments
- should reach a justified conclusion.

(12 marks plus 3 SPaG marks)

Punishment

Aims of punishment

 Protection

A key purpose of punishment is to keep criminals away from society so they can't hurt others. Christians agree that protecting society is important. Human life is sacred as God created it.

Retribution

Punishment should make criminals pay for what they have done wrong.

- In Christianity, God is a god of justice, so making criminals pay for what they have done wrong seems just.

- The Old Testament has a teaching 'eye for eye, tooth for tooth' (Exodus 21:24). This seems to suggest ideas of retribution.

- Many Christians, however, feel there is a difference between retribution and revenge.

Deterrence

The purpose of a deterrent is to discourage someone from breaking the law. Christians agree that punishment is good if it helps stop someone from reoffending or committing a crime in the first place.

MUGGER GETS FIVE YEARS

A serial mugger was sentenced yesterday at Newtown county court to

Reformation

Punishment shows the criminal what they have done wrong and gives them the opportunity to change. This could mean educating them or providing skills/a job so they don't need to turn to crime.

- Jesus taught about the importance of agape love (selfless and unconditional love) and Christians believe this is needed in order for a person to have a new start.

- Even when Jesus was on the cross, he forgave the criminals crucified alongside him. This demonstrates the importance of giving criminals the chance to ask for forgiveness and to reform.

Biblical teaching about punishment

Christianity teaches that punishment is necessary when a person has done wrong.

Christians also believe that a person will face God after death and have to account for their actions. This is believed to determine their afterlife.

For in the same way you judge others, you will be judged, and with the measure you use, it will be measured to you. (Matthew 7:2)

Then they will go away to eternal punishment, but the righteous to eternal life. (Matthew 25:46)

Brothers and sisters, if someone is caught in a sin, you who live by the Spirit should restore that person gently. But watch yourselves, or you also may be tempted. (Galatians 6:1)

These quotes teach that everyone will be judged, both on Earth and in heaven, and warn against being tempted while helping others.

First, consider reasons why reformation might be more important than the other aims of punishment, developing each argument. Then consider alternative arguments. Finish with a well-justified conclusion.

Now try this

'Reformation is the most important aim of punishment.' Evaluate this statement. In your answer you:

- should give reasoned arguments in support of this statement
- should give reasoned arguments to support a different point of view
- should refer to religious arguments
- may refer to non-religious arguments
- should reach a justified conclusion.

(12 marks plus 3 SPaG marks)

Punishment

Punishment has a number of key aims: protection, retribution, deterrence, and reformation.

Aim of punishment	What is it?	Muslim response
Protection	To protect society by keeping dangerous criminals locked away so they cannot hurt others.	• Strongly support, believing protection of people in society is vital. • Could be seen as justice (see Surah 4:135).
Retribution	Punishment makes criminals pay for their crime.	Muslims believe punishment should enable justice (see Surah 57:25).
Deterrence	Anything that discourages someone from breaking the law, e.g. information about the punishment for a crime.	• Muslims support maintaining order and justice. • Some punishments in the Qur'an discourage others from crime (see Surah 5:41).
Reformation	Punishment shows the criminal what they have done wrong and gives them time to reform. This could include education or providing skills or a job so they become a law-abiding citizen.	• Islam teaches that Allah is forgiving, so Muslims should try to apply this teaching in their lives. • It is important to give someone a chance to change their behaviour and become a better person (see Surah 4:26–28).

Qur'anic teachings about punishment

The Qur'an gives specific instructions for particular crimes. Stricter punishments are considered to be last resorts.

> Allah wants to make clear to you [the lawful from the unlawful] and guide you to the [good] practices of those before you and to accept your repentance. (Surah 4:26)

This Qur'anic quote shows that Islam teaches that fair punishment is important, but that those who do wrong need to be given the opportunity to repent and change.

Worked example

'Protecting people in society should be the main aim of punishment.'

Evaluate this statement. In your answer you:
- should give reasoned arguments in support of this statement
- should give reasoned arguments to support a different point of view
  - should refer to religious arguments
  - may refer to non-religious arguments
  - should reach a justified conclusion.

(12 marks plus 3 SPaG marks)

Most Muslims agree that protecting people is important when punishing criminals. For example, it is not fair to put other people at risk. Surah 4 states that fair punishment is important.

Other Muslims may see punishment as having other aims, including reformation of the criminal. Surah 4 also teaches that forgiveness is important, so we should give criminals the chance to see why their behaviour is wrong and to change. Islam teaches that Allah is forgiving so Muslims believe they should also try to be forgiving towards others in their lives.

This is the beginning of a student's answer, which offers a reason to agree with the statement and a reason to disagree with it. To continue, the student needs to add more reasons in support of and against the statement. These could include Christian as well as Muslim views, and non-religious arguments. The student then needs to offer a justified conclusion.

Now try this

Explain **two** religious beliefs about the aims of punishment.

Refer to sacred writings or another source of religious belief and teaching in your answer. **(5 marks)**

Had a look ☐ Nearly there ☐ Nailed it! ☐

The treatment of criminals

Although Christians recognise the importance of the aims of punishment, forgiveness and fairness, they may disagree about the treatment of criminals.

Divergent Christian attitudes about the treatment of criminals

Human rights

- Christians recognise that all humans deserve to have human rights because God created all humans equal.
- Christians accept criminals deserve to be punished, which may involve the removal of some human rights (for example their freedom), but this is seen as just. Basic human rights, for example to food and water, should be upheld.

> ... you are all one in Christ Jesus. (Galatians 3:28)

Fair trial

- This is where the person accused of the crime has both the evidence against them and a defence for them put forward.
- Christians believe justice is important and support a fair trial.

> Does our law condemn a man without first hearing him to find out what he has been doing? (John 7:51)

Trial by jury

- A group of people decide whether a person is guilty based on evidence.
- The Bible teaches the importance of being fair, so Christians support making an informed, objective decision in this way.

> Do not pervert justice or show partiality. Do not accept a bribe, for a bribe blinds the eyes of the wise and twists the words of the innocent. (Deuteronomy 16:19)

Use of torture

- The Bible appears to acknowledge the use of torture.
- Most Christians today do not support the use of torture. They may argue that all life is sacred and that violence is wrong.
- Some Christians may consider that if torturing a person could save many lives, it may be justified as a last resort.

> ... handed him over to the jailers to be tortured. (Matthew 18:34)

Prison

- Most Christians believe prisons protect society, deterring others from crime and allowing prisoners time to reform.
- Many Christians would be concerned about the welfare of criminals, for example no overcrowding, access to sanitary facilities.

> ... remember those who are in prison, as though in prison with them. (Hebrews 13:3)

Corporal punishment

- This is physical punishment such as caning or flogging. It is illegal in the UK.
- Christians do not support corporal punishment, as it is seen as getting revenge through hurting a prisoner. Christians follow the example of Jesus, who taught about forgiveness.
- Christians support punishment that brings justice. The criminal should be treated with respect, as all life is sacred.

> Love your neighbour as yourself. (Matthew 22:39)
> Do to others as you would have them do to you. (Luke 6:31)

Community service

- This is voluntary work where a criminal helps their local community in some way, for example by removing graffiti or litter, so local people see this as justice.
- Many Christians support this form of punishment, believing it helps to reform and educate criminals.
- Some Christians believe community service may have a better outcome than prison.

> This view could be supported by **situation ethics**, whereby each individual situation is considered separately.

Now try this

Give **two** religious beliefs about corporal punishment. **(2 marks)**

The treatment of criminals

Muslims believe that it is important to treat criminals in a fair way.

Divergent Muslim attitudes about the treatment of criminals

Human rights

Some Muslims accept criminals should be punished for their crimes, which may involve the removal of some human rights (for example, their freedom), but this is seen as justice.

Fair trial

Most Muslims believe justice is important, so criminals have the right to a fair trial, where both sides of the case are considered. They believe the laws of the state should be recognised and upheld, and crimes punished.

Trial by jury

Trials need to be conducted fairly, and a jury would work to achieve this. Muslims would see this as just and in line with Islamic teachings on fairness.

Use of torture

Some Muslims believe it is wrong to inflict pain. Criminals are human and, as Allah created all humans, they are sacred and should be treated respectfully.

Prison

- Many Muslims support prison's role in protecting society from criminals and the reformation of criminals.
- Many Muslims believe prison ensures justice.
- Some Muslims support prisoners' rights and humane treatment, believing all life is Allah's sacred creation.

Corporal punishment

- Some Muslims support its use.
- Others believe it is wrong to cause another pain, even criminals, as human life is sacred.

Community service

- Most Muslims support the reformation of criminals, as forgiveness is important.
- Islam teaches that Allah will judge all Muslims after death on how they have lived. If a criminal recognises their crime, seeks forgiveness and makes amends through good works, this will help with their afterlife.

Human rights are the fundamental rights of every person, to basic necessities such as water, food and shelter and the right to a fair trial.

O you who have believed, be persistently standing firm in justice, witnesses for Allah, even if it be against yourselves or parents and relatives. (Surah 4:135)

There might be instances where situation ethics could be applied and questions asked: What is the best course of action for the greater good? Is torture justifiable?

The [unmarried] woman or [unmarried] man found guilty of sexual intercourse – lash each one of them with a hundred lashes, and do not be taken by pity for them in the religion of Allah, if you should believe in Allah and the Last Day. And let a group of the believers witness their punishment. (Surah 24:2)

And cooperate in righteousness and piety, but do not cooperate in sin and aggression. And fear Allah; indeed, Allah is severe in penalty. (Surah 5:2)

Allah wants to make clear to you [the lawful from the unlawful] and guide you to the [good] practices of those before you and to accept your repentance. (Surah 4:26)

Some Muslims may believe that if someone has done wrong, their freedoms and human rights should be limited. Shari'ah law is very clear about those who have been convicted being given punishments, and some Muslims may accept appropriate retaliation against those whose guilt has been proven.

Now try this

Give **two** religious beliefs about how criminals should be treated. **(2 marks)**

You need to state **two** different beliefs held by religious believers. These can either be from the same religion or from different religions.

Forgiveness

The nature of forgiveness

Forgiveness is to stop blaming someone for what they have done, accept that they are sorry and work towards **reconciliation** (bringing people back together after conflict). Ideas of forgiveness are important to Christians: Jesus taught about forgiveness through the Lord's Prayer and through his actions towards others. He forgave those who crucified him before he died on the cross.

> For if you forgive other people when they sin against you, your heavenly Father will also forgive you. But if you do not forgive others their sins, your Father will not forgive your sins. (Matthew 6:14–15)
>
> Do not judge, and you will not be judged. Do not condemn, and you will not be condemned. Forgive, and you will be forgiven. (Luke 6:37)
>
> Father, forgive them, for they do not know what they are doing. (Luke 23:34)

Restorative justice

Restorative justice brings together the offender and the victim of a crime to try to restore peace. Prison Fellowship, a Christian organisation, runs a victim awareness programme called Sycamore Tree. This explores the effect of crime on victims and their families. Victims of crime come and talk to offenders as part of the programme.

Worked example

Give **two** religious beliefs about forgiveness. **(2 marks)**

Many Christians believe the Bible teaches that they should forgive others, even when this is difficult. They also believe God helps them to do this.

This answer states **two** different beliefs as the question requires. Remember that you can also give two different beliefs from Islam for this question or one from Christianity and one from Islam.

Forgiveness for offenders

Offenders can be reintegrated within their local community, sometimes through Christian organisations such as street pastors or the Prison Fellowship, by providing them with an education and the opportunity to learn vocational skills. They may also be asked to pay back into their community, for example by helping to improve their local area.

It is important to Christians that offenders realise the wrongness of their actions and make retribution to those whom they have wronged. Forgiveness and reformation are seen as central to this because they help to unite people as a community.

See page 106 for more on retribution and reformation.

These prisoners are carrying out community service, to help make amends for their crimes.

Importance of restorative justice and forgiveness

1 Jesus died on the cross to bring forgiveness and reconciliation between God and humanity.

2 Christians should try to forgive others, even when it is difficult – God helps them to do this.

3 Seeing the effects of crime on victims may help change offenders' behaviour

4 The Bible teaches that it is important to settle conflicts, forgive and reconcile wherever possible.

> ... if you hold anything against anyone, forgive him. (Mark 11:25)
>
> Be kind and compassionate to one another, forgiving each other, just as in Christ God forgave you. (Ephesians 4:32)

Now try this

Explain **two** religious beliefs about the importance of forgiveness for criminals.
Refer to sacred writings or another source of religious belief and teaching in your answer. **(5 marks)**

Forgiveness

Forgiveness is accepting someone's apology for his or her misdeed and moving on.

Importance of forgiveness

Muslim teachings say that:

- Allah is compassionate and merciful and forgives people so Muslims should too
- if a person truly repents, then they should be forgiven
- people should try to forgive those who have wronged, as Muhammad taught
- Islam is a religion of peace
- a killer may be forgiven if they pay compensation to the family (Qur'an)
- on the Day of Judgement people will be judged on their behaviour and those who repent will be forgiven.

Importance for offenders

Reintegrated into the community

Gain skills and education from the punishment

Carry out community service to make amends for wrong

A way of protecting the ummah

Ease tensions in the community because victims can see justice has been done

O you who have believed, indeed, among your wives and your children are enemies to you, so beware of them. But if you pardon and overlook and forgive – then indeed Allah is Forgiving and Merciful. (Surah 64:14)

Restorative justice

Restorative justice is an attempt to bring together the offender and victim of a crime to try to restore peace and allow a community and individuals to heal.

Worked example

Explain **two** religious beliefs about why it is important for criminals to be forgiven.
Refer to sacred writings or another source of religious belief and teaching in your answer. **(5 marks)**

Muslims believe that Allah is 'forgiving and merciful' (Surah 64:14) and wants them also to be forgiving. Therefore Muslims will try to forgive criminals who are sorry for what they have done.

Islam is also a religion of peace – Muslims believe Allah intends people to live in harmony. Forgiveness allows all members of the ummah to understand that a person is sorry and accept them back into society.

For the first belief, the student gives a developed explanation and successfully quotes from the Qur'an. The second part of the answer offers a different belief to the first that is also developed.

Before you answer this question, consider examples of things that could be forgiven and things that could not be forgiven. Use these to develop your arguments before giving a justified conclusion at the end. You can include both Christian and Muslim arguments or just focus on one religion in your answer. You can also refer to non-religious arguments.

Now try this

'We should always forgive.'
Evaluate this statement. In your answer you:

- should give reasoned arguments in support of this statement
- should give reasoned arguments to support a different point of view
- should refer to religious arguments
- may refer to non-religious arguments
- should reach a justified conclusion.

(12 marks plus 3 SPaG marks)

111

The death penalty

There are many arguments – religious, non-religious and ethical – that support or are against the use of the death penalty (capital punishment).

The death penalty

The death penalty is execution, where the life of a condemned prisoner is taken away. The death penalty has been abolished completely in the UK, although it still exists in some countries, including China, Iran, Saudi Arabia and some states in the USA.

Purpose of the death penalty

1 To provide punishment for the most severe crimes committed.

2 To act as a deterrent to other criminals.

3 To make victims feel as though punishment has been given.

4 To make sure that the offender cannot commit the same crime again.

Arguments for the death penalty

- The Old Testament teaches that the death penalty should be sought for some crimes.
- Jesus never taught the death penalty was wrong.
- The Christian Church used the death penalty in the Middle Ages for those who challenged the authority of the Church.
- St Paul teaches in the New Testament to obey the laws of the country – this could include the death penalty.

Whoever sheds human blood, by humans shall their blood be shed; for in the image of God has God made mankind. (Genesis 9:6)

Arguments against the death penalty

- The overall message from Christianity is to love and forgive others, and capital punishment goes against this.
- Jesus taught that revenge was wrong.
- Human life is sacred.
- Most Christian denominations have spoken out against capital punishment.

You shall not murder. (Exodus 20:13)
You have heard that it was said, 'Eye for eye, and tooth for tooth.' But I tell you, do not resist an evil person. If anyone slaps you on the right cheek, turn to them the other cheek also. (Matthew 5:38–39)

Alternative views

- Humanists generally oppose the death penalty, as they believe any killing is wrong. Error is also possible.
- Atheists may support or oppose the death penalty. Some may think the most severe crimes, such as murder, justify this punishment; others may think the use of the death penalty means the criminal escapes rather than is given justice (a long prison sentence).
- Some non-religious people may adopt **situation ethics**, that you need to look at each individual case to decide the best action.

Ethical arguments

☑ The theory of **utilitarianism** is based on a principle that the best action is the one that brings the greatest happiness to the greatest number. It could be argued that giving a convicted criminal the death penalty would protect many more people in society.

☑ In contrast, ethical arguments based on the **sanctity of life** idea would state that life should be protected at all costs and so would reject the death penalty.

Now try this

Explain **two** religious beliefs that show the death penalty should not be supported.
Refer to sacred writings or another source of religious belief and teaching in your answer.   **(5 marks)**

You can answer from a Christian or Muslim perspective.
You can reference teachings or writings by paraphrasing or by direct quotation.

The death penalty

There are arguments both for and against the use of the death penalty (capital punishment) in Islam.

Purposes of the death penalty

1 To offer a punishment for the most severe crimes committed.

2 To act as a deterrent for other criminals.

3 To make victims feel as though punishment has been given and to offer closure for the victim's family.

4 To make sure that the offender cannot commit the same crime again.

5 To give a chance for the offender to repent by facing up to what they have done.

A protest against the death penalty.

Muslim attitudes to the use of capital punishment

In support of capital punishment	Arguments against capital punishment
• The Qur'an says the death penalty can be used for certain crimes. • Shari'ah law agrees with the Qur'an. • Muhammad made statements suggesting he agreed with the death penalty. • When Muhammad was the ruler of Medinah, he sentenced people to death for committing murder.	• The scholars of Shari'ah law do not agree when or how the death penalty should be applied, showing there are differences in opinion. • The Qur'an states that capital punishment is one option – but it is not the only option. • Strict conditions given by the Qur'an about capital punishment are often not met. • Some Muslims may use the argument that life is special and sacred and it is not the place of humans to take it away in any circumstances. • If there is no capital punishment in the country they live in, then they accept this law.

Muslim teachings on capital punishment

In Hadith (Sahih Muslim 16:4152), it suggests that the death penalty can be used for the crimes of murder and for Muslims who refuse to do their Islamic duty. The Qur'an also indicates that the death penalty can be for crimes of rape, homosexual acts and apostasy (when someone works against Islam).

Non-religious attitudes

Humanists and atheists generally oppose the use of the death penalty, as they believe premeditated killing is wrong – even when carried out by the state. There is also the possibility of error. When situation ethics are applied, some may believe that in certain circumstances capital punishment might be the better option.

Now try this

Your answer can include Christian and Muslim arguments or just focus on one religion. You can also refer to non-religious arguments.

'The death penalty should not be supported.'
Evaluate this statement. In your answer you:
- should give reasoned arguments in support of this statement
- should give reasoned arguments to support a different point of view

- should refer to religious arguments
- may refer to non-religious arguments
- should reach a justified conclusion.

(12 marks plus 3 SPaG marks)

Religion, crime and punishment: Contrasting beliefs

A requirement of one type of examination question is to explain two contrasting or similar religious beliefs about three possible topics – for Theme E, these topics are corporal punishment, the death penalty and forgiveness. The question may ask you to refer to the main religious tradition in Britain, which is Christianity, sometimes compare religious to non-religious beliefs and sometimes to give two contrasting beliefs from two religious traditions. This page helps you to compare and contrast these beliefs.

Christian beliefs about corporal punishment

- Many Christians would not support corporal punishment, as they believe all humans are entitled to human rights, which includes the right not to be harmed.

- Christianity teaches that all life is sacred and the use of corporal punishment appears to contradict this.

- Many Christians recognise that when a crime has been committed, an appropriate punishment is fair and should be expected. Yet they do not necessarily agree that this should be a physical punishment.

- Christianity teaches about the importance of reforming a criminal and making them realise that the actions they did were wrong – this can be achieved through imprisoning and educating a criminal, not physically hurting them.

Islamic beliefs about corporal punishment

- Islam is a religion of peace, so many Muslims would not support the harming of criminals, even though they had done wrong.

- Muslims believe all life is special as it is Allah's creation, so many believe in fair and just punishment that does not harm anyone.

- Islam teaches that it is important for a person to be given the opportunity to reform. This will not necessarily happen with the use of physical punishment.

- Muslims believe Allah created all people so all people deserve equality and human rights, which some feel means not using corporal punishment.

Beliefs about the death penalty

Some Christians agree with the use of the death penalty for the most serious of crimes, such as murder, as this is a view promoted in the Old Testament section of the Bible.

Christianity upholds the sanctity of life argument, which says life is special as it is God's creation, so taking life through the death penalty is seen as wrong.

Christianity

Some Christians support the use of the death penalty because the Christian Church in the Middle Ages used it for those who challenged its authority.

Many Christians today support the view that the death penalty is wrong, as the overall message from Christianity is one of love and forgiveness.

Some Muslims support the use of the death penalty for the most serious crimes, as the Qur'an supports this view.

Muslims support the view that all human life is sacred, as it is Allah's creation, which means they do not support the death penalty as it ends life.

Islam

There are teachings in the Hadith from Muhammad that suggest the death penalty is acceptable, so Muslims may support its use for the most serious crimes.

Many Muslims today argue that although the death penalty is one possible option as a punishment, the Qur'an does not say it is the only option, so other forms of punishment should be considered.

Religion, crime and punishment: Contrasting beliefs

Beliefs about forgiveness

Christian beliefs	Islamic beliefs
Forgiveness is important for Christians and Christianity has many teachings on it.	Muslims believe Allah is merciful and forgives people, so they believe they should try to apply this to their lives too.
Christians believe Jesus died on the cross to bring forgiveness and reconciliation between God and humanity, so many Christians believe they should also try to be forgiving in their lives.	Most Muslims believe they should forgive others, especially if they are sorry for the crimes they have committed.
Christians believe God is forgiving and that he helps them to try to be forgiving towards others in their lives, so many Christians believe forgiveness and the opportunity to change are important aims of punishment.	Islam is a religion of peace, and many Muslims believe they should be forgiving towards others to achieve peace in the world.
The Bible teaches it is important to settle conflicts, forgive and reconcile, especially when crimes have been committed.	Muslims are taught that Allah will judge them on their behaviour after death and that those who repent will be forgiven.

Worked example

Explain **two** similar beliefs in contemporary society about the forgiveness of criminals.

In your answer you must refer to one or more religious traditions. **(4 marks)**

Christians believe forgiveness of criminals is important in helping them to reform. This is reinforced through the example and teachings of Jesus, who showed forgiveness when he was on the cross towards those who crucified him.

Muslims also believe forgiveness is important as they believe Allah is merciful and they should try to be forgiving towards others in their lives. Forgiving a criminal when they have done something wrong puts this belief into action.

> Read the question carefully to ensure you know what you are being asked. Here, you are being asked to consider two **similar** religious beliefs.

> Here, the student gives similar beliefs from a Christian and Muslim perspective. Each belief is detailed and explained.

> Each question requires you to give a detailed explanation. Make sure you compare **two** religious beliefs that are **different** – these could be from the same religion or from different religious traditions, e.g. Christianity and Islam.

Now try this

1 Explain **two** contrasting beliefs in contemporary British society about corporal punishment.

In your answer you should refer to the main religious tradition of Great Britain and one or more other religious traditions. **(4 marks)**

2 Explain **two** contrasting beliefs in contemporary British society about why the use of the death penalty is wrong.

In your answer you should refer to the main religious tradition of Great Britain and one or more other religious traditions. **(4 marks)**

Prejudice and discrimination

Christian teaching states that prejudice and discrimination are wrong, but this teaching is not always fully put into practice. Prejudice and discrimination can lead to problems in society. **Positive discrimination** is one way of tackling these.

Christian teachings on prejudice and discrimination

Prejudice and discrimination are wrong because:

 Christians believe all humans are equal – they were all 'made in the image of God'

 Christians teach agape (selfless) love, which supports the idea of treating all people in the same way

 Christians follow the example of Jesus, who did not discriminate

④ the 'do to others what you would have them do to you' (Matthew 7:12) teaching suggests discrimination is wrong

⑤ the Parable of the Good Samaritan demonstrates ideas of helping others, not treating them differently.

> To show partiality in judging is not good. (Proverbs 24:23)
>
> God does not show favouritism – they added nothing to my message. (Galatians 2:6)
>
> There is neither Jew nor Gentile, neither slave nor free, nor is there male and female, for you are all one in Christ Jesus. (Galatians 3:28)

Treatment of women

Examples of gender inequality in Christianity:

- Catholic Christians only allow men to hold church positions, for example bishop, priest, pope.
- St Paul taught 'Women should remain silent in the churches. They are not allowed to speak, but must be in submission, as the law says' (1 Corinthians 14:34).

Examples of support for gender equality:

- Since 2015, the Church of England has allowed female bishops.
- Many Christian organisations (for example, Christian Aid, Tearfund) promote gender equality.

See page 50 for more on Christianity and gender prejudice and discrimination.

Treatment of homosexuals

- Teachings of equality suggest homosexuals should be allowed to marry.
- Some Christians believe 'love is love' regardless of the sex of the people.
- Many churches welcome homosexuals.
- Traditionally some Christians believe marriage should only be between a man and a woman, and that same-sex relationships are wrong, as they don't produce children naturally.
- Some churches do not accept homosexuals.

See pages 36 and 42 for more on Christian responses to homosexuality.

Problems in society

Prejudice and discrimination can lead to a lack of trust in communities, resulting in violence or isolation leading to fear and depression. Minority groups may have restricted access to facilities.

Positive discrimination

Positive discrimination is when people from minority racial groups are given preferential treatment, for example in job interviews, to ensure a range of races are represented. Some people see this as unethical – as unfair as negative discrimination – while others feel it is necessary to achieve racial equality.

Now try this

Give **two** religious beliefs about why racial discrimination is wrong.　**(2 marks)**

Prejudice and discrimination

Muslim teachings

Muslims believe prejudice and discrimination are wrong because:

1 Allah created all humans – they are equal although not the same. All people, however, deserve equal treatment and respect

2 Muhammad taught about the importance of treating everyone equally in his final sermon.

> We have created you from male and female and made you peoples and tribes that you may know one another. (Surah 49:13)

This quote shows the belief that all humans were created equally by Allah. This is a key teaching when considering why Muslims believe prejudice and discrimination are wrong.

Treatment of women

Men and women are seen to have different roles in Islam.

- Men are providers, who are seen to protect women.
- Women raise the children and look after the home.

These roles are seen to complement each other.

> All people are equal … as the teeth of a comb. (Hadith)

See page 51 for more on Islam and gender prejudice and discrimination.

Treatment of homosexuals

Islam traditionally teaches that homosexuality is wrong, as:

- homosexual couples cannot have children naturally, which is the purpose of marriage
- same-sex relationships are seen to threaten the family unit and the stability of society.

There are many examples of Muslims who are homosexual being rejected by other Muslims. For example, their family refuses to have anything to do with them because they claim it is impossible to be both Muslim and homosexual.

See pages 37 and 43 for more on Muslim responses to homosexuality.

Racial discrimination

1 Muslims believe everyone was made equal by Allah.

2 The Qur'an teaches: 'And of His signs is the creation of the heavens and the Earth and the diversity of your languages and your colours. Indeed in that are signs for those of knowledge' (Surah 30:22). This suggests that Islam recognises there is diversity between people in terms of race, but they are all equal.

3 Muslims recognise that diversity between people can cause problems in society and lead to conflict.

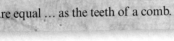

Racial discrimination occurs when a person is treated differently because of their race, colour, descent, national or ethnic origin or immigrant status. It includes both positive and negative discrimination.

Malcolm X (1925–65)

- Malcolm X was an African-American Muslim who campaigned for racial equality.
- He became a minister for the radical Nation of Islam organisation to try to spread the message for a 'Black people only state'.
- In his speeches, Malcolm X said that his followers should not start violence but should defend themselves if attacked. Some Muslims today may share his view.
- Some Muslims today believe that equality should be achieved by entirely peaceful methods.

Now try this

Explain **two** religious beliefs about racial discrimination. Refer to sacred writings or another source of religious belief and teaching in your answer. **(5 marks)**

Equality and freedom of religious belief

Christian teachings on equality

Christians believe humans are equal because:

 all humans were made in God's image

② God loves everyone equally

③ the Parable of the Good Samaritan teaches Christians to care for everyone equally

④ Jesus treated everyone the same – even people who at the time were treated as outcasts, such as the poor, lepers, Gentiles and criminals.

> There is neither Jew nor Gentile, neither slave nor free, nor is there male and female, for you are all one in Christ Jesus. (Galatians 3:28)

Freedom of religious belief

• Most Christians support religious freedom.

• Jesus taught, 'treat others as you would want to be treated'.

• Jesus did not judge anyone – he simply moved on from people who rejected his religious message (Luke 9:52–6). He also spoke to a Samaritan woman even though Jews would not associate with Samaritans (John 4:7–27).

• Some Christians are afraid that new laws and attitudes, including acceptance of religious freedom, threaten Christianity.

• Some Christians believe their religion is the true faith, so are less accepting of others.

Freedom of religious expression

• Most Christians believe people should be able to express their religion freely – including religious clothing, food and prayer.

• Most Christians recognise that the ability of religious believers to express their faith does not affect the rights of others.

At times, Christians have not been allowed to express their religion freely. For example:

• Nadia Eweida was sent home for wearing her crucifix when she worked for an airline.

• Nurse Sarah Kuteh was sacked in 2016 after discussing Christianity with patients and offering to pray with them.

Human rights

Human rights are basic rights and freedoms to which everyone is entitled. Most Christians believe:

• Bible teachings support human rights

• all humans are God's creation and so are sacred

• God loves everyone equally, so all people should be treated equally.

This inspires Christians to work for a fair world.

> ... whatever you did for one of the least of these brothers and sisters of mine, you did for me (Matthew 25:40)

Divergent Christian responses

Some Christians, such as Desmond Tutu and Martin Luther King Jr, feel that when the law is in conflict with their conscience over human rights, it is right to challenge the law.

Other Christians support **situation ethics**, and think that each individual situation should be considered separately.

Problems for Christians

Sometimes there is a conflict between Christian principles and human rights. For example, some Christians are opposed to homosexuality and female priests. Other Christians may argue that such views go against human rights and fail to value equality.

Now try this

Explain **two** religious beliefs about freedom of expression.
Refer to sacred writings or another source of religious belief and teaching in your answer.

(5 marks)

Equality and freedom of religious belief

Equality

Islam teaches that Allah created all people equally, although not the same. This suggests differences between people are not important.

> Among His signs is the creation of the heavens and the earth, and the difference of your languages and colours. (Surah 30:22).

- Muslims are all part of the ummah, so are united regardless of colour and nationality.
- Many practices in Islam show equality: completion of Hajj; praying at the same time every day; all wearing white garments, etc.
- Muhammad's final sermon before his death spoke of equality and tolerance.

Religious freedom

Religious freedom is a fundamental human right that creates the conditions for peace, and peace is an important idea within Islam. Muslims believe that community is important – demonstrated by the ummah.

> There shall be no compulsion in [acceptance of] the religion. (Surah 2:256)

This quote shows that Muslims believe religious freedom is important.

Freedom of religion and belief

Limited religious freedom

Some believe that Islam is the only true faith and the only religion exclusively correct.

Some believe they have a mission to lead non-Muslims to Allah.

Some hold that Islam has the whole truth but other religions have parts of the truth.

Some accept that all righteous people will be favoured by Allah and, therefore, it does not matter which religion a person belongs to.

Maximum religious freedom

Freedom of religious expression

Many Muslims believe people should be able to express their faith freely. At times Muslims have been unable to do this. In France and Austria, the wearing of any sort of face veil has been banned. Some school uniform policies do not allow traditional forms of Islamic dress.

Some minority Muslim groups hold extreme views and persecute and kill other Muslims because they are seem to be the 'wrong type'.

Most Muslims agree that human rights need to be upheld. Yet some (e.g. same-sex marriage) may conflict with teachings.

Muslim views on human rights

Islam teaches that all humans were created equal by Allah, and Muhammad tried to demonstrate the fair treatment of all people. The Qur'an has teachings that support human rights.

Muslims may find there is conflict between a human right and a law within Islam. They may also see a conflict between a human right and a law of the country they live in, and countries may have laws that result in inequality.

Non-religious views include the belief that every person should be treated fairly, and the importance of upholding people's rights.

Now try this

'Everyone has a responsibility to stand up when human rights are denied.'

Evaluate this statement. In your answer you:

- should give reasoned arguments in support of this statement
- should give reasoned arguments to support a different point of view
- should refer to religious arguments
- may refer to non-religious arguments
- should reach a justified conclusion.

(12 marks plus 3 SPaG marks)

Social justice

Social justice means equal distribution of wealth, opportunities and privileges in society.

Wealth and opportunity in the UK and world

Wealth and money are not distributed equally in the UK or the world. Smaller numbers of people hold larger amounts of wealth, meaning that many people live in poverty. It is also fair to suggest that people living in poverty face fewer opportunities in life as a result.

Christian teachings

- Christians have a duty to work for social justice, as this reflects Bible teachings and the example set by Jesus.

- 'Love your neighbour as yourself' (Mark 12:31) – meaning Christians should help others.

- All humans are equal, as they were made in the image of God.

- Christians believe they should stand up for the rights of others.

- The Bible teaches that Christians have a responsibility to help those less fortunate. 'Whoever is generous to the poor lends to the Lord, and he will repay him for his deed' (Proverbs 19:17).

> The Synod [believes] that, as a matter of common humanity and of our mutual interest in survival, the world requires a new and more equitable system of economic relationships between nations. (General Synod of the Church of England, 1981)
>
> *Rich nations* have a grave moral responsibility toward those (less fortunate). (Catechism of the Catholic Church 2439)

Statements of belief relating to social justice.

> The King will reply, 'Truly I tell you, whatever you did for one of the least of these brothers and sisters of mine, you did for me.' (Matthew 25:40)

Jesus compared helping another person to helping him directly.

The Church and social justice

1. Many Christians promote ideas of social justice in their local communities.

2. Many Christians try to educate others about the unfairness of social injustice and how to tackle it.

3. Churches try to address issues of social injustice by providing food banks and help for those who need it.

4. Many Christians and churches are involved in charity work, to raise awareness of social justice issues and money to support them. Christian Aid, Christians Against Poverty (CAP) and CAFOD are examples of Christian charities. Turn to pages 18 and 126 to remind yourself of some of the work done by Christian charities.

Christians may favour the use of situation ethics, such as 'doing the most loving thing', an idea promoted through the example of Jesus.

The importance of the Church working for social justice

Jesus said 'the poor you will always have with you'. This suggests there will always be those who are considered poor, and that Christians should aim to help them whenever they can. Helping others will lead to reward in heaven – which many Christians see as the ultimate goal. This also reflects Jesus' example and Christian teachings such as 'treat others as you would like to be treated'.

Make sure you develop each argument fully – use examples and teachings to support the points you make. Remember to give a justified conclusion and to check your answer for SPaG when complete.

Now try this

'We should all work for social justice.'
Evaluate this statement. In your answer you:

- should give reasoned arguments in support of this statement
- should give reasoned arguments to support a different point of view

- should refer to religious arguments
- may refer to non-religious arguments
- should reach a justified conclusion.

(12 marks plus 3 SPaG marks)

Social justice

Justice in society is the equal distribution of wealth, opportunities and privileges.

Wealth and opportunity in the UK and world

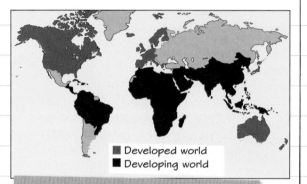

■ Developed world
■ Developing world

Wealth and opportunity are not distributed equally among people in the UK, nor in the rest of the world. Small numbers of people hold very large amounts of wealth, resulting in many people living in poverty. Wealth gives these people far greater opportunities in life than the majority of people worldwide.

Muslim teachings about social justice

Muslims believe:

✓ they have a duty to work for social justice

✓ Allah is always watching and they will be judged after death by Allah on their actions

✓ all humans are equal as they were made equal by Allah

✓ everyone is human and is entitled to human rights

✓ the Qur'an teaches Muslims they should work for social justice

✓ in Shari'ah law, which promotes social justice

✓ in the Five Pillars, which promote social justice – Zakah (charity) and Sawm (fasting) are done to sympathise with the poor in society

✓ that each situation should be taken individually and appropriate help given – this could be seen to be applying the ethical theory of situation ethics, which means the action taken in each individual situation is what is most loving.

The Qur'an and social justice

Those who follow the Messenger, the unlettered prophet, whom they find written in what they have of the Torah and the Gospel, who enjoins upon them what is right and forbids them what is wrong and makes lawful for them the good things and prohibits for them the evil and relieves them of their burden and the shackles which were upon them. So they who have believed in him, honored him, supported him and followed the light which was sent down with him – it is those who will be the successful. (Surah 7:157)

This quote talks of the importance of helping others through social justice in order to relieve the inequality within the world.

Worked example

Give **two** ways in which religious believers work for social justice.   **(2 marks)**

Muslims give Zakah (2.5%) to charity. Islamic charities such as Islamic Relief to help those affected after natural disasters.

Here, the student states **two** different things that Muslims can do to work for social justice. They are concise and direct, with each idea in a separate sentence.

Now try this

Give each belief then develop it further by giving additional information. Make sure you include a quote or paraphrase a teaching (summarise it in your own words), to link to the beliefs you present.

Explain **two** religious beliefs about why religious believers work for social justice.
Refer to sacred writings or another source of religious belief and teaching in your answer.   **(5 marks)**

Components 2A and 2B

Responsibilities of wealth

Many Christians see wealth as a gift from God, yet believe that spiritual wealth has far greater value than material wealth. Poverty causes great suffering in the world and most Christians believe that it is important to try to reduce poverty.

Christian teachings on poverty and wealth

- Christians believe they should follow the example of Jesus, who showed compassion for others.

- Christians do not believe it is wrong to be wealthy, but that it is important to gain wealth honestly and that you should use it to help others. The Parable of the Sheep and the Goats (Matthew 25:31–46) talks of God separating out people for reward and punishment based on whether they helped others in their lives.

Anyone who has two shirts should share with the one who has none, and anyone who has food should do the same. (Luke 3:11)

Go, sell everything you have and give to the poor, and you will have treasure in heaven. (Mark 10:21)

For I was hungry and you gave me something to eat, I was thirsty and you gave me something to drink, I was a stranger and you invited me in, I needed clothes and you clothed me. (Matthew 25:35–36)

These teachings show Christians that wealth is not important and that they have a duty to use their wealth to care for others.

The right attitude to wealth

The Ten Commandments teach Christians how to approach wealth.

You shall not covet your neighbour's house. You shall not covet your neighbour's wife, or his male or female servant, his ox or donkey, or anything that belongs to your neighbour. (Exodus 20:17)

Covet means to envy. This passage teaches Christians to be content with what they have. Material wealth is a gift from God, but it is not as important as spiritual wealth.

The uses of wealth

Christians believe it is important to use their wealth correctly.

- ✓ Wealth shouldn't be used selfishly but unselfishly to look after each other.

- ✓ Many Christians choose to **tithe** – to give 10 per cent of their earnings to the Church for charity purposes.

- ✓ Christians support charities like Christian Aid, which work to try to end poverty.

Duty to help the poor

Christians believe they have a duty from God to care for others, especially those in poverty.

The Parable of the Good Samaritan told by Jesus demonstrates the Christian idea of helping others.

Love your neighbour as yourself. (Matthew 22:39)

Do to others as you would have them do to you. (Luke 6:31)

Jesus' teachings show the importance of compassion and caring for others.

Christian actions to reduce poverty

1. Most Christians promote ideas of helping each other and working for social justice.

2. Many Christians try to educate others about the unfairness of poverty.

3. Churches address poverty by providing food banks and help for those who need it.

4. Many Christians do charity work to raise money to help those in poverty and increase awareness of social justice. Christian Aid, Christians Against Poverty (CAP) and CAFOD are examples of Christian charities.

Organisations like the Trussell Trust provide food banks to help those in poverty.

Now try this

Give **two** ways that religious believers can help those living in poverty. **(2 marks)**

This question tests your recall – you need to state **two** pieces of information, each in a short sentence. These can be from the same religion or from different religions.

Responsibilities of wealth

Components 2A and 2B

Islam teaches that wealth is a gift from Allah and should not be wasted. Many Muslims believe they have a duty to care for others and one way of doing this is to help those living in poverty and help to tackle the causes of poverty.

Causes of poverty in the UK and world

Poverty is caused by a combination of factors. Some of the common causes of poverty are:

1. low-paid work
2. unemployment
3. family breakdowns or illnesses
4. inadequate social benefits
5. rapid population growth leading to overpopulation
6. war and political instability
7. high national debt

8. lack of education and opportunity
9. discrimination and social inequality
10. environmental problems or natural disasters.

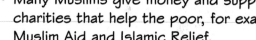

Islamic charities work in the UK and all over the world to tackle the challenge of poverty.

The right attitude to wealth

Islamic teachings state that Muslims should:

- act responsibly with wealth by helping those in need
- understand that all possessions belong to Allah and disapprove of greed and waste
- help individuals according to their needs.

The uses of wealth

- Muslims pay Zakah – 2.5% of their annual wealth is used to help the poor and needy.
- Muslims are encouraged to choose to give sadaqah, which is voluntary charity.
- Many Muslims give money and support to charities that help the poor, for example Muslim Aid and Islamic Relief.
- Muslims avoid gambling and lending for profit.

Muslims are taught that Allah expects them to show concern for others.

All Muslims are part of the ummah, and Islam teaches that they should care for each other as they were all made equal by Allah.

Righteousness is [in] one who believes in Allah, the Last Day, the angels, the Book, and the prophets and gives wealth, in spite of love for it, to relatives, orphans, the needy, the traveller, those who ask [for help], and for freeing slaves. (Surah 2:177)

Duty of Muslims to help tackle poverty

O mankind, indeed We have created you from male and female and made you peoples and tribes that you may know one another. (Surah 49:13)

Muslims believe Allah has given them the responsibility of being good khalifahs, which means to take care of Allah's creation – this is seen to include humans, who were created by Allah.

Muslims believe they have duties given to them by Allah – one of the Five Pillars is Zakah. Zakah is believed to purify the poor, because it means they are not tempted to be jealous.

The Earth is green and beautiful, and Allah has appointed you his stewards over it. (Hadith)

Establish Salah and pay Zakah, and whatever good you send ahead of you to the Hereafter for yourselves, you shall find it with Allah; surely Allah is watching all your actions. (Surah 2:110)

Now try this

Use the quotes above to help develop your explanations.

Explain **two** religious beliefs about the duty of religious believers to tackle poverty.
Refer to sacred writings or another source of religious belief and teaching in your answer.   **(5 marks)**

Exploitation of the poor

To exploit a person means to take advantage of them. Often those in society who are poor or living in poverty can easily be taken advantage of by others due to their desperate circumstances. Christian teachings clearly state that this is wrong.

1 Unfair pay

Unfair pay is when a person is not paid fairly for something. For example, it is unfair to pay someone a wage they cannot survive on. UK law recognises this by providing a 'living wage', which is the minimum hourly wage considered sufficient to maintain a normal standard of living in the UK.

Fair pay is different to equal pay – which is paying different people the same amount for doing the same job.

How the poor are exploited

2 Excessive interest on loans

A loan is money that is borrowed and paid back with interest. For example, if you borrow £5000 and the interest rate is 8.0%, you will be charged £400 in interest on top of repaying the loan of £5000. Some companies offer loans with excessive amounts of interest to be paid back. This makes it very hard for people struggling financially to pay off their debts.

3 People trafficking

This is the practice of illegally transporting people from one country to another, typically for forced labour, sexual exploitation or organ trafficking. It is understood as modern slavery.

Christian responses

1 Fair pay

- Christianity teaches that God created every human and therefore no one should be taken advantage of by not being paid fairly, as justice and equality are important.
- Christianity has a long history associated with **fair trade** – paying labourers a fair living wage. Today, fair trade has global reach and represents Christian values of fairness.

2 Excessive interest on loans

- Christianity teaches that money is a gift from God and should be earned honestly in a way that does not harm others.
- Most Christians would not support excessive interest rates, as they would feel people are being exploited, which is unacceptable.

3 Human trafficking

- Christians would not accept human trafficking under any circumstances, as they believe all human life is sacred and so all people should be treated well.
- Most Christians would also believe that human trafficking goes against agape love and the teachings of Jesus.

...I am filled with power, with the spirit of the Lord, and with justice and might. (Micah 3:8)

There is neither Jew nor Gentile, neither slave nor free, nor is there male and female, for you are all one in Christ Jesus. (Galatians 3:28)

So God created mankind in his own image, in the image of God he created them; male and female he created them. (Genesis 1:27)

Do to others as you would have them do to you. (Luke 6:31)

Love your neighbour as yourself. (Mark 12:31)

The International Labour Organization (ILO) estimates that around 40 million people worldwide are trapped in modern slavery.

Now try this Make sure you read all possible answers before making your selection.

Which **one** of the following is a term used to describe modern slavery?

A human trafficking ☐ **B** fair pay ☐ C equality ☐ **D** justice ☐ **(1 mark)**

Exploitation of the poor

Islam teaches the importance of caring for each other, which means not exploiting or taking advantage of people.

Muslim responses to how people are exploited

Way humans are exploited	Muslim view and response
Unfair pay – people not being paid fairly for the work they do. Factories where workers work long hours for little pay are known as 'sweatshops'.	• Islam teaches that Allah made all humans, so everyone is special. • Most Muslims do not support people being taken advantage of by not being paid fairly for the work they do. • Many Muslims believe money should be earned honestly so that people can live an honest and fair life. • Ideas of justice and equality are also important in Islam. O, you who have believed, be persistently standing firm in justice, witnesses for Allah, even if it be against yourselves or parents and relatives. Whether one is rich or poor, Allah is more worthy of both. (Surah 4:135)
Excessive interest on loans – money loaned with high interest rates added on top. A 'loan shark' is a moneylender who charges extremely high interest rates.	• Lending money in Islam is forbidden if the lender benefits from interest (known as riba). And whatever you give for interest to increase within the wealth of people will not increase with Allah. But what you give in Zakah, desiring the countenance of Allah – those are the multipliers. (Surah 30:39) • Muslims are encouraged to share money and help others rather than exploit people through taking high amounts of money from them. • When people do owe money, Muslims are encouraged to be sympathetic towards them. And if someone is in hardship, then [let there be] postponement until [a time of] ease. But if you give [from your right as] charity, then it is better for you, if you only knew. (Surah 2:280) • If Muslims do wish to lend money, there are Muslim banks with special facilities so Muslims can borrow money without the bank making interest on it.
Human trafficking – illegally moving people from one place to another, typically for forced labour or sexual exploitation.	• Muslims accept the sanctity of life argument – they believe that life is sacred as it was created by Allah. O mankind, indeed We have created you from male and female and made you peoples and tribes that you may know one another. Indeed, the most noble of you in the sight of Allah is the most righteous of you. Indeed, Allah is Knowing and Acquainted. (Surah 49:13) • Islam teaches that humans have a duty to care for each other so most Muslims would agree that any form of human trafficking is wrong.

Globally, the average cost of a slave is about £70. Around 80% of those trafficked are female and half are children.

Now try this

'Everyone should work to stop exploitation of the poor.'
Evaluate this statement. In your answer you:
- should give reasoned arguments in support of this statement
- should give reasoned arguments to support a different point of view
- should refer to religious arguments
- may refer to non-religious arguments
- should reach a justified conclusion.

(12 marks plus 3 SPaG marks)

Ensure you cover all aspects that this question requires. You can use the bullet points as a checklist to help you.

Poverty and charity

Christian teachings on poverty

- Helping the poor and needy is believed by Christians to gain favour with God.

> Give generously to them and do so without a grudging heart; then because of this the Lord your God will bless you in all your work. (Deuteronomy 15:10)

- Many Christians believe that looking after God's creation includes taking care of people, and that to do so honours God.

> Whoever oppresses the poor shows contempt for their Maker, but whoever is kind to the needy honours God. (Proverbs 14:31)

- Jesus taught that the poor are just as important as those with money and wealth.

> Blessed are you who are poor, for yours is the kingdom of God. (Luke 6:20)

Christian teachings on charity

- Christianity teaches compassion to all.

> Be kind and compassionate to one another, forgiving each other, just as in Christ God forgave you. (Ephesians 4:32)

- Jesus taught about the importance of helping others through parables such as the Good Samaritan.
- The Bible says that everything belongs to God, so should be shared.

> The heavens are yours, and yours also the earth; you founded the world and all that is in it. (Psalm 89:11)

How can the poor help themselves?

It may be easier for people living in poverty to help themselves if they live in relative rather than absolute poverty.

Christians may argue that the poor can:

- seek opportunities to work
- accept help offered but not rely on it as a permanent solution to their problems.

Christians may try to help people become self-sufficient, for example by providing training or tools rather than giving them money.

- The Parable of the Talents states that people are given the opportunity to use what God has given to them (which include their skills) to increase what they have.

> The United Nations defines **absolute poverty** as severe deprivation of basic human needs including food, safe drinking water, sanitation, health, shelter, education and information. **Relative poverty** is defined in terms of living standards, so varies from one country to another.

> So take the talent from him and give it to him who has the ten talents. For to everyone who has will more be given, and he will have an abundance. (Matthew 25:28)

Christian charities

1 CAFOD (Catholic Agency for Overseas Development)

CAFOD works in over 40 countries with people of all faiths to end poverty, and focuses on sustainable development rather than aid, especially at times of disaster.

2 Christian Aid

- It is a charity supported by Protestant denominations in the UK and aims to end poverty through tackling the causes of poverty.
- It helps in emergency situations such as natural disasters.

Now try this

> Develop each belief and link it to what holy books such as the Qur'an or Bible say on the issue.

Explain **two** religious beliefs about helping the poor. Refer to sacred writings or another source of religious belief and teaching in your answer.   **(5 marks)**

> Some Christians prefer to support charities rather than give money directly to the poor, because they may fear that a person could use money unwisely, e.g. for drink or drugs.

Poverty and charity

Muslim teachings on poverty

Islam teaches that those who help others will gain favour with Allah.

> The generous man is near God, near Paradise, near men and far from Hell, and the ignorant man who is generous is dearer to God than a worshipper who is miserly. (Hadith)

> [true] righteousness is [in] one who believes in Allah, the Last Day, the angels, the Book, and the prophets and gives wealth, in spite of love for it, to relatives, orphans, the needy, the traveller, those who ask [for help], and for freeing slaves. (Surah 2:177)

This quote teaches that caring for the poor and needy is honourable and righteous.

Islamic teachings on charity

1 Muslims help others through the third pillar of Islam – Zakah. They give 2.5% of their annual earnings to charity to help those living in poverty.

2 Muslims are taught that they have a duty to care for other Muslims, as they all are part of the ummah (the Muslim community).

3 Muslims are also encouraged to perform sadaqah, which is any good deed done for others. This could include giving a donation to charity.

> And establish prayer and give Zakah, and whatever good you put forward for yourselves – you will find it with Allah. Indeed, Allah of what you do, is Seeing. (Surah 2:110)

How can the poor help themselves?

- The majority of Muslims feel that working to help others is the best way of putting Muslim teachings into action.
- Yet while charity is important in Islam, Muslims believe that this should not be expected nor relied on for survival. Through the work of charities such as Muslim Aid, Muslims try to offer support to those living in poverty by helping them to become more self-sufficient.
- Many Muslims believe that while people have a responsibility to help others, those experiencing hardship need to be proactive in looking for ways to help themselves, such as opportunities to better their financial situation by actively searching for work or utilising their current talents.

Muslim charities

1 **Muslim Aid**
- works in deprived areas of the world to help relieve poverty
- responds in emergency situations to provide emergency relief and aid through medical care, clean water, food and shelter
- offers sustainable solutions, so people can support themselves in future.

2 **Islamic Relief**
- provides emergency relief in natural disasters
- supports those considered weakest in society, such as women and orphans
- focuses on education and health, to ensure the poor have equal rights.

Muslim charities help all people in need, although they may concentrate their efforts on those who belong to the Muslim faith.

Now try this

'It is important for those living in poverty to help themselves overcome their difficulties.'
Evaluate this statement. In your answer you:
- should give reasoned arguments in support of this statement
- should give reasoned arguments to support a different point of view

Try to show in your answer the importance of those living in poverty helping themselves as well as the responsibility people have to care for others. Make sure that you cover all the requirements of the bullet points within your answer.

- should refer to religious arguments
- may refer to non-religious arguments
- should reach a justified conclusion.

(12 marks plus 3 SPaG marks)

Had a look ☐   Nearly there ☐   Nailed it! ☐

Religion, human rights and social justice: Contrasting beliefs

A requirement of one type of examination question is to explain two contrasting or similar religious beliefs about three possible topics – for Theme F, these topics are the status of women in religion, the uses of wealth and freedom of religious expression. The question may ask you to refer to the main religious tradition in Britain, which is Christianity, sometimes to compare religious to non-religious belief, and sometimes give to two contrasting beliefs from two religious traditions. This page helps you to compare and contrast these beliefs.

Christian beliefs about the status of women in religion

- Christianity teaches that all humans – both men and women – are equal, as they were all made equal 'in the image of God' (Genesis 1:26).
- Christians follow the example of Jesus, who did not discriminate between men and women, and treated women as equal to men.
- Catholics only allow men to hold the positions of bishop, priest, deacon and pope, as they believe that these roles represent Jesus, who was male. This shows the status of women in the Catholic Church is still not equal.
- The Protestant Church allows female bishops, showing equality of position between men and women in the Church.

Islamic beliefs about the status of women in religion

- Islam teaches that men and women are equal though not the same.
- Muhammad taught about the importance of treating everyone equally in his final sermon, suggesting that there is equality between men and women in Islam.
- Men and women are seen to have different roles within Islam – men provide for and protect the family, while women are seen to have the role of raising the children and looking after the home.
- While men and women are given different roles in Islam, they are seen to complement each other and therefore be equal.

Beliefs about the uses of wealth

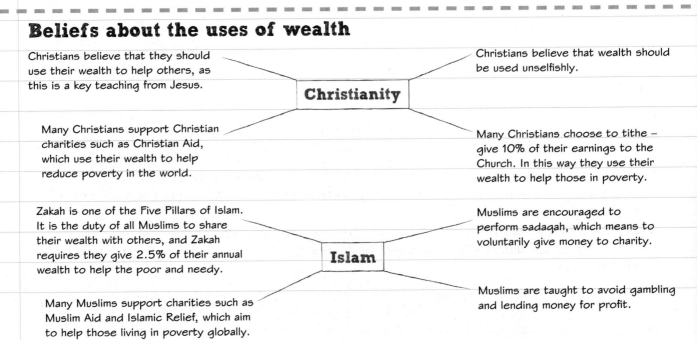

Christians believe that they should use their wealth to help others, as this is a key teaching from Jesus.

Christians believe that wealth should be used unselfishly.

Christianity

Many Christians support Christian charities such as Christian Aid, which use their wealth to help reduce poverty in the world.

Many Christians choose to tithe – give 10% of their earnings to the Church. In this way they use their wealth to help those in poverty.

Zakah is one of the Five Pillars of Islam. It is the duty of all Muslims to share their wealth with others, and Zakah requires they give 2.5% of their annual wealth to help the poor and needy.

Islam

Muslims are encouraged to perform sadaqah, which means to voluntarily give money to charity.

Many Muslims support charities such as Muslim Aid and Islamic Relief, which aim to help those living in poverty globally.

Muslims are taught to avoid gambling and lending money for profit.

Religion, human rights and social justice: Contrasting beliefs

Beliefs about freedom of religious expression

Christian beliefs	Islamic beliefs
Most Christians believe anyone of any religion should be free to express their faith and practise their religion.	Most Muslims believe that all believers of all religions should be able to practise their religion freely.
Some Christians believe that all religions are equally valid and, as everyone is equal, all should be free to follow and practise their faith.	Some Muslims believe that Allah will favour all righteous people and therefore it does not matter what religion a person belongs to.
Some Christians believe only Christianity contains the 'true' message, so while they may respect others religions, some Christians believe they have a duty and responsibility to share their faith with others.	Some Muslims believe that Islam is the one true faith and correct religion, and that it is their duty to share their faith and lead others to Allah.
Some Christians believe that Christianity in today's world is at threat from secular (non-religious) ideas as well as the growing nature of other religions.	Some Muslims believe Islam has the whole truth, but that other religions have parts of the truth, so respect and recognise the idea of religious freedom.

Worked example

Explain **two** similar beliefs about the use of wealth by religious believers. In your answer you must refer to one or more religious traditions.

(4 marks)

Christians and Muslims both believe that wealth should be used unselfishly to help others, especially the poor and needy, as this is a duty given by God.

Christians and Muslims also believe it is important to make regular financial donations to help the poor and needy in society. Christians may tithe, which is giving 10% of their earnings to the Church, while Muslims give Zakah, which is 2.5% of their earnings, to the mosque. In this way, they use their wealth to help the poor.

> Read the question carefully, to ensure you know what you are being asked. Here it asks for two **similar** beliefs. These can be from within one religion or from two different religions.

> This student answer gives **two** similar, detailed beliefs about how wealth should be used correctly. The student refers to beliefs from both Christianity and Islam.

Now try this

> Remember that men and women may be given different roles but can still be considered to be equal.

1 Explain **two** contrasting beliefs in contemporary British society about the status of women.
   In your answer, you should refer to the main religious tradition of Great Britain and one or more other religious traditions. **(4 marks)**

2 Explain **two** contrasting beliefs in contemporary British society about freedom of religious expression.
   In your answer, you should refer to the main religious tradition of Great Britain and one or more other religious traditions. **(4 marks)**

> Make sure you identify **two** ways that are different and develop each one by giving further information or perhaps an example.

John's preparation for Jesus' ministry

The Bible contains four Gospels – Matthew, Mark, Luke and John – which are found in the New Testament.

> The word 'gospel' originates from the Old English term 'god spel', meaning 'good news'.

St Mark's Gospel

1 St Mark's Gospel is similar to the Gospels of Matthew and Luke. Collectively the are known as the Synoptic Gospels, as they describe events from a similar point of view.

2 St Mark's Gospel was probably written in Rome between 65CE and 75CE.

3 The actual author of St Mark's Gospel is unknown.

4 An early Christian wrote that St Mark was the 'interpreter of Peter' but had not known Jesus personally – perhaps he received the information from Peter.

5 St Mark's Gospel tells of the **ministry** of Jesus – his works and teachings – from his baptism to his death, burial and discovery of the empty tomb.

The importance of St Mark's Gospel

Christians believe:

- St Mark wrote his Gospel because key people who knew Jesus and remembered his stories were dying, so the stories had to be preserved.

- The Gospels are seen as the 'Word of God' so have great authority and value for Christians.

- They give clues about who Jesus was, the example he set and how he lived.

- In the 19th century, many scholars came to see that St Mark's Gospel was written first and that elements of St Matthew's and St Luke's Gospels were based on it.

John's preparation for Jesus' ministry

> Here, Jesus is given the titles of 'Messiah' and recognised as the 'Son of God'.

> The 'good news' of St Mark's Gospel begins with the prophecy of a messenger who has been sent in anticipation of the coming of Jesus.

The beginning of the good news about Jesus the Messiah, the Son of God, as it is written in Isaiah the prophet: 'I will send my messenger ahead of you, who will prepare your way... a voice of one calling in the wilderness, "Prepare the way for the Lord, make straight paths for him."'

> John is seen to be preparing the way for Jesus so his teaching and example may be accepted by others.

And so John the Baptist appeared in the wilderness, preaching a baptism of repentance for the forgiveness of sins. The whole Judean countryside and all the people of Jerusalem went out to him. Confessing their sins, they were baptised by him in the Jordan River. John wore clothing made of camel's hair, with a leather belt around his waist, and he ate locusts and wild honey. And this was his message: 'After me comes the one more powerful than I, the straps of whose sandals I am not worthy to stoop down and untie. I baptise you with water, but he will baptise you with the Holy Spirit.' (Mark 1:1–8)

> This is a vivid description of John. However, it is clear that John's role is that of a servant – he is one called to serve in order to prepare the way for Jesus.

> John holds a significant role in bringing his message – he is preparing the way for the Son of God.

Now try this

1 Which **one** of the following is a name given to Jesus?
   A powerful man ☐   **B** Messiah ☐   **C** Mark ☐   **D** disciple ☐   **(1 mark)**
2 Give **two** reasons why John is important to the early ministry of Jesus.   **(2 marks)**

Jesus' baptism and temptation

St Mark's Gospel begins the story of the life of Jesus not with Jesus' birth, as the Gospels of St Matthew and St Luke do, but with his baptism.

The baptism of Jesus

At that time Jesus came from Nazareth in Galilee and was baptised by John in the Jordan. Just as Jesus was coming up out of the water, he saw heaven being torn open and the Spirit descending on him like a dove. And a voice came from heaven: 'You are my Son, whom I love; with you I am well pleased.' (Mark 1:9–11)

This passage reflects ideas of the Trinity – God as Father, Son and Holy Spirit. The voice of God is heard, the spirit descends through the representation of the dove, and Jesus as the Son of God is baptised. See page 3 for more on the Trinity.

John baptises Jesus in the Jordan River. As Jesus was baptised, he heard a voice and a dove appeared.

The temptation of Jesus

After John baptises Jesus, Jesus spends 40 days in the wilderness, where he is tempted by the devil.

At once the Spirit sent him out into the wilderness, and he was in the wilderness forty days, being tempted by Satan. He was with the wild animals, and angels attended him. (Mark 1:12–13)

This passage states that Jesus was tempted, but does not describe the three ways in which this happened, as the Gospels of Matthew and Luke do. Yet St Mark's version does give an important message: in the baptism of Jesus, when the voice from heaven says 'with you I am well pleased', many Christians understand this to be the spirit of God blessing Jesus for what he would go on to face in the wilderness.

Angels Ministering to Christ in the Wilderness by Matteo Rosselli (1578–1650)

The baptism of Jesus also shows that he identifies with sinners, as his baptism symbolises the entrance of followers into Christianity even through Jesus himself had no sin.

Jesus' baptism by John shows the truth of the prophecy of Jesus as Messiah – he is publically recognised by John as the Son of God and the one the Christians are waiting for.

Importance of Jesus' baptism and temptation

Jesus coming to John to be baptised also demonstrates his approval of John performing baptisms – this is especially important later, when the authority of John is challenged.

The temptation of Jesus in the wilderness is important in showing that all Christians need to resist temptation and follow the true path of God.

The baptism of Jesus reflects Christian understanding of God through the representation of the Trinity – Father, Son and Holy Spirit.

Now try this

1 Which **one** gives the number of days Jesus spent in the wilderness when he was tempted by the devil?
   A 3 days ☐ **B** 60 days ☐ **C** 40 days ☐ **D** 10 days ☐   **(1 mark)**

2 Explain **two** ways in which St Mark's account of the baptism of Jesus is important for Christians today. You must refer to St Mark's Gospel in your answer.   **(5 marks)**

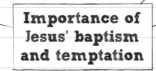

You can reference St Mark's Gospel by paraphrasing or by direct quotation.

Miracles of Jesus I

There are many stories about Jesus in St Mark's Gospel that indicate the actions Jesus performed and the kind of person he was. These stories give important truths about Jesus as the Son of God, as well as demonstrating the power of God and the importance of having faith.

The paralysed man (Mark 2:1–12)

- A paralysed man is brought to Jesus and Jesus forgives him for his sins.
- The crowd watching think only God can forgive sins and accuse Jesus of **blasphemy**.

> Blasphemy is speaking disrespectfully about God – in this case, the crowd thought Jesus was pretending to be God.

- Jesus asks if it is easier to forgive sins or make a paralysed man walk.
- The man gets up and walks, proving that Jesus, as the Son of God, has authority to forgive sins on Earth.

> When Jesus saw their faith, he said to the paralysed man, 'Son, your sins are forgiven.' (Mark 2:5)
>
> But I want you to know that the Son of Man has authority on earth to forgive sins. (Mark 2:10)

> The first quote is the words spoken by Jesus to the paralysed man, while the second details the purpose of Jesus forgiving the man, rather than just making him walk. He wants to demonstrate his power on Earth.

Jairus' daughter (Mark 5:21–24, 35–43)

- Jairus, a synagogue official, begs Jesus to heal his daughter.
- When Jesus arrives, the girl is apparently already dead but Jesus revives her.
- This miracle shows the importance of faith, through Jairus asking Jesus for help.

> He pleaded earnestly with him, 'My little daughter is dying. Please come and put your hands on her so that she will be healed and live.' (Mark 5:23)
>
> Jesus told him, 'Don't be afraid; just believe.' (Mark 5:36)
>
> The child is not dead but asleep. (Mark 5:39)

> These quotes show the power of God through the miracles of Jesus in healing physical illness. Faith is seen to be 'active', as Jairus needs to take a 'step of faith' in order to believe in the power of Jesus.

The rejection at Nazareth (Mark 6:1–6)

> 'Where did this man get these things?' they asked. 'What's this wisdom that has been given him? What are these remarkable miracles he is performing? Isn't this the carpenter? Isn't this Mary's son...' (Mark 6:2–3)
>
> He could not do any miracles there, except lay his hands on a few sick people and heal them. He was amazed at their lack of faith. (Mark 6:5–6)

> In Mark 6:1–6, Jesus is unable to perform miracles because the people do not have faith. This again shows the central importance of faith in Christianity.

Now try this

1 Give **two** reasons why faith is shown to be important in the miracles performed by Jesus. **(2 marks)**

2 Explain **two** ways in which St Mark's stories about the miracles performed by Jesus are important today. You must refer to St Mark's Gospel in your answer. **(5 marks)**

> State each way then develop it – this could be done by using the stories of the paralysed man or Jairus' daughter from St Mark's Gospel.

Miracles of Jesus II

There are many miracles performed by Jesus in the Gospels. A famous one is the feeding of the five thousand, recorded in all four Gospels and emphasised by many Christians as showing the power of God through Jesus controlling nature.

Feeding of the five thousand (Mark 6:30–44)

> Taking the five loaves and the two fish and looking up to heaven, he gave thanks and broke the loaves. Then he gave them to his disciples to distribute to the people. He also divided the two fish among them all. They all ate and were satisfied, and the disciples picked up twelve basketfuls of broken pieces of bread and fish. The number of the men who had eaten was five thousand.
> (Mark 6:41–44)

Jesus is described as giving thanks before breaking the loaves. Many Christians see this as similar to actions performed in the Eucharist service, during which bread is broken and shared to remember Jesus' sacrifice for our sins and his actions at the Last Supper. For more on the Eucharist, see page 12.

Jesus is believed to have performed the miracle of feeding five thousand people with only five loaves of bread and two fish – and there was even food left over. This shows God's power through Jesus, controlling nature and inspiring awe and wonder in those who witnessed it.

The importance of miracles for Christians

Christians believe that miracles:

- prove the existence of God as a greater being who is involved with and acts in the world
- show God cares for his creation
- show he wants to be involved in the world
- provide people with the comfort that God is ever-present and close.

Jesus performing miracles as described in the Gospel of Mark would have had great importance for his early followers in confirming faith. However, today some Christians may not give much emphasis to these accounts as modern science can offer alternative explanations.
For more on the importance of miracles for Christians, see page 72.

Non-religious beliefs

Non-religious communities may not give the accounts of miracles in St Mark's Gospel any importance because:

- ✓ they do not believe the stories in St Mark's Gospel are factual accounts of what happened
- ✓ there could be other scientific explanations that do not refer to God
- ✓ they may not believe that miracles happen or, even if they do, that God causes them.

Philosophers such as David Hume and Richard Swinburne reject the existence of miracles, arguing that there could be scientific explanations not understood at the time or that witnesses may have been mistaken.

Make sure you include all aspects required by the question – you can use the list as a checklist.

Now try this

'The power of God is proven through the miracles performed by Jesus.' Evaluate this statement.
In your answer you:

- should give reasoned arguments in support of this statement
- should give reasoned arguments to support a different point of view
- should refer to St Mark's Gospel
- may refer to non-religious arguments
- should reach a justified conclusion.

(12 marks plus 3 SPaG marks)

Caesarea Philippi and the transfiguration

The later ministry of Jesus includes the conversation at Caesarea Philippi, where the disciples recognise Jesus for the first time as the **Messiah**, and the **transfiguration** of Jesus.

Conversation at Caesarea Philippi (Mark 8:27–33)

> Jesus and his disciples went on to the villages around Caesarea Philippi. On the way he asked them, 'Who do people say I am?' They replied, 'Some say John the Baptist; others say Elijah; and still others, one of the prophets.' 'But what about you?' he asked. 'Who do you say I am?' Peter answered, 'You are the Messiah.'
>
> He then began to teach them that the Son of Man must suffer many things and be rejected by the elders, the chief priests and the teachers of the law, and that he must be killed and after three days rise again. (Mark 8:27–31)

Meaning

- Christians recognise this account in St Mark's Gospel as the first open acceptance from the disciples of Jesus as the Messiah. The disciples have witnessed Jesus' miracles and preaching, but this is seen as a turning point in his ministry.
- Jesus then goes on to predict his death and what will happen to him.

Importance

- This event is important for the disciples, as they now know that Jesus is the Messiah.
- This event is important for Christians today because it shows the person Jesus was in accepting that he was to die on the cross to save the sins of the world.
- After this event, the ministry of Jesus becomes more private and focused on his disciples. See page 136 for more about Jesus as the Messiah.

The transfiguration of Jesus

> After six days Jesus took Peter, James and John with him and led them up a high mountain, where they were all alone. There he was transfigured before them. His clothes became dazzling white, whiter than anyone in the world could bleach them. And there appeared before them Elijah and Moses, who were talking with Jesus. ... Then a cloud appeared and covered them, and a voice came from the cloud: 'This is my Son, whom I love. Listen to him!' Suddenly, when they looked around, they no longer saw anyone with them except Jesus. As they were coming down the mountain, Jesus gave them orders not to tell anyone what they had seen until the Son of Man had risen from the dead. (Mark 9:2–9)

Meaning

- God speaks to Peter, James and John and declares Jesus to be his Son and that they should listen to him.
- Jesus' clothes turn white – Christians believe this symbolises Jesus' divinity.

Importance

- The transfiguration is seen as unique, as a miracle is performed (the prophets Elijah and Moses appear) yet Jesus does not perform it.
- Jesus is understood through the transfiguration to show human meeting divine.
- The transfiguration shows Jesus being recognised as the Son of God.
- The transfiguration reflects Jesus' teachings about eternal life, as Moses and Elijah, who died centuries before, return to be part of the miracle.

Now try this

1 Which **one** of the following terms is used when Jesus is seen with the prophets Moses and Elijah and the voice of God is heard confirming Jesus as God's son?

A baptism ☐ B resurrection ☐ C transfiguration ☐ D crucifixion ☐ **(1 mark)**

2 Explain **two** ways in which Mark's account of the conversation at Caesarea Philippi is important for Christians today.

You must refer to St Mark's Gospel in your answer. **(5 marks)**

Passion prediction and James and John's request

In his later ministry, Jesus took on the role of a teacher to his disciples. He was able to rely on them more and trust them through sharing information about important events.

Jesus' passion prediction (Mark 10:32–34)

They were on their way up to Jerusalem, with Jesus leading the way, and the disciples were astonished, while those who followed were afraid. Again he took the Twelve aside and told them what was going to happen to him. 'We are going up to Jerusalem,' he said, 'and the Son of Man will be delivered over to the chief priests and the teachers of the law. They will condemn him to death and will hand him over to the Gentiles, who will mock him and spit on him, flog him and kill him. Three days later he will rise. (Mark 10:32–34)

Jesus took the disciples into his confidence and shared with them details about what would happen to him. This was the third time Jesus shared this knowledge with them and told them not to share it with anyone else.

The request of James and John (Mark 10:35–45)

Then James and John, the sons of Zebedee, came to him. 'Teacher,' they said, 'we want you to do for us whatever we ask.' 'What do you want me to do for you?' he asked. They replied, 'Let one of us sit at your right and the other at your left in your glory.' 'You don't know what you are asking,' Jesus said. 'Can you drink the cup I drink or be baptised with the baptism I am baptised with?' 'We can,' they answered. Jesus said to them, 'You will drink the cup I drink and be baptised with the baptism I am baptised with, but to sit at my right or left is not for me to grant. These places belong to those for whom they have been prepared.'
(Mark 10:35–40)

After Jesus shared the prophecy of what would happen to him for a third time, James and John made their request. Jesus replied that in order to be 'great' in the Kingdom of God, they need to be the 'least' (humble) on Earth, but the brothers did not understand. He told James and John off for seeking their own glory and trying to make the disciples jealous.

They show Jesus trying to prepare the disciples for what was going to happen to him. They show that even though the disciples followed Jesus, they did not truly understand the sacrifice that he was going to have to make. Jesus was trying to prepare them for what would happen.

Importance of these events

Many Christians today take hope from these teachings, which show the disciples failing to fully understand what Jesus was telling them. Just as the disciples did not understand the importance of what Jesus was trying to tell them, when modern Christians fail in their lives, there is hope that this, too, is all right.

Now try this

You need to state **two** different reasons – you are not required to explain them.

Give **two** reasons why Jesus shared his passion prediction with the disciples.

(2 marks)

The story of Bartimaeus

The story of Bartimaeus in Mark 10:46–52 appears at first to be the story of another healing miracle. Yet it provides important insight into Jesus and some of the names he is given. Bartimaeus shows his faith in his acceptance that Jesus representing God in human form can help him.

Bartimaeus gains his sight (Mark 10:46–52)

> Bartimaeus' sight is restored because he has complete faith that Jesus is able to heal him.

As Jesus and his disciples, together with a large crowd, were leaving the city, a blind man, Bartimaeus (which means 'son of Timaeus'), was sitting by the roadside begging. When he heard that it was Jesus of Nazareth, he began to shout, 'Jesus, Son of David, have mercy on me!' Many rebuked him and told him to be quiet, but he shouted all the more, 'Son of David, have mercy on me!' Jesus stopped and said, 'Call him.' So they called to the blind man, 'Cheer up! On your feet! He's calling you.' Throwing his cloak aside, he jumped to his feet and came to Jesus. 'What do you want me to do for you?' Jesus asked him. The blind man said, 'Rabbi, I want to see.' 'Go,' said Jesus, 'your faith has healed you.' Immediately he received his sight and followed Jesus along the road. (Mark 10:46–52)

In this story, various names are used to describe Jesus, including Jesus of Nazareth Son of David, and Rabbi. Other names that are used to describe Jesus include Son of Man, Son of God and Messiah.

Significance of the titles given to Jesus

In St Mark's Gospel, Jesus is called by a number of titles, each of which gives clues about him.

Title	Significance
Jesus of Nazareth	Nazareth is the town where Jesus grew up and began his teaching and ministry.
Son of David	• Jesus was born in Bethlehem, also known as the city of David. • God promised David – the rightful King of Israel – that his throne would be established forever. This suggests Jesus is the rightful King of the Jews.
Son of God	• This title is used for Jesus only after his death. It is significant that Jesus does not refer to himself this way and it is only after his death that he is recognised as the Son of God, as seen in the idea of the Trinity. • After Jesus' baptism, the words 'You are my Son, whom I love; with you I am well pleased' are used.
Rabbi	A rabbi is a Jewish teacher or scholar. The use of this term for Jesus shows the authority he was seen to have as well as the respect others had for his teachings.
Son of Man	• This is the title Jesus uses when referring to himself. • It represents the idea that Jesus felt ordinary human emotions and had been born to a woman (Mary).
Messiah	• Although Jesus saw himself as the Messiah, he was not what most people expected due to his humble and simple approach. • After telling the disciples at Caesarea Philippi that he is the Messiah, they recognise Jesus as the Christ.

> Remember: 'Messiah' means someone who has been chosen to lead the world and save it. The Greek translation of Messiah is 'Christ'.

Turn to page 131 for more on Jesus' baptism. See page 134 for more on Jesus' conversation with his disciples at Caesarea Philippi.

Now try this

> There are many names you could include – you only need to give two.

1 Give **two** names used to describe Jesus.   **(2 marks)**

2 Explain **two** ways in which the names given to Jesus are important for Christians today. You must refer to St Mark's Gospel in your answer.   **(5 marks)**

The entry into Jerusalem

Jesus' entry into Jerusalem marks the beginning of the week known as 'the Passion' – the week prior to Jesus' crucifixion. As Jesus and his disciples knew that he was going to die there, many expected him to enter quietly and without fuss.

The entry into Jerusalem (Mark 11:1–11)

As they approached Jerusalem and came to Bethphage and Bethany at the Mount of Olives, Jesus sent two of his disciples, saying to them, 'Go to the village ahead of you, and just as you enter it, you will find a colt tied there, which no one has ever ridden. Untie it and bring it here. If anyone asks you, "Why are you doing this?" say, "The Lord needs it and will send it back here shortly."'

They went and found a colt outside in the street, tied at a doorway. As they untied it, some people standing there asked, 'What are you doing, untying that colt?' They answered as Jesus had told them to, and the people let them go. When they brought the colt to Jesus and threw their cloaks over it, he sat on it. Many people spread their cloaks on the road, while others spread branches they had cut in the fields. Those who went ahead and those who followed shouted, 'Hosanna!', 'Blessed is he who comes in the name of the Lord!', 'Blessed is the coming kingdom of our father David!', 'Hosanna in the highest heaven!'

Jesus entered Jerusalem and went into the temple courts. He looked around at everything, but since it was already late, he went out to Bethany with the Twelve.

(Mark 11:1–11)

Jesus entered Jerusalem riding on a donkey (or a colt, as it is described in St Mark's Gospel), and people lay down palm branches and their coats for him.

Jesus' enters Jerusalem

How might Jesus have entered?	How did he enter?
Unnoticed and secretly	In front of witnesses, not afraid to face people
Unhappy and fearful of the fate he knew awaited him	Happy and cheerful – shouts of joy and celebration
As a 'king' he should enter on an animal that represents this	He rode on the back of a donkey and people laid down their cloaks for him

The titles Jesus is given

- Jesus is given the title 'Lord' in Mark 11:1–11, which suggests ideas of power, kingship and authority.
- Christians in the 1st century would have considered titles important, because they show Jesus' roles and significance to their religion.
- Christians today recognise the importance of the titles given to Jesus as they include the idea that he was both human (on Earth) and divine (the Son of God).

You could consider the benefits of having more than one title in trying to capture Jesus' many roles and aspects. Yet how could this also cause confusion? Include a range of viewpoints and refer to what St Mark's Gospel says before reaching a well-justified conclusion.

Now try this

1 Give **two** reasons why Jesus' entry into Jerusalem is important to Christians. **(2 marks)**

2 'Jesus should only have one title to cause less confusion.'
Evaluate this statement. In your answer you:
- should give reasoned arguments in support of this statement
- should give reasoned arguments to support a different point of view
- should refer to St Mark's Gospel
- may refer to non-religious arguments
- should reach a justified conclusion.

(12 marks plus 3 SPaG marks)

The Last Supper

Christians give special importance to the last week in the life of Jesus. St Mark's Gospel reflects this importance too, as five chapters are devoted to Jesus' death and the events that led up to it, as well as a whole chapter on the resurrection of Jesus.

The Last Supper (Mark 14:12–26)

This famous painting by Leonardo da Vinci (1498) imagines Jesus at the Last Supper.

> … Jesus took bread, and when he had given thanks, he broke it and gave it to his disciples, saying, 'Take it; this is my body.' Then he took a cup, and when he had given thanks, he gave it to them, and they all drank from it. 'This is my blood of the covenant, which is poured out for many,' he said to them. (Mark 14:22–24)

Jesus shared bread and wine with his disciples at the Last Supper. He told them the bread represented his body and the wine, his blood.

Eucharist/Holy Communion

Christians re-enact the Last Supper through the **sacrament** of the Eucharist, also known as Holy Communion, Mass or the Lord's Supper.

- ✓ Catholics believe in **transubstantiation** – the bread and wine actually become the physical body and blood of Jesus.
- ✓ Protestants accept the bread and wine as **symbolic** of the body and blood of Jesus – they are shared in remembrance of him.

See page 12 for more on the sacrament of the Eucharist and page 11 for more on sacraments.

Jesus' prophesy

During the Passover meal shared with his disciples, Jesus revealed two prophesies:

- **one of the disciples would betray him** – Jesus does not say who this disciple is
- **the disciple Peter would deny knowing Jesus three times** – a claim Peter refuses to believe.

> Truly I tell you, one of you will betray me – one who is eating with me. (Mark 14:18)

See page 139 for details of Jesus' betrayal.

Importance of the Last Supper

Importance to the followers of Jesus	Importance to Christians today
• It was the last meal shared between Jesus and his disciples before Jesus' death. • Jesus predicted that one of his disciples would betray him and another deny him. • Jesus shared the ceremonial representation of the bread and wine, so that it could be passed on. • The Last Supper took place during the Jewish festival of Passover, so was a 'Passover meal' – two symbols (the bread and the wine) were given new significance.	• It marks the beginning of the events of the crucifixion and resurrection of Jesus, which are central to Christianity. • Jesus' instructions about remembering him and his sacrifice are still practised today in the sacrament of the Eucharist/Holy Communion. The bread and wine unite all Christians in this ceremony. • The Last Supper allows Christians to remember Jesus' sacrifice and to celebrate him overcoming death.

Now try this

Make sure you explain each point you make and that they are **contrasting** ways.

Explain **two** contrasting ways in which Christians today understand the words 'Take it; this is my body'.

(4 marks)

Jesus in Gethsemane and the trial

Jesus in Gethsemane (Mark 14:32–52)

1 After the Last Supper, Jesus goes to the Garden of Gethsemane with his disciples.

They went to a place called Gethsemane, and Jesus said to his disciples, 'Sit here while I pray.' (Mark 14:32)

2 Before he prayed, Jesus, knowing his fate, told Peter, James and John of his sadness. He then prayed to God to change his outcome, although he accepted this could not happen.

He took Peter, James and John along with him, and he began to be deeply distressed and troubled. 'My soul is overwhelmed with sorrow to the point of death,' he said to them. 'Stay here and keep watch.' Going a little farther, he fell to the ground and prayed that if possible the hour might pass from him. 'Father,' he said, 'everything is possible for you. Take this cup from me. Yet not what I will, but what you will.' (Mark 14:33–36)

3 Returning to his disciples and finding them sleeping, Jesus woke them to accept his fate.

Returning the third time, he said to them, 'Are you still sleeping and resting? Enough! The hour has come. Look, the Son of Man is delivered into the hands of sinners. Rise! Let us go! Here comes my betrayer!' (Mark 14: 41–42)

4 Judas betrayed him 'with a kiss' – this is the signal that tells the guards who they should arrest.

Now the betrayer had arranged a signal with them: 'The one I kiss is the man; arrest him and lead him away under guard.' Going at once to Jesus, Judas said, 'Rabbi!' and kissed him. (Mark 14:45–46)

5 One of the disciples used violence when Jesus was arrested but Jesus urged them to show peace. Jesus was arrested and led away.

The men seized Jesus and arrested him. Then one of those standing near drew his sword and struck the servant of the high priest, cutting off his ear. (Mark 14:44–45)

See page 86 for Jesus' response to this violent act.

The trial before the Jewish authorities (Mark 14:53, 57–65)

They took Jesus to the high priest, and all the chief priests, the elders and the teachers of the law came together. (Mark 14:53)

Then some stood up and gave this false testimony against him. (Mark 14:57)

Again the high priest asked him, 'Are you the Messiah, the Son of the Blessed One?' 'I am,' said Jesus. 'And you will see the Son of Man sitting at the right hand of the Mighty One and coming on the clouds of heaven.' (Mark 61–62)

The high priest tore his clothes. 'Why do we need any more witnesses?' he asked. 'You have heard the blasphemy. What do you think?'

They all condemned him as worthy of death. (Mark 14:63–64)

The trial is biased against Jesus, with some testifying falsely against him.

Once again, Jesus is given titles: Messiah; the Son of the Blessed One; Son of Man.

Jesus is sentenced to death for blasphemy – the crime of speaking against God – because he confirms that he is the Messiah.

The Garden of Gethsemane brings true the prophecy that Jesus made at the Last Supper, which is that one of the disciples will betray him.

Importance of these events

The trial is seen as illegal, with false evidence being presented and the trial taking place at night. Jesus is also asked if he is the 'Messiah', and although he appears to confirm that he is, this is misinterpreted as him admitting the charge of blasphemy. This means that Jesus is not given the opportunity to defend himself or offer any evidence against the crime for which he is convicted.

Now try this

1 Which **one** of the following is the name of the disciple who betrayed Jesus?
   A Judas ☐   **B** John ☐   **C** Peter ☐   **D** James ☐   **(1 mark)**

2 Give **two** reasons why Jesus going to the Garden of Gethsemane was important.   **(2 marks)**

The trial before Pilate, the crucifixion and burial

The trial before Pilate (Mark 15:1–15)

After the trial before the Jewish authorities, St Mark's Gospel details how Jesus was taken to Pontius Pilate, the ruler of Judea. There, Pilate had to decide what was to happen to Jesus.

Christ in front of Pilate by Mihály Munkácsy (1881)

> So they bound Jesus, led him away and handed him over to Pilate. 'Are you the king of the Jews?' asked Pilate. 'You have said so,' Jesus replied. (Mark 15:1–2)

Pilate seemed to think Jesus was not guilty. As it was the Jewish festival of Passover, Pilate referred to an old tradition of releasing a prisoner. His prisoners were Jesus and a murderer called Barabbas. Pilate used this tradition to ask the crowd who to release. The crowd asks for Barabbas, so Pilate had no choice but to sentence Jesus to death.

The crucifixion (Mark 15:21–41)

> They brought Jesus to the place called Golgotha (which means 'the place of the skull'). Then they offered him wine mixed with myrrh, but he did not take it. And they crucified him. It was nine in the morning when they crucified him. The written notice of the charge against him read: THE KING OF THE JEWS. (Mark 15:22–25)

Jesus was crucified at Golgotha. His crime was claiming to be 'King of the Jews', which was written above him.

> At noon, darkness came over the whole land until three in the afternoon. And at three in the afternoon Jesus cried out in a loud voice, 'Eloi, Eloi, lema sabachthani?' (which means 'My God, my God, why have you forsaken me?'). (Mark 15:33–34)

> The curtain of the temple was torn in two from top to bottom. And when the centurion, who stood there in front of Jesus, saw how he died, he said, 'Surely this man was the Son of God!' (Mark 15: 38–39)

The sky became dark before Jesus died. Once the curtain tore in two, some recognised the real truth of who Jesus was – the Son of God.

The burial of Jesus (Mark 15:42–47)

> So as evening approached, Joseph of Arimathea, a prominent member of the Council, who was himself waiting for the kingdom of God, went boldly to Pilate and asked for Jesus' body. Pilate was surprised to hear that he was already dead. Summoning the centurion, he asked him if Jesus had already died. When he learned from the centurion that it was so, he gave the body to Joseph. So Joseph bought some linen cloth, took down the body, wrapped it in the linen, and placed it in a tomb cut out of rock. Then he rolled a stone against the entrance of the tomb. (Mark 15:42–46)

The burial customs mentioned in St Mark's Gospel reflect what would have happened at the time.

Interpretations of Jesus' death

Christians may see Jesus' death as:

- ✓ a divine sacrifice that represents God's love for humanity
- ✓ a sacrifice
- ✓ the victory of good over evil
- ✓ the price being paid for the forgiveness of humanity.

Now try this

Remember to present **two** different understandings.

1. Give **two** burial customs that happened to Jesus. **(2 marks)**
2. Explain **two** ways in which Christians interpret the account of the crucifixion of Jesus in St Mark's Gospel. **(4 marks)**

The empty tomb

Jesus' resurrection is given a whole chapter in St Mark's Gospel. Various references are not included in the chapter (such as the vision of Jesus resurrected or mention of the male disciples) that are found in other Gospel accounts.

The empty tomb (Mark 16:1–8)

When the Sabbath was over, Mary Magdalene, Mary the mother of James, and Salome bought spices so that they might go to anoint Jesus' body. Very early on the first day of the week, just after sunrise, they were on their way to the tomb and they asked each other, 'Who will roll the stone away from the entrance of the tomb?'

But when they looked up, they saw that the stone, which was very large, had been rolled away. As they entered the tomb, they saw a young man dressed in a white robe sitting on the right side, and they were alarmed.

'Don't be alarmed,' he said. 'You are looking for Jesus the Nazarene, who was crucified. He has risen! He is not here. See the place where they laid him. But go, tell his disciples and Peter, "He is going ahead of you into Galilee. There you will see him, just as he told you."'

Trembling and bewildered, the women went out and fled from the tomb. They said nothing to anyone, because they were afraid.

St Mark's Gospel explains that the full burial of Jesus could not take place, as it was the day before the Sabbath. We are told that the women go to anoint the body of Jesus after the Sabbath, but when they arrive the tombstone has been moved and the tomb is empty.

Understanding the empty tomb

1 Evidence of the resurrection

St Mark's Gospel provides evidence of the miracle of Jesus' resurrection, including:

- three female witnesses – the fact there are three witnesses and not just one gives strength to their account
- the actual timing of when the women visited the tomb
- the vision of the man dressed in white at the tomb and the message to go to the disciples. Many Christians interpret this message as coming from an angel sent by God.

2 Significance of the young man's message

- The message to tell the disciples is significant: Jesus has risen, as he himself prophesised.

See page 135 for details of Jesus' prophecy about his death and resurrection.

- The young man's message is that Jesus will be waiting for the disciples in Galilee.

Many Christians today accept the findings of modern science. The resurrection appears to go against this, which leads some to question the truth of the resurrection.

Difference in interpretation of Jesus' resurrection

The Gospel accounts give different information about the resurrection. For example, some accounts reference resurrection visions where Mary Magdalene, followers of Jesus or even the disciples witness the event. However, St Mark's Gospel does not mention any visions.

Many Christians point to the fact that the resurrection is evidence of a miracle – an event that seems impossible. For many Christians, having faith in Jesus and God means accepting things that sometimes science cannot explain.

Remember to give **two** different beliefs in your answer. You simply need to state what St Mark's Gospel says. For example, you could mention the empty tomb, the man dressed in white or the women visiting the tomb.

Now try this

Give **two** Christian beliefs according to St Mark's Gospel about the empty tomb of Jesus.   **(2 marks)**

The Kingdom of God I

The 'Kingdom of God' is emphasised in all of the Gospels and is a key element in the teachings of Jesus. Christians believe that when Jesus began his ministry, God's Kingdom arrived on Earth.

The Kingdom of God

After John was put in prison, Jesus went into Galilee, proclaiming the good news of God. 'The time has come,' he said. 'The Kingdom of God has come near. Repent and believe the good news!' (Mark 1:14–15)

Truly I tell you, I will not drink again from the fruit of the vine until that day when I drink it new in the Kingdom of God. (Mark 14:25)

The first quote was spoken by Jesus at the start of his ministry, where he proclaimed the good news of the Kingdom of God.

The second quote contains the words spoken by Jesus at the Last Supper, giving significance to this last supper – and the Kingdom of God being heaven.

Different interpretations of the Kingdom of God

Christian understanding of the Kingdom of God differs. Some Christians see it as a physical place, while others see it as a state of being with God.

1 Present reality

In the Gospel of Luke, the Pharisees asked Jesus when the Kingdom of God would come. Jesus replied, 'the Kingdom of God is in your midst'. Some Christians interpret this to mean that part of the Kingdom of God is present in the world. Christians believe they have a duty to share their religion with others and bring them to the shared Kingdom of God.

2 Future hope

The Kingdom of God could be understood as yet to come. Jesus taught that when the final judgement after death comes, all those who accept God as King will be in the Kingdom of God; those who have not accepted him with be outside of it.

Different Christian understandings of the Kingdom of God

3 Personal inner state

One interpretation of the Kingdom of God is that it is within people – in their hearts. In this sense, it is an individual response to accept the existence of the Kingdom of God.

4 A community

The Kingdom of God can be understood as a community of people who share the beliefs and teachings shared by Jesus at its core.

The greatest commandment (Mark 12:28–34)

'Love the Lord your God with all your heart and with all your soul and with all your mind and with all your strength.' ... 'Love your neighbour as yourself.' There is no commandment greater than these.' (Mark 12:30–31)

- Jesus teaches that the greatest commandment is to love God and to love one another. This teaching is central to Christianity.
- Christians believe that it is through the love of God in sending Jesus that they were able to 'know' God and they should reciprocate this through showing love to others.
- Christianity teaches the importance of agape love – the highest form of love, which is understood as selfless or unconditional love. For Christians, it is accepted to be the love of God for humanity, his creation and the love humanity has towards God.

Now try this

1 Give **two** reasons why the Kingdom of God taught in St Mark's Gospel is important to Christians. **(2 marks)**

2 Explain **two** contrasting Christian beliefs about the Kingdom of God as shown in St Mark's Gospel. **(4 marks)**

You must give **two** contrasting beliefs. For example, you could explain the idea of the Kingdom of God being a present reality and then explain how the Kingdom of God is also a future hope.

The Kingdom of God II

Entry to the Kingdom of God

Christians believe you need to do certain things or live your life in a particular way in order to be able to enter the Kingdom of God, as explained in St Mark's Gospel.

Jesus and the children (Mark 10:13–16)

> Truly I tell you, anyone who will not receive the kingdom of God like a little child will never enter it. (Mark 10:15)

Jesus makes it clear that in order to enter the Kingdom of God you must accept it like a child – with open trust and gratitude, rather than with an adult's suspicion or doubt.

The rich man (Mark 10:17–27)

> It is easier for a camel to go through the eye of a needle than for someone who is rich to enter the kingdom of God. (Mark 10:25)

Jesus taught that being wealthy is not important; rather, it is how you use your wealth, perhaps by showing love to others, that you gain entry to the Kingdom.

Parables about the Kingdom of God

Parables (stories that have an important meaning) in St Mark's Gospel help Christians to understand the Kingdom of God more easily.

 1 Parable of the Sower (Mark 4:1–20)

In this parable, Jesus describes a sower sowing seed and how the seed falls in different areas.

> As he was scattering the seed, some fell along the path, and the birds came and ate it up. Some fell on rocky places, where it did not have much soil. It sprang up quickly, because the soil was shallow. But when the sun came up, the plants were scorched, and they withered because they had no root. Other seed fell among thorns, which grew up and choked the plants, so that they did not bear grain. Still other seed fell on good soil. It came up, grew and produced a crop, some multiplying thirty, some sixty, some a hundred times. (Mark 4:4–8)

The message of this parable is that those who hear God's message are like the different types of soil. Many people will hear God's word (represented by the seed) but will not be able to receive it because they won't listen or understand, or get distracted. Only those whose hearts are open are able to receive God's love.

 2 Parable of the Growing Seed (Mark 4:26–29)

> He also said, 'This is what the kingdom of God is like. A man scatters seed on the ground. Night and day, whether he sleeps or gets up, the seed sprouts and grows, though he does not know how. All by itself the soil produces grain – first the stalk, then the head, then the full kernel in the head. As soon as the grain is ripe, he puts the sickle to it, because the harvest has come.' (Mark 4:26–29)

This parable suggests that the Kingdom of God (represented by the seed) grows gradually but there is no stopping it. The seed continuing to grow unaided suggests that God achieves his aims even when humans are absent or unaware of what he is doing. The final harvest suggests that Christians will one day realise the benefits of God's Kingdom.

3 Parable of the Mustard Seed (Mark 4:30–34)

> What shall we say the kingdom of God is like, or what parable shall we use to describe it? It is like a mustard seed, which is the smallest of all seeds on earth. Yet when planted, it grows and becomes the largest of all garden plants, with such big branches that the birds can perch in its shade. (Mark 4:30–32)

This parable reinforces the idea of the Kingdom of God being like a community of believers that is continually growing.

Now try this

Explain **two** ways in which St Mark's telling of Jesus' parables helps Christians today understand the Kingdom of God. You must refer to St Mark's Gospel in your answer. **(5 marks)**

Jesus' relationships: Women

There are various stories in St Mark's Gospel where Jesus meets with people from different groups in society that were generally not treated well or given any status or importance. These include women, who were viewed at that time as inferior to men and treated disrespectfully.

Jesus' relationships with women

The status and role of women in the time of Jesus was severely limited in most cultures at the time. Jewish law and custom meant women had little or no authority, and they were largely confined to their father or husband's homes.

In contrast, Jesus seemed to support a radical change in the treatment of women, appearing to challenge many centuries of Jewish law and custom. Some of these included:

- talking to foreign women, which was considered inappropriate – custom required men to only speak to women within their families
- using terminology that appears to give equality between men and women – for example, referring to a woman as a 'daughter of Abraham'
- accepting women into his inner circle of trusted people – his disciples were mentioned alongside women, including Mary Magdalene
- challenging the poor treatment of women.

The anointing at Bethany (Mark 14:1–9)

St Mark's Gospel tells how a woman anointed Jesus by pouring a jar of expensive oil over his head. This was considered a blessing and was done during religious rituals, yet her actions were described as wasteful. She was also criticised because Jesus did not know her and yet she touched him. However, Jesus defended her:

'Leave her alone,' said Jesus. 'Why are you bothering her? She has done a beautiful thing to me… She poured perfume on my body beforehand to prepare for my burial. Truly I tell you, wherever the gospel is preached throughout the world, what she has done will also be told, in memory of her.' (Mark 14:6, 8–9)

The widow at the treasury (Mark 12:41–44)

In this story, Jesus praises a woman for her offering, which although less than those made by wealthy people, is worth much more since she has given all she has to live on.

Jesus sat down opposite the place where the offerings were put and watched the crowd putting their money into the temple treasury. Many rich people threw in large amounts. But a poor widow came and put in two very small copper coins, worth only a few cents.

Calling his disciples to him, Jesus said, 'Truly I tell you, this poor widow has put more into the treasury than all the others. They all gave out of their wealth; but she, out of her poverty, put in everything – all she had to live on.' (Mark 12:41–44)

Now try this

Give **two** reasons why teachings about Jesus' attitude towards women in St Mark's Gospel is important for Christians.   **(2 marks)**

Remember, you just need to state **two** different reasons when answering this question – there is no need for you to explain each idea in detail.

Jesus' relationships: Gentiles and tax collectors

Some of the stories in St Mark's Gospel emphasise the relationship Jesus had with **Gentiles** and tax collectors – two groups who were treated badly in society at that time. Association with Gentiles was considered to make you impure, while tax collectors were seen as dishonest and unclean.

> **Gentile** is a term to describe a person who is not Jewish.

The Greek woman's daughter (Mark 7:24–30)

In this parable, a non-Jewish woman begs Jesus to drive the evil spirit from her daughter. Jesus tells her that the 'children' (Jews) must be 'fed' first – meaning his healing powers are intended for them. She replies that surely the 'dogs' (non-Jews) can have the scraps the children do not want. For this answer, Jesus heals her daughter; the woman has faith Jesus' power is for everyone, and he accepts her argument.

> … a woman whose little daughter was possessed by an impure spirit came and fell at [Jesus'] feet. The woman was a Greek, born in Syrian Phoenicia. She begged Jesus to drive the demon out of her daughter. 'First let the children eat all they want,' he told her, 'for it is not right to take the children's bread and toss it to the dogs.' 'Lord,' she replied, 'even the dogs under the table eat the children's crumbs.' Then he told her, 'For such a reply, you may go; the demon has left your daughter.' She went home and found her child lying on the bed, and the demon gone. (Mark 7:25–30)

The call of Levi (Mark 2:13–17)

Jesus ate a meal with Levi, a tax collector. Doubts are raised about why Jesus was associating with people who are considered dishonest and unclean, due to their role of being tax collectors. Jesus challenged this stereotype by arguing that his role was to save the sinners.

> When the teachers of the law who were Pharisees saw [Jesus] eating with the sinners and tax collectors, they asked his disciples: 'Why does he eat with tax collectors and sinners?' On hearing this, Jesus said to them, 'It is not the healthy who need a doctor, but the sick. I have not come to call the righteous, but sinners.' (Mark 2:16–17)

Significance of Jesus' attitudes

Stories such as those in the examples above are important because:

- ✓ Jesus set the example of not discriminating against any group of people; he showed that he came to save everyone
- ✓ Jesus began to challenge typical stereotypical views of various groups within society
- ✓ Jesus' behaviour put many of his teachings, such as loving everyone and treating people how they would like to be treated, into action.

Worked example

Give **two** examples from St Mark's Gospel of how Jesus treated those disregarded by society.
(2 marks)

Jesus challenged the view that Gentiles were not to be mixed with by healing the daughter of a non-Jewish woman.

Jesus also challenged traditional views of tax collectors, who were considered unclean, by sitting and sharing a meal with them. This was considered inappropriate as eating with them would, in turn, make you also unclean.

Now try this

Explain **two** ways in which Jesus' treatment of those disregarded by society is shown to be important in St Mark's Gospel.
You must refer to St Mark's Gospel in your answer.

(5 marks)

Jesus' relationships: The sick

There are many stories of Jesus healing people in St Mark's Gospel. Sick people would have been isolated in society and their illnesses often thought of as a punishment from God.

The man with leprosy (Mark 1:40–45)

In the 1st century, there were strict rules about how lepers should be treated so the disease did not spread: 'They must live alone' (Leviticus 13:46). A man with leprosy begs Jesus to heal him, which he does.

> A man with leprosy came to [Jesus] and begged him on his knees, 'If you are willing, you can make me clean.' Jesus ... reached out his hand and touched the man. 'I am willing,' he said. 'Be clean!' Immediately the leprosy left him and he was cleansed. (Mark 1:40–42)

This story shows how Jesus was willing to help sick people – despite rules about isolating them from others. This shows his willingness to love and help everyone.

The demon-possessed boy (Mark 9:14–29)

This story of healing happens after Jesus' disciples are unable to cure a boy with an evil spirit.

> A man in the crowd answered, 'Teacher, I brought you my son, who is possessed by a spirit that has robbed him of speech. Whenever it seizes him, it throws him to the ground. He foams at the mouth, gnashes his teeth and becomes rigid. I asked your disciples to drive out the spirit, but they could not.' (Mark 9:17–18)

Some people today believe the boy in this story was not possessed but epileptic. **Epilepsy** is a brain disorder that causes seizures.

Jesus tells the boy's father that his son can be cured if he shows faith. The father says he has faith, but needs help to overcome his 'unbelief'. Jesus then casts the evil spirit out.

This story shows the important role that faith played in Jesus' miracles.

Worked example

'People should follow the example set by Jesus of treating everyone equally.'
Evaluate this statement. In your answer you:
- should give reasoned arguments in support of this statement
- should give reasoned arguments to support a different point of view
- should refer to St Mark's Gospel
- may refer to non-religious arguments
- should reach a justified conclusion.

(12 marks plus 3 SPaG marks)

Some people may agree with the statement, as St Mark's Gospel gives many examples of how Jesus tried to treat all people equally. Examples include Jesus healing the epileptic (demon-possessed) boy (Mark 9:14–29) and the man with leprosy (Mark 1:40–45) where Jesus showed others not to be afraid of the sick but to try to help them. In the 1st century women were considered inferior, yet Jesus still praised them for their actions, as seen in the examples of the widow at the treasury (Mark 12: 41–44). Many Christians believe that they should follow Jesus' example.

The student needs to continue by giving at least one more argument, then give reasoned arguments that disagree with the statement – perhaps by thinking about why some people in society may not deserve fair treatment, as seen from other stories in St Mark's Gospel. Finally, they need to give a reasoned conclusion.

Now try this

Write your own answer to the worked example question.

Faith and discipleship I

St Mark's Gospel describes the call of the disciples, the role they played, and their importance in preaching the Gospel to others.

The call of the first disciples (Mark 1:16–20)

- The word 'disciple' means 'follower'. It is often used to describe Jesus' twelve followers from the Gospels. It is also a term used generally to mean any Christian.
- Another term used to describe the twelve disciples is 'apostles'. This term describes their role as teachers who spread the word of God.
- Alongside the twelve apostles, Jesus had other followers, which included women.

'Come, follow me,' Jesus said, 'and I will send you out to fish for people.' (Mark 1:17)

This quotation shows Jesus speaking to his twelve disciples and identifying their specific role in gathering more people to follow his teachings.

The mission of the Twelve (Mark 6:7–13)

Calling the Twelve to him, he began to send them out two by two and gave them authority over impure spirits. These were his instructions: 'Take nothing for the journey except a staff – no bread, no bag, no money in your belts. Wear sandals but not an extra shirt. Whenever you enter a house, stay there until you leave that town. And if any place will not welcome you or listen to you, leave that place and shake the dust off your feet as a testimony against them.' They went out and preached that people should repent. They drove out many demons and anointed many sick people with oil and healed them. (Mark 6:7–13)

This passage details the role and rules of Jesus' twelve followers. They were:

- given authority over evil spirits
- told what to take with them and what to wear
- given instructions to stay where they were welcome and leave where they were not
- told to share Jesus' stories and to preach the good news to those who would listen
- given the role of healing others, following the example of Jesus.

The commission and ascension (Mark 16:14–20)

After the resurrection of Jesus, he shared with his eleven disciples their continued mission. He urged them to preach the Gospel.

'Go into all the world and preach the gospel to all creation. Whoever believes and is baptised will be saved, but whoever does not believe will be condemned. And these signs will accompany those who believe: In my name they will drive out demons; they will speak in new tongues; they will pick up snakes with their hands; and when they drink deadly poison, it will not hurt them at all; they will place their hands on sick people, and they will get well.' (Mark 16:15–18)

- Some fundamental Christians believe that the twelve apostles could actually speak in different languages, drive out demons and drink poison.
- Many Christians today believe Jesus' instructions are symbolic of the greater mission each Christian has to share their faith with others. They do not believe the account literally.

Jesus' followers were given the gift of being able to speak in tongues in order to preach. This is when they were filled with the Holy Spirit and could communicate in many languages.

You need to **apply** your knowledge to answer this question successfully. Why might Christians find it difficult to accept that only some people are saved? What other Christian teachings may contradict this belief?

Now try this

Give **two** reasons why some Christians may find it difficult to follow the teaching in St Mark's Gospel that 'whoever believes and is baptised will be saved but whoever does not believe will be condemned.' **(2 marks)**

Faith and discipleship II

St Mark's Gospel highlights both the challenges and rewards of being one of Jesus' twelve disciples. This is seen through the example of one of the disciples, Peter. St Mark's Gospel also emphasises the importance of having faith, as shown through the story of the woman with a haemorrhage.

The cost and rewards of being a disciple (Mark 8:34–38, 10:28–31)

Jesus told the disciples that although they faced persecution, they would be rewarded with eternal life.

'Whoever wants to be my disciple must deny themselves and take up their cross and follow me.' (Mark 8:34)

The disciples faced various challenges, such as giving up aspects of their lives to follow Jesus. This is important even today as Christians face various challenges because of their faith.

'Truly I tell you,' Jesus replied, 'no one who has left home or brothers or sisters or mother or father or children or fields for me and the gospel will fail to receive a hundred times as much in this present age...' (Mark 10:29–30)

Jesus tells the disciples they will have to give up things now but will receive so much more in the future.

Peter's denials (Mark 14:27–31, 66–72)

Peter was one of the first disciples to be called to the ministry of Jesus. Jesus predicted at the Last Supper that Peter, one of his most trusted disciples and eventual leader of the early Christian Church, would deny knowing Jesus – which comes true.

Jesus answered, 'today – yes, tonight – before the rooster crows twice you yourself will disown me three times.' (Mark 14:30)

[Peter] swore to them, 'I don't know this man you're talking about.' Immediately the rooster crowed the second time. Then Peter remembered the word Jesus had spoken to him: 'Before the rooster crows twice you will disown me three times.' And he broke down and wept. (Mark 14:71–72)

These passages demonstrate the difficulty Peter faced in being a disciple. Christians today recognise that Jesus chose Peter to be a disciple, despite knowing what Peter would eventually do in denying him. Christians today take comfort from this, knowing that while they try to follow Jesus' example, they cannot be expected to achieve this in all aspects.

The woman with a haemorrhage (Mark 5:24–34)

While Jesus was on his way to Jairus' house, a woman from the crowd with severe bleeding touched his cloak. She was healed, through her faith that Jesus could heal her.

A woman was there who had been subject to bleeding for twelve years. She had suffered a great deal under the care of many doctors and had spent all she had, yet instead of getting better she grew worse. When she heard about Jesus, she came up behind him in the crowd and touched his cloak, because she thought, 'If I just touch his clothes, I will be healed.' Immediately her bleeding stopped and she felt in her body that she was freed from her suffering ... He said to her, 'Daughter, your faith has healed you. Go in peace and be freed from your suffering.' (Mark 5:25–29, 34)

Now try this

In order to answer this question successfully, you need to consider your knowledge of Peter as a disciple as well as the rewards and challenges faced by the disciples in general.

1 Give **two** ways in which being a disciple was seen as a challenge in St Mark's Gospel. **(2 marks)**

2 'It was rewarding to be a disciple in the time of Jesus.'
Evaluate this statement. In your answer you:
- should give reasoned arguments to support this statement
- should give reasoned arguments to support a different point of view
- should refer to St Mark's Gospel
- may refer to non-religious arguments
- should reach a justified conclusion.
(12 marks plus 3 SPaG marks)

Answers

CHRISTIANITY

Key beliefs

1 The nature of God I
B Omnipotent

2 Evil and suffering
Answers may vary, but you may include some of the following evidence and arguments.

Arguments in support:
- Letting people suffer is seen as cruel; when humans do this to each other, they are criticised for it. It is hard to justify God's existence when nothing is done to help those who suffer, especially those who are innocent, such as children.
- Suffering may have a purpose, but the extent of suffering in the world seems excessive. Allowing people to continually suffer seems mean and suggests God cannot exist, as he would want to help his creation.
- The presence of evil and suffering in the world challenges both the existence and nature of God. If he existed, it is difficult to understand why he does not prevent it.

Arguments in support of other views:
- Christians argue that God gave humans free will and, therefore, in order for people to be free, God cannot interfere in the world and stop suffering.
- Some Christians accept that there may be a purpose to suffering that they do not understand. Humans are not as great as God, as shown by his nature, and should not question what he does.
- Christians may view suffering as a test and opportunity to respond with compassion in the world. They use the example of Job, who had his faith tested, and they look to charity and prayer to help them cope with evil and suffering.

You will be awarded marks for accurate spelling and punctuation, the effective use of grammar to convey meaning and the use of a wide range of specialist terminology.

3 The nature of God II
1   For example:
- The Trinity is the three parts of God.
- The three parts of the Trinity are God as Father, Son and Holy Spirit.
- The Trinity is the three roles of God.
- The Father is the powerful creator of the world.
- The Son is Jesus, who came to Earth in human form.
- The Holy Spirit is the invisible part of God acting within the world.

2   Your answer must include relevant, accurate references to scripture or sacred writings. For example:
- One aspect of the Trinity is God as Father: the Father is the powerful creator of everything; he created the universe with a single command of his word (Nicene Creed, John 1:1).
- One aspect of the Trinity is God as the Son: the Son is Jesus Christ who came to Earth in human form to redeem the sins of the world (Mark 1:9).
- One aspect of the Trinity is God as the Holy Spirit: this is the invisible power of God acting within the world, which guides and inspires Christians (Matthew 28:19).

4 Creation
Answers may vary, but you may include some of the following evidence and arguments.

Arguments in support:
- Fundamental Christians believe the Bible is the word of God and, therefore, only accept what it says. God chose to create the universe and planned it as the Bible says.
- Fundamental Christians do not accept scientific theories about how the world was created as they conflict with the Bible. As the Big Bang theory and theory of evolution are not mentioned in the Bible, they must be wrong.
- Fundamental Christians believe that the world was created in six 24-hour days with God creating something different on each day as the Bible says. The Bible comes directly from God and therefore cannot be wrong.

Arguments in support of other views:
- Liberal Christians believe the Bible offers more of a mythical account of how the universe was created. Although it is the word of God, it needs to be updated to fit with modern ideas of the world.
- Liberal Christians believe science and the Bible together can explain the creation of the universe. Science explains *how* the world was created, while the Bible explains *why* it was created.
- Liberal Christians believe science and the Bible are not in conflict. God created the world but used the Big Bang and theory of evolution to do so.

You will be awarded marks for accurate spelling and punctuation, the effective use of grammar to convey meaning and the use of a wide range of specialist terminology.

5 The afterlife
For example:
- Those who fear hell are motivated to try to please God to avoid it – for example, they will try to help others as they believe this is what the Church teaches they should do to reach heaven.
- They will put their faith in God that he will ensure fair judgement is given after death. Christians believe God is just and will act in a fair and unbiased way to judge whether each person deserves to go to heaven or hell.
- They will understand that death is not the end and try to follow the example of Jesus, as his resurrection is their evidence of an afterlife. They will try to follow the teachings of Jesus, such as 'love your neighbour'.

Jesus Christ and salvation

6 Jesus as the Son of God
1   **D** Incarnation
2   Your answer must include relevant, accurate references to scripture or sacred writings. For example:
- Jesus is God in human form: Christians believe in the Trinity and one part of this is Jesus, the Son of God; the birth of Jesus fulfilled the prophecy of Christ coming to Earth as Saviour to save the sins of the world (1 Timothy 3:36).

- Jesus is both human and divine: the Bible details how Jesus was born to a human mother Mary. In addition, he was able to perform miracles and forgive sins, showing he was divine. (John 21:17).
- The Nicene Creed explains the Incarnation: it talks of Jesus being the only Son of God who came down from heaven and was made human (Nicene Creed).

7 Crucifixion, resurrection and ascension

1 **A** resurrection
2 For example:
- The prophecy about Jesus was proven to be true.
- They show that Jesus was incarnate.
- They demonstrate Jesus is worthy of worship and respect.
- They demonstrate Christian beliefs about life after death.
- They show that God loves his creation.
- They help Christians understand the sacrifice Jesus made for them.

8 Salvation and atonement

You may refer to any contrasting ways, e.g. from Catholic, Orthodox and Protestant traditions. Answers could include:
- Jesus' death as a divine sacrifice represents God's love for humanity. Christians believe that the death of Jesus atoned for original sin, which was brought into the world when Adam and Eve disobeyed God in the Garden of Eden. The sacrifice of Jesus repaired the broken relationship between God and humanity.
- Jesus' death represents the price being paid for the forgiveness of humanity. Christians believe that in order to be able to achieve redemption, Jesus had to die. Following the way and example of Jesus today means people can also achieve salvation.
- Jesus' death is a victory of good over evil. Jesus was used as the ransom to prevent the devil having hold over humanity; it shows that evil will not win.

Worship and festivals

9 Forms of worship

You may refer to any contrasting ways, e.g. from Catholic, Orthodox and Protestant traditions. Answers could include:
- Liturgical worship: Christians worship according to a set pattern; Catholics and Anglicans often follow this type of worship; worship happens on a regular basis (usually a Sunday); set prayers will be used; often the Book of Common Prayer will be used; prayer will be led by a priest or minister; the Eucharist/Holy Communion/Mass is an example of a service; the Bible may be used, a sermon will be given, hymns will be sung, prayers will be said.
- Non-liturgical worship: less formal than liturgical worship; denominations such as Methodist and Pentecostal follow this; there is no set pattern of worship; worship can be unscripted and improvised; may be charismatic worship; can involve clapping, singing and the use of music; emphasises the Holy Spirit; may involve speaking in tongues.
- Private worship: may involve Christians praying alone; could spend time reading the Bible to understand more fully its meaning and significance; could involve a retreat where Christians simply focus on prayer; may involve being silent.

10 Prayer

Answers may vary, but you may include some of the following evidence and arguments.
Arguments in support:
- Individual Christians can choose how they want to worship and pray in private; in public worship they have to follow set prayers and actions that everyone is doing; private worship allows for prayer to be more personal.
- Private prayer can be understood to have more meaning as Christians individually decide what to say and do; they cannot copy what others do as in public prayer; they can develop a more meaningful relationship with God.
- Jesus told his disciples in Matthew 6:6 to pray in private; this allows them time to reflect and not to show off; it has meaning as it is following the teaching of Jesus.
Arguments in support of other views:
- Public worship allows Christians to feel more supported than in private worship; they are part of a community sharing their faith; they do not have to struggle to pray and worship by themselves.
- Public worship means everyone is performing the set prayers and actions, so know what to do; there will be someone to lead the prayers; praying with others together gives the prayers more meaning.
- Both forms of prayers are equally valid and needed as they suit different occasions: at times, Christians may want to offer personal prayers alone to God and on other occasions share their faith; both have equal meaning and relevance to Christianity.
You will be awarded marks for accurate spelling and punctuation, the effective use of grammar to convey meaning and the use of a wide range of specialist terminology.

11 Baptism

1 **A** full immersion
2 For example:
- The person is able to understand the meaning of baptism.
- The person is making the choice for himself or herself.
- They may be confirming their commitment to Christianity made as a child.
- They are able to make their own testimony.
- They show acceptance of Jesus in their lives.
- It follows the method of Jesus being baptised.

12 Eucharist

You may refer to any contrasting ways, e.g. from Catholic, Orthodox and Protestant traditions. Answers could include:
- Catholics: call the Eucharist service 'Mass'; believe in transubstantiation, where the bread and wine actually become the body and blood of Jesus; call Christ's presence in the bread and wine the 'real' presence.
- Orthodox: understand the Eucharist service as a sacrament but refer to it as a 'mystery'; believe that the bread and wine becomes the body and blood of Jesus but do not pretend to be able to understand how it does this; refer to the change in the bread and wine as a divine mystery.
- Baptist: accept the Eucharist, referring to it as 'the Lord's supper'; understand it as a remembrance of the suffering of Jesus and mark it using the words he used at the Last Supper; do not accept there is any presence of Jesus in the wine and bread – it is only symbolic.

13 Pilgrimage

1 For example:
- They can visit places of religious significance to Christianity.
- They can feel closer to God.
- It is tradition in the religion.
- They can visit places such as Iona, where prayers have been answered.
- They can visit places such as Lourdes, where miracles are believed to have happened.
- They can have time to reflect on their religion.

2 You may refer to any contrasting examples, e.g. from Catholic, Orthodox and Protestant traditions. Answers could include:

Pilgrimage to Lourdes:
- Pilgrims go to Lourdes because of the healing miracles that happened there.
- They go to visit the place Bernadette Soubirous saw a vision of the Virgin Mary.
- They may pray for a miracle for themselves.
- It is especially important to Catholics.
- They may attend a Mass service or the torchlight Marian evening procession.
- Many attend the grotto where Bernadette had the vision.

Pilgrimage to Iona:
- Pilgrims spend time praying and studying the Bible.
- They can attend a retreat.
- They can spend time in quiet reflection.
- They can remember the saints who lived there.
- They can visit the abbey church and monastery.

14 Celebrations

1 For example:
- Easter remembers the death and crucifixion of Jesus.
- It celebrates the resurrection of Jesus.
- It reinforces the Christian belief in the afterlife.
- It brings the Christian community together.
- It is an opportunity to share with others through giving cards and Easter eggs.
- Jesus is central to the religion and it celebrates his role within Christianity.

2 Answers may vary, but you may include some of the following evidence and arguments.

Arguments in support:
- Christmas brings people in the Christian community together.
- They attend Midnight Mass together to remember the incarnation of God through Jesus.
- They will share in the traditions of a meal and being together.
- The birth of Jesus marks the start of the Christian religion.
- The life of Jesus is central to the Christian faith.
- Nativity plays are put on to mark the importance of the birth of Jesus.
- Christmas is a time for ideas of helping and caring for others to be promoted.
- Often people will send cards and gifts to mark the occasion.
- People may try to think of those in society who are less well-off and include them in the celebrations.

Arguments in support of other views:
- The significance of Christmas has been lost, as some believe society is becoming secular.
- Christmas is less about Jesus and more about presents.
- The true religious meaning of Christmas is being forgotten.
- Some may argue that Christmas has importance but other Christian teachings are more important.
- Ideas of charity work and helping others are practically more beneficial.
- They can have a positive impact on the world more than celebrating Christmas.
- Some may argue that it is the death of Jesus celebrated through the festival of Easter that is more important.
- Easter marks the death and resurrection of Jesus rather than his birth.
- Easter gives hope of an afterlife.

You will be awarded marks for accurate spelling and punctuation, the effective use of grammar to convey meaning and the use of a wide range of specialist terminology.

The role of the Church

15 The church in the local community

1 For example:
- Work of street pastors on the streets in the community.
- Food banks.
- They hold social events such as coffee mornings.
- They hold Bible study groups.
- They celebrate rites of passage.
- They celebrate festivals.

2 Your answer must include relevant, accurate references to scripture or sacred writings. For example:
- Food banks provide stocks of food for those who are in need in the local community; food vouchers may be issued so it can be fairly distributed.
- It puts the principle taught by Jesus of 'Love your neighbour' into action through providing food in times of need.
- Food banks ensure that those who are struggling to feed their family can do so.
- Food packages of non-perishables can be made up for those who need it.
- It puts into action the idea of helping others promoted in the Parable of the Sheep and Goats in Matthew 25.
- In emergency situations, food banks can provide emergency food parcels; this is seen through organisations such as the Trussell Trust.
- It puts into action the principles of 'treating others as you would like to be treated', which was taught by Jesus.

16 Sharing faith

1 **D** missionary
2 Your answer must include relevant, accurate references to scripture or sacred writings. For example:
- Christians have a duty to share their faith with others: faith can be shared locally, nationally and globally through opportunities provided such as charity work, projects and missionary work; doing so follows teachings in the Bible such as Matthew 28:19, which says that 'they should make disciples of all nations'.

- The Holy Spirit can be seen acting within the world through evangelism: Christians believe that evangelical work is how God stays close to his creation and acts within the world; passages in the Bible such as John 20:22 talk of 'receiving the Holy Spirit'.
- Christians are expected to share the Gospel to follow the example of Jesus: just as Jesus shared his faith with his disciples and fishermen, Christians should follow his example; passages from the Bible such as Matthew 4:19 tell of Jesus putting this teaching into practice.

17 Importance of the worldwide Church I

1 For example:
  - Praying for the persecuted.
  - Helping the persecuted to escape the country where they are being persecuted and become refugees.
  - Giving practical help through charity organisations.
  - Educating others about the persecution.
  - Putting pressure on authorities to help stop the persecution.
2 Your answer must include relevant, accurate references to scripture or sacred writings. For example:
  - Jesus taught us to 'love one another'.
  - Christians believe they have a duty to care for each other and work for reconciliation.
  - They should try to support each other and work together for peace (John 13:34).
  - The Bible teaches about the importance of forgiveness: this is shown through the example of Jesus forgiving those who have done wrong.
  - Showing forgiveness towards others will help to bring reconciliation between people (Mark 11:25).
  - The Bible teaches to 'love your enemies and pray for those who persecute you'; this means to work to help those who persecute others – this could be done through helping them to understand the reasons why they persecute and change their behaviour (Matthew 5:44).

18 Importance of the worldwide Church II

For example:
- They respond after a disaster.
- They offer practical help after landslides, typhoons, earthquakes, tsunamis, etc.
- They offer food, water, shelter and medical care to those people who have lost everything.
- They help educate people about human injustices.
- They raise awareness of human rights and campaign when rights have been denied.
- They work in places where women may be treated as inferior or people are targeted for their religious beliefs.
- They help local communities to become self-sufficient.
- They provide education and tools so that they can begin to take care of themselves.
- They help set up resources so people have access to them to survive.

ISLAM
Key beliefs

19 The six articles of faith in Sunni Islam

1 For example:
  - Tawhid (belief in the Oneness of Allah).
  - Belief in angels.
  - Authority of the holy books.
  - Prophethood.
  - Belief in supremacy of Allah's will.
  - Belief in life after death.
2 For example:
  - Belief in life after death may influence them to try to please Allah.
  - They would wish to be rewarded in paradise and not punished in hell.
  - They may avoid things such as drinking alcohol and place importance on things such as performing the Five Pillars of Islam.
  - Belief in the authority of the holy books may encourage them to read them more frequently.
  - They may read the Qur'an, their main holy book daily.
  - They will try to follow the Qur'an's teachings to please Allah.
  - Belief in Tawhid will make them want to submit to Allah in everything they do.
  - They will ensure they pray five times a day to Allah and show commitment to him.
  - They will try to recite daily the Shahadah, which contains the belief of Tawhid.

20 The five roots of Usul ad-Din in Shi'a Islam

Answers may vary, but you may include some of the following evidence and arguments.
Arguments in support:
- Tawhid (the belief in the Oneness of Allah) is at the heart of the Islamic faith for both Sunni and Shi'a Muslims.
- It is in both the six articles of faith and the five roots of Usul ad-Din, showing it is important.
- Tawhid is often understood to underpin all other beliefs; for example, belief in the afterlife and Day of Judgement is in both the six articles and the five roots and directly links to Allah judging humans in the afterlife.
- Tawhid affects every action a Muslim performs.
- Awareness of Allah watching them and being part his creation will affect how Muslims behave and act in their lives.
Arguments in support of other views:
- There are many other beliefs other than Tawhid in Islam that are equally important.
- The six articles and five roots contain shared beliefs such as life after death and prophethood, which will also impact on the lives of Muslims.
- Islam is a religion of beliefs and practices so one belief is no more important than actions.
- Muslims are expected to perform the Five Pillars of Islam, which are all actions and duties, showing they are important.
- Muslims may argue that a belief in the afterlife is more important than Tawhid, as this will dictate how they behave in order to be rewarded.

- Muslims wish to achieve paradise and will therefore try to achieve this, so this has a greater impact on their individual lives.

You will be awarded marks for accurate spelling and punctuation, the effective use of grammar to convey meaning and the use of a wide range of specialist terminology.

21 The Oneness and nature of God

For example:
- Muslims may be influenced to recite the Shahadah daily.
- The Shahadah says 'There is no God but Allah'.
- Muslims show their commitment through this key belief.
- Muslims will be aware of their daily actions.
- They believe everything they do is linked to the concept of Allah.
- They want to please him so will try to live as he wants.
- Muslims will feel united to all other Muslims in the world.
- Sunni Muslims have Tawhid in the six articles of faith and Shi'a Muslims have it in the five roots of Usul ad-Din.
- Muslims will feel the ummah (Muslim community) is strengthened.

22 Angels

1 For example:
- Angels act as messengers between Allah and humans.
- They watch over humans.
- They are one of the six articles of faith for Sunni Muslims.
- They have unique roles.
- They help Muslims understand how to live their lives.
- It was the angel Jibril who brought the Qur'an to Muslims through Muhammad.

2 Your answer must include relevant, accurate references to scripture or sacred writings. For example:
- Angels were created out of light: the Qur'an describes them as messengers with wings (Surah 35:1).
- Angels are given individual unique roles: Jibril was the angel given the task of sharing the Qur'an from Allah to Muhammad (Surah 2:97).
- Angels are seen to be messengers between Allah and Prophets: they praise God but have no free will (Surah 2:97–98).

23 al-Qadr and Akhirah

For example:
- Muslims will want to live their lives according to the belief that their future is predetermined.
- They know Allah will judge them on the Day of Judgement.
- They want to please Allah so they will be rewarded after death.
- Muslims will be constantly aware of their thoughts, beliefs and actions.
- They will want to follow the duties Allah has given them.
- They will try to perform the Five Pillars.
- Muslims will believe it is important to help others.
- The Qur'an teaches them that this is how Allah wants them to behave.
- They believe this will bring favour with Allah.

Authority

24 Risalah (prophethood)

1 For example:
- Adam
- Ibrahim
- Muhammad
- Isa
- Musa
- Ishmail

2 For example:
- They are a channel of communication between Allah and humanity.
- They have brought important messages from Allah.
- They have brought holy books.
- They are named in the Qur'an.
- They show Muslims how to live their lives.
- They confirm the nature of Allah through their messages.

25 The holy books

1 For example:
- They use them as a source of authority.
- When they have an issue or a problem, they will look to teachings contained in them; for example, if they want to know whether divorce is acceptable or not.
- They will use them in daily worship.
- They will recite words from the Qur'an in prayer.
- They help them to understand and connect to Allah.
- They will use them to receive the messages from Allah.
- There have been many prophets who have connected Allah to humanity; for example, Muhammad brought the message of the Qur'an.

2 Your answer must include relevant, accurate references to scripture or sacred writings. For example:
- The Qur'an contains the literal, unchanged words of Allah: the Qur'an was revealed to Muhammad through the angel Jibril and Muslims do not accept translations; its meaning should be understood in its original language as it was recited (Surah 53–5).
- The Qur'an is a form of direct revelation from Allah: it was revealed to Muhammad through the angel Jibril over a period of 23 years. Muhammad's last sermon, Surah 53:4–5, says it was revelation from Allah.
- The Qur'an is intended to be recited and Qur'an means 'recitation': as Muhammad was illiterate, he recited and learned the words by heart (Surah 96:1).

26 The Imamate in Shi'a Islam

Your answer must include relevant, accurate references to scripture or sacred writings. For example:
- The Imamate possess the same characteristics as Prophets: they were appointed by Allah and given the role to lead Islam after the death of Muhammad. Surah 2:124 shows this when Allah appointed Ibrahim as an 'imam'.
- Allah loves his creation and left the Imamate to guide and lead Muslims: Shi'a Muslims do not accept that Allah would abandon them, and after the death of Muhammad, imams were appointed to continue the leadership role (Hadith Silsilat al-ahaadeeth al-saheehah predicts the final imam will return).

- The imams are not prophets but should be treated respectfully and protected: they are not prophets as they have not received revelation but are considered to be infallible human beings who justly rule over the Muslim community (Surah 21:73 says the imams were chosen and guided).

Worship

27 The Five Pillars and the Ten Obligatory Acts

1 **D** khums
2 For example:
   - Both include Salah (prayer).
   - Both include Zakah (charity).
   - Both include Hajj (pilgrimage).
   - Both include Sawm (fasting).
   - Both are seen to unite Muslims.
   - Both are seen to support Muslims in the practice of their faith.

28 The Shahadah

Answers may vary, but you may include some of the following evidence and arguments.

Arguments in support:
- The Shahadah is the first of the Five Pillars of Islam, suggesting it is the most important, as it comes before all other pillars and is given prominence as the first pillar.
- The Shahadah is considered to underpin all other pillars; it contains the central belief of acceptance in Allah, who is at the centre of the religion of Islam.
- The Shahadah is spoken daily, makes up part of the adhan (call to prayer), is whispered into the ears of newborn babies and should be spoken before death; speaking it at these key points in life shows its importance.

Arguments in support of other views:
- Islam teaches that the pillars are all equally important; they are all considered to be duties and practices performed for Allah, which is expected of all Muslims.
- Salah (prayer) could be considered more important than the Shahadah, as this happens five times a day and is regular communication with Allah; it is a practical way of developing a personal relationship with him.
- Zakah and Sawm are considered to be the pillars where Muslims can have the most impact in the world; these two pillars help others – especially the poor and needy – whereas the Shahadah is a personal and individual proclamation of faith.

You will be awarded marks for accurate spelling and punctuation, the effective use of grammar to convey meaning and the use of a wide range of specialist terminology.

29 Salah I

Your answer must include relevant, accurate references to scripture or sacred writings. For example:
- Salah is compulsory prayer five times a day: this is the second of the Five Pillars and is a duty for every Muslim to complete (Surah 20:13 tells Muslims to 'worship [Allah] and offer prayer').
- Muhammad established regular prayer: he taught about this to his followers and commanded them to direct their prayer to Allah (Surah 1:1–4 says 'Oh Allah how perfect you are and praise be to You').

- Islam teaches that regular prayer will help Muslims act as Allah intended: Muslims understand that they will be judged by Allah after death and regular prayer will help them to achieve heaven rather than hell (Hadith Al-Albani, Sahih al-Jami says that Muslims will be brought to account for the prayers they have offered on the Day of Judgement).

30 Salah II

1 **A** Jummah
2 You may refer to any contrasting ways. Answers could include:

Sunni Muslims:
- They perform prayer five times a day at set times/they do not combine prayers.
- They prostrate themselves directly onto the clean floor or prayer mat/they do not have anything between them and the ground.
- They complete their prayers by moving their head from right to left, to show respect.

Shi'a Muslims:
- They can combine their prayers.
- They combine two of the five prayers and pray three times a day.
- They do not prostrate themselves directly onto the ground or mat, but place their forehead onto a natural material such as wood.
- They raise their hands three times at the end of completing prayers, to show submission to Allah.

Duties and festivals

31 Sawm

1 Those who do not have to fast during Sawm and why, for example:
   - elderly Muslims, as it may affect their health
   - young children, as their bodies are still developing and need food
   - pregnant women, as it would be dangerous to their baby
   - those on long journeys, as they need food for energy
   - Muslims who are unwell, as it may affect their health.

2 Your answer must include relevant, accurate references to scripture or sacred writings. For example:
   - It is one of the Five Pillars of Islam: it is therefore a duty for Muslims to perform it and shows a Muslim is obeying Allah (Surah 2:183 says 'fasting is prescribed for you').
   - It has many benefits, including helping Muslims to develop self-discipline, and offering sympathy for the poor: Muslims can spend time in reflection on their personal faith and connection to Allah as well as gaining understanding of the poverty faced by some people in the world (Surah 2:183 says 'fasting is prescribed for you').
   - It helps Muslims to remember the importance of the Qur'an being revealed: Sawm commemorates the Night of Power, when Muhammad received his religious experience and revelation of the Qur'an (Surah 96:1–5 teaches Muslims to 'recite', which is what Muhammad was told to do when the Qur'an was revealed).

32 Zakah and khums

Answers may vary, but you may include some of the following evidence and arguments.

Arguments in support:

- Zakah is the third pillar of Islam and is a duty for all Muslims; giving Zakah means submitting to Allah, so is a good way of serving him.
- Zakah is used to help the most poor and needy in society, which is understood as something that Allah has commanded; the Qur'an teaches the importance of helping others.
- Muslims believe that after death Allah will judge them on the way they have lived their lives and they will be rewarded or punished; giving Zakah means they will find favour with Allah.

Arguments in support of other views:

- Allah is at the centre of the Islamic faith and Salah – compulsory prayer – may be considered to be a better way of serving him directly, as developing a relationship with Allah is important.
- Muslims would give all five of the Five Pillars of Islam importance in serving Allah; no one pillar is considered to be more important than another, as they are all duties from Allah.
- Giving time and volunteering or working for a charity organisation such as Muslim Aid may have a bigger impact than giving Zakah once a year; some Muslims may argue that there are better ways to serve Allah in the world.

You will be awarded marks for accurate spelling and punctuation, the effective use of grammar to convey meaning and the use of a wide range of specialist terminology.

33 Hajj

1 For example:.
- They perform Tawaf.
- They run between the hills of Safa and Marwa.
- They put on ihram.
- They stone the devil at Mina.
- They sacrifice an animal.
- They complete the 'Stand' on Mount Arafat.

2 For example:
- All Muslims put on ihram; this shows unity and equality before Allah.
- The state of ihram means they are getting into the right frame of mind to complete Hajj for Allah.
- Muslims perform Tawaf; this demonstrates unity of all Muslims in submission to Allah.
- All Muslims move in the same direction around the Ka'aba in harmony.
- They complete the 'Stand' on Mount Arafat to praise Allah; standing in the sun in the heat reminds Muslims of the Day of Judgement and this is a time for Muslims to reflect on what they have done wrong and ask Allah for forgiveness.

34 Jihad

1 **C** to struggle

2 Answers may vary, but you may include some of the following evidence and arguments.

Arguments in support:

- Greater jihad is emphasised as more important in the Qur'an; one hadith says that Prophet Muhammad returned from war saying, 'You have come from the Lesser Jihad to the Greater Jihad – the striving of a servant (of Allah) against his desires' (Hadith).
- Greater jihad is considered to be a personal and individual struggle on a daily basis to overcome temptation; it is more difficult and challenging to stay committed to Islam rather than to declare war.
- Greater jihad has a wider impact on the life of a Muslim as it can involve daily acts that Muslims complete, such as following the Five Pillars and rules of Islam.

Arguments in support of other views:

- Muslims do not take lesser jihad lightly; it is a difficult decision to take to go to war to defend Islam and there are strict conditions for lesser jihad that need to be met.
- There may be occasions when Islam or Allah is threatened, which could include Muslims being prevented from practising their faith; in such circumstances, defending Islam as a whole takes on great importance.
- The Qur'an talks in Surah 2 and 22 of lesser jihad, showing it has equal, if not more importance than greater jihad; it also contains teachings on the conditions needed to declare lesser jihad.

You will be awarded marks for accurate spelling and punctuation, the effective use of grammar to convey meaning and the use of a wide range of specialist terminology.

35 Festivals and commemorations

1 For example:
- They allow Muslims to remember past events and important people within Islam.
- They help to strengthen the ummah.
- Muslims can share their beliefs together.
- They give them a sense of identity and belonging.
- They allow Muslims time to celebrate Islam and mark important days.

2 For example:
- They will attend the Mosque.
- Special prayers will be said.
- Muslims will be reminded of the reasons why they fasted during Ramadan.
- They will sacrifice an animal. It will be shared with family and friends and the poor and needy.
- They will share a special meal to symbolise the breaking of the fast.
- They will exchange gifts and cards.
- They may wish each other Id Mubarak, which means Happy Id.
- Homes will be decorated and they will share foods and gifts with each other.

Theme A: Relationships and families

Sex, marriage and divorce

36 Sexual relationships (Christianity)

For example:
- God intended sex to only happen within marriage.
- Some may take a vow of chastity.
- Sex is a gift to be saved for marriage.
- The purpose of sex is to have children within a stable marriage.
- Religious believers think they will be rewarded for staying sexually pure until after marriage.

37 Sexual relationships (Islam)

Answers may vary, but you may include some of the following evidence and arguments.

Arguments in support:
- Some Christians follow traditional arguments against homosexuality because they believe God intended marriage to be between one man and one woman. They consider marriage a stable environment to procreate and raise children, which same-sex couples cannot do naturally. Reference may be made to Genesis 2:24, Romans 1:27 or 1 Corinthians 6:9–10.
- Many Muslims are against homosexuality and accept teachings from the Qur'an that say it is unnatural as homosexual relationships do not produce children naturally, which is a key purpose of marriage. They may also believe that homosexual relationships threaten the stability of the Islamic society.
- Many religious believers will not accept homosexual relationships because they are not what God intended/ marriage was intended for one man and one woman.
- Many religious believers feel that a homosexual couple cannot have children naturally/being able to have children naturally is a key belief about the purpose of relationships within religion, especially for married relationships.
- Religious couples may feel that sacred texts support heterosexual relationships.

Arguments in support of other views:
- Some Christians are more tolerant of homosexuality, believing that all humans were created in God's image and that feelings of love between same-sex couples should be celebrated. They may accept that homosexuality is natural and not a choice.
- Some modern Muslims are more tolerant of homosexuality, believing it is not a choice and that those who engage in homosexual relationships should not be excluded from society.
- Many religious believers as well as non-religious believers may feel that as society has changed, so too have beliefs about homosexuality.
- It is no longer illegal to be homosexual in the UK.
- It is illegal to discriminate against someone because of their sexual orientation in the UK.
- Today some people recognise that homosexuality is not a choice – it is the way a person is born.
- Many people feel that love should be recognised and celebrated whether it is between a heterosexual or homosexual couple.

You will be awarded marks for accurate spelling and punctuation, the effective use of grammar to convey meaning and the use of a wide range of specialist terminology.

38 Contraception (Christianity)

You may refer to any contrasting beliefs. Answers could include:

Christianity:
- There are contrasting beliefs within Christianity. Catholics teach that the use of artificial contraception is against the purpose of marriage, which is to procreate. They believe that every sexual act should be open to the possibility of creating new life. They may use the teaching of Genesis 9:7 to support this view. They may accept some forms of natural contraception such as the rhythm method.
- Other Christians (for example, Church of England) accept the use of contraception for the purpose of family planning. They may believe that forms of contraception do not go against God's teachings and that sexual relationships are for pleasure as well as procreation.

Islam:
- Some Muslims will accept the use of contraception if it is to preserve the life of the mother, protect the well-being of the current family unit or to plan when a Muslim couple have their children.
- Many Muslims oppose any method of contraception that could be considered an early abortion.
- Some Muslims oppose the use of artificial contraception, as they believe it goes against Allah's plans for humanity, but they may allow natural methods of contraception, as this is what Islamic sources of authority promote.

39 Contraception (Islam)

Your answer must include relevant, accurate references to scripture or sacred writings. For example:

Christianity:
- Many Christians believe that Bible teachings show they have a responsibility to procreate and have children. Some Christians may apply these teachings to the issue of contraception, and suggest that the use of contraception is wrong as it prevents procreation. They may refer to Genesis 9:7 to support their views.
- Some Christians may point towards the fact that there is no direct teaching on the issue of contraception in the Bible, and therefore suggest that although the main purpose of sex is procreation, the use of contraception is sensible for family planning as it means every child is wanted and can be provided for. They may refer to teachings such as Genesis 1:27 to show that as all humans are 'made in the image of God' they should be cared for properly.

Islam:
- In Islam there may be divided views and teachings used to support beliefs about contraception. Many Muslims believe Prophet Muhammad did not support natural forms of contraception such as the withdrawal method, and use Sahih al-Bukhari 34:432 to support this view, believing that the purpose of sex is procreation and for a married couple to have a family.

- Some Muslims may believe that the use of contraception helps a married couple plan their family and can be used to protect the life of the mother if it is in danger from having another pregnancy, or the lives of other children within the family unit. A teaching in Islam that supports this view is Sahih al-Bukhari 62:136, which appears to suggest that natural contraception was common practice during the time of Muhammad.

40 Marriage (Christianity)
For example:
- To provide companionship, friendship and support.
- To enjoy a sexual relationship.
- To procreate.
- To make a lifelong commitment in a stable relationship.
- To make a contribution to society.
- To strengthen society.

41 Marriage (Islam)
Answers may vary, but you may include some of the following evidence and arguments.
Arguments in support:
- Marriage is sacred to Christians, as it is a sacrament made in front of God. Many Christians believe it is part of God's plan for couples to take the gift of marriage and live together in order to have a sexual relationship and children. Many Christians see marriage as a stable environment in which a couple can have children and raise them as Christians.
- Marriages in Islam are often arranged and it is seen as a social contract where two families are united – having children and raising them as Muslims is a key part of this. Many Muslims believe that Allah created man and woman for each other so that they can have a sexual relationship and raise a family.
- Having a sexual relationship and children are seen as natural steps after a couple are married.
- Many religious believers feel that marriage provides the best environment to have a family and raise children appropriately.
- Out of all the purposes of marriage, having children is considered the most important and part of the role of men and women within the family unit.

Arguments in support of other views:
- Many Christians recognise that marriage has many purposes, including having children, providing support and stability to the family unit and society generally, and all are equally important.
- Muslims recognise that having a family can provide stability to the Muslim community, which is important.
- Marriage is about more than just children.
- The couple are making a commitment to each other.
- Some people may not be able to have children.
- Same-sex couples cannot have children naturally.
- Other purposes of marriage may be equally or more important.
- Many people in today's society may choose to cohabit rather than marry and still have children. These relationships may be just as successful as marriages and couples may still have children and raise them appropriately.

You will be awarded marks for accurate spelling and punctuation, the effective use of grammar to convey meaning and the use of a wide range of specialist terminology.

42 Different relationships (Christianity)
B cohabitation

43 Different relationships (Islam)
For example:
- Same-sex marriage is seen as not what Allah intended.
- Marriage should be between one man and one woman.
- A key purpose of marriage is to have children, which same-sex couples cannot do naturally.
- Many religious believers do not support same-sex marriage taking place in holy buildings.
- Same-sex marriage can be seen as unnatural.

44 Divorce and remarriage (Christianity)
For example:
- Remarriage may not be accepted if divorce is not supported.
- Marriage is intended to be for life to one person.
- Remarriage may be encouraged to provide stability to a family unit.
- It may be up to individual leaders to decide whether to conduct a remarriage in a holy building.
- Remarriage may be seen to give stability to society if a previous relationship has broken down beyond repair.

45 Divorce and remarriage (Islam)
Your answer must include relevant, accurate references to scripture or sacred writings. For example:
Christianity:
- Catholics do not recognise divorce because marriage is intended to be for life. Jesus said that divorce was wrong and would break the promises made as a sacrament before God. Catholics may accept an annulment under certain circumstances. References that may be included to support these views are Mark 10:9 and Matthew 19:8–9.
- Protestants allow divorce as a last resort, as they recognise that it may sometimes be necessary. They believe that people can make mistakes but God is forgiving. In addition, UK law allows divorce.
Islam:
- Islam teaches that divorce should be a last resort after all attempts to reconcile have been tried. Muslims have to undergo a waiting period to ensure the woman is not pregnant. While divorce is allowed, Muslims believe it is not encouraged and is hated by Allah. Islam provides guidelines for Muslims to follow when considering divorce. References may include Surah 2:226 or Surah 2:227.

Families and gender equality

46 Families (Christianity)
A nuclear

47 Families (Islam)
Answers may vary, but you may include some of the following evidence and arguments.
Arguments in support:
- Many Christians believe parents have a duty to raise their children and introduce them to the Christian faith. Many Christians believe the family is a place where teaching can happen and the family unit can attend church and share their faith together. Children can also be introduced to Christianity through rites of passage such as baptism, which would not happen unless they were brought up this way.

- Muslims are taught that family is the foundation of Islamic society. Many Muslims believe that family provides stability and security and gives a good environment to raise children within the Islamic faith. Parents in an Islamic family are seen to have the role of educating their children within the Islamic faith and teaching them how to be good Muslims, through the parents acting as role models.
- For religious believers, raising their children within a faith is important.
- It helps to continue and grow the faith, which some believers feel is a duty given to them by God.
- All religions teach ideas of good morals and include teachings such as helping others.
- Raising a child within this environment means they are brought up with good morals.
- The family unit provides security and stability to raise children.
- Many religions believe parents have a responsibility and role of educating their children to contribute to the stability of society.

Arguments in support of other views:
- While many Christians recognise the importance of the family unit in raising children, they also accept that the family has other important aspects, such as teaching children the difference between right and wrong and giving them a stable upbringing.
- Islam teaches that the family is a place where children can care for their elderly parents, so for many Muslims this is seen as an important role of the family.
- Many people may not be brought up in a religious family and still find faith in their own way, so family is not the only place where faith can be taught.
- Family gives an ideal environment to raise children with good morals and teach them to be good citizens, which has nothing to do with religion.
- Many non-religious believers feel that faith should not be forced on children and that children should not be brought up in a religious environment for this reason.

You will be awarded marks for accurate spelling and punctuation, the effective use of grammar to convey meaning and the use of a wide range of specialist terminology.

48 Contemporary issues (Christianity)

For example:
- Men and women were both made by God to be equal.
- Traditional roles can complement each other.
- Today men and women can both earn a living and take care of children.
- Ideas of men providing and women caring for children may be outdated.
- Some religious believers may prefer traditional roles that suit physical abilities.

49 Contemporary issues (Islam)

Answers may vary, but you may include some of the following evidence and arguments.
Arguments in support:
- Some teachings in the Bible suggest inequality between men and women. Passages such as Genesis 2:18 suggest that woman should be a helper for man, which suggests inequality. Catholics do not allow female priests, which is another example of inequality within Christianity.

- Many Muslims follow traditional teachings of men being the providers in the family and women being the caregivers of children and the home. In addition, men also are expected to attend the mosque, while women are not.
- There are examples in religion where there appears to be inequality; for example, in Islam men are often perceived as superior; in some Christian denominations only men can be priests.
- Many people today may still see inequality between jobs and rates of pay between men and women, which supports the view that men and women are not equal/treated the same.

Arguments in support of other views:
- Many Christians believe that men and women were both made by God in his image, meaning they are equal and should be treated this way.
- Many Christians recognise that in the past, male and female roles were not the same but that developments in society have led to greater equality between the sexes. This can be seen within the Church of England, where men and women can hold the same positions of authority, for example there are now female bishops.
- Many Muslims believe that men and women are equal, although not the same. While many Muslims follow traditional teachings of men being the providers in the family and women being the caregivers of children and the home, many Muslims believe these roles to be equally important and to complement each other.
- Many modern Muslims believe that both men and women can hold all roles in society and that this suggests complete equality.
- While men and women may be suited to different roles, many religious believers feel these roles complement each other and together allow society to function.
- In modern society, men and women can have the same jobs and be recognised in the same way.
- Religious believers point to religious teachings that show men and women were made in the same way by God, which supports views of equality.
- Some non-religious as well as religious believers see traditional roles of men as providers and women as based in the home as outdated, believing in equality between the sexes.

You will be awarded marks for accurate spelling and punctuation, the effective use of grammar to convey meaning and the use of a wide range of specialist terminology.

50 Gender prejudice and discrimination (Christianity)

B gender discrimination

51 Gender prejudice and discrimination (Islam)

For example:
- Everyone was created equal by God.
- Males and females will be judged in the same way after death.
- Men and women have the same duties and responsibilities.
- Religious teachings suggest equality between genders is important.
- Men and women can hold the same jobs and positions of responsibility within religion.

52–53 Relationships and families: Contrasting beliefs (Christianity and Islam)

1 You may refer to any contrasting beliefs. Answers could include:

Christianity:

- Some Christians follow traditional arguments against homosexuality because they believe God intended marriage to be between one man and one woman. They consider marriage a stable environment in which to procreate and raise children, and same-sex couples cannot do this naturally. Reference may be made to Genesis 2:24, Romans 1:27 or 1 Corinthians 6:9–10.
- Other Christians are more tolerant of homosexuality, believing all humans were created in God's image and that feelings of love between same-sex couples should be celebrated. They may accept that homosexuality is natural and not a choice.

Islam:

- Many Muslims are against homosexuality. They may accept teachings from the Qur'an that say it is unnatural because homosexual relationships do not produce children naturally, which is a key purpose of marriage. They may also believe that homosexual relationships threaten the stability of Islamic society.
- Some modern Muslims are more tolerant of homosexuality, believing it is not a choice and that those who engage in homosexual relationships should not be excluded from society.

2 You may refer to any contrasting beliefs. Answers could include:

Christianity:

- Catholicism teaches that the use of artificial contraception goes against the purpose of marriage, which is to procreate. Many Catholics believe that every sexual act should be open to the possibility of creating new life. They may use the teaching of Genesis 9:7 to support this view. They may accept some forms of natural contraception such as the rhythm method.
- Other Christians (for example, Church of England) accept the use of contraception for the purpose of family planning. They may believe that contraception does not go against God's teachings, and that sexual relationships are for pleasure as well as procreation.

Islam:

- Some Muslims accept the use of contraception if it is to preserve the life of the mother, protect the well-being of the current family unit or to plan when a Muslim couple have their children. Many Muslims oppose any method of contraception that could be considered an early abortion. Some Muslims oppose the use of artificial contraception, as they believe it goes against Allah's plans for humanity, but they may allow natural methods of contraception, as this is what Islamic sources of authority promote. They may reference Sahih al-Bukhari 34:432 or 62:136.

Theme B: Religion and life
Origins and value of the universe

54 Origins of the universe (Christianity)
C Big Bang theory

55 Origins of the universe (Islam)

1 For example:
- Many believe God used science to create the universe.
- God created the Big Bang, which created the universe.
- Scientific theories are part of God's plan in creating the universe.
- Interpretation of the 'days' as periods of time allows for the scientific theory of evolution.
- Science explains how the universe was created and religion why it was created.

2 Your answer must include relevant, accurate references to scripture or sacred writings. For example:

Christianity:
- Many Christians today accept both the story of Creation in the Bible and scientific accounts of the creation of the universe. They may see no conflict between these ideas, believing the Big Bang and evolution to be part of God's plan. They may refer to Genesis 1, which explains the Christian Creation story and shows how scientific theories can be incorporated into this.
- Other Christians may take a literal interpretation of the Christian Creation story as contained in Genesis 1 and reject all scientific discoveries of the Big Bang and evolution as they are not mentioned in this account.

Islam:
- Islam teaches that Allah created the universe and everything within it. The Qur'an tells how Allah created the universe in six 'days'. Muslims may refer to Surah 39:62 or Surah 7:54 to support this belief, believing that what is in the Qur'an is a literal account of how the universe was created.
- Some Muslims may support both scientific explanations and the explanation in the Qur'an of how the universe was created. They may refer to passages such as Surah 51:47 that talk of 'expansion' in the universe, and see this as supporting the Big Bang theory.

56 The value of the world (Christianity)

For example:
- Duty of stewardship.
- Humans were made to have dominion over the Earth and to look after it.
- Earth is a gift from God to be looked after.
- The Earth does not belong to humanity but to God.
- God wants humanity to look after the world for future generations.

57 The value of the world (Islam)

Your answer must include relevant, accurate references to scripture or sacred writings. For example:

Christianity:

- Christians believe God gave humans the responsibility of stewardship, which means they should act as 'caretakers' of the Earth and protect it for future generations. To support these views they may refer to the Apostles' Creed, which states that God created the world, or to Psalm 24:1, which recognises that the world belongs to God and should be returned to him in the state it was given.

Islam:

- Islam teaches that Allah is the creator of the world and humans are on Earth as trustees or vicegerents. Muslims are understood to be khalifahs (the Arabic term for stewards), who have a responsibility to care for the world as it belongs to Allah. They may refer to Surah 30:26, Surah 35:39 or the Hadith that says 'Allah has appointed you his stewards'.

58 The natural world (Christianity)

You may refer to any contrasting beliefs. Answers could include:

Christianity:

- Some Christians believe that animal experimentation may be acceptable if it is used to save human lives or to further knowledge for advances in medical treatment, because the Bible states humans are superior to animals.
- Other Christians may believe that as animals are part of God's creation, they should not be used in animal experimentation. This view is also supported by God giving humans the duty of stewardship, so they may care for his creation – which includes animals.

Islam:

- Many Muslims support animal experimentation if it can be used to save human lives, because Islam teaches that humanity is at the top of Allah's creation.
- Some Muslims may argue that Allah gave humanity the duty of being khalifahs and taking care of his creation, which includes animals, so they may believe that animal experimentation is cruel and unnecessary.

59 The natural world (Islam)

Answers may vary, but you may include some of the following evidence and arguments.

Arguments in support:

- Many Christians believe that animal experimentation is acceptable if it is used responsibly to save human lives. The Bible includes teachings such as Genesis 1:26, which states that humans are superior to animals as they were 'made in the image of God', so it may seem acceptable to use animals to save human lives.
- Christians may see animals as part of God's creation. They may argue that as long as animals are treated humanely and their suffering kept to a minimum, it is acceptable to use them to further human knowledge and advance medical treatment for humans.
- Many Muslims believe that humans are at the top of Allah's creation and therefore animals can be used in experiments if they are intended to help develop knowledge or to save human lives.

- Muslims may believe that some animal experimentation is justifiable if it helps to preserve human life, but that these animals should be cared for and their suffering kept to a minimum, as Allah gave humanity the duty of being khalifahs and taking care of his creation.
- Some non-religious believers may hold that animals are there for humans to use and if experiments help to develop human knowledge and survival then this is a good thing. As they hold no religious beliefs about animals, they may not see anything wrong in using them to make life easier for humans.

Arguments in support of other views:

- Some Christians may believe that as animals are part of God's creation, they are special and should not be used in experiments. They may view some experiments as harmful to animal life and the cause of unnecessary suffering.
- Many Christians believe that God gave humans the duty of stewardship, meaning they have a responsibility to care for his creation and not harm it. Some Christians may use this argument to suggest that animal experimentation is wrong and that alternatives should be used that do not cause animals to suffer.
- Islam teaches that Allah created animals as part of his creation so they should be cared for. Some Muslims may argue that since many animal experiments are cruel and painful, any that are not necessary to saving human life (e.g. those carried out to test cosmetics) should not be done at all.
- Some non-religious believers may have concerns if animals are used in animal experimentation because they may feel that this is not how animals should be treated. They do not believe that God created animals, but may feel that unnecessary suffering should not be caused.

You will be awarded marks for accurate spelling and punctuation, the effective use of grammar to convey meaning and the use of a wide range of specialist terminology.

Origins and value of human life

60 Origins of human life (Christianity)

For example:

- Evolution is wrong as it is not contained in holy books.
- Evolution contradicts accounts in holy books.
- Evolution suggests God does not exist.
- Evolution is part of God's plan.
- God used evolution to create humans in the world.

61 Origins of human life (Islam)

Answers may vary, but you may include some of the following evidence and arguments.

Arguments in support:

- Many Christians believe there is no conflict between the biblical account of Creation and Darwin's theory of evolution. They may accept that evolution is part of God's plan for humanity.
- Special Agenda IV Diocesan Synod is a Christian document that attempts to bring together ideas of evolution and traditional biblical teachings about the creation of humanity, to show they can work together.
- Many Muslims today hold that science offers a more believable account of how humans were created. They may accept that they need to adapt their beliefs to accept what both religion and science argue. They may believe that Allah is the origin of human life but that evolution is the tool he used to achieve this.

Arguments in support of other views:
- Some Christians believe that the theory of evolution conflicts with religious beliefs about the origins of humanity. They may argue that evolution goes against belief in God creating humanity, as detailed in Genesis. Furthermore, the theory of evolution does not require belief in God, as it suggests species evolved to their current forms by chance.
- Some Muslims believe traditional Qur'anic accounts such as Surah 32:7–8, which states that Allah created humans from clay. The scientific theory of evolution does not support this account, so some Muslims would reject evolution, arguing that it is in conflict with their teachings.
- Non-religious believers might argue that religious Creation stories in holy books are not relevant, as scientific knowledge has developed to provide a detailed and factual account of the universe. They might suggest that only scientific theories such as evolution should be accepted, as there is proof of these ideas.

You will be awarded marks for accurate spelling and punctuation, the effective use of grammar to convey meaning and the use of a wide range of specialist terminology.

62 Sanctity and quality of life (Christianity)

Your answer must include relevant, accurate references to scripture or sacred writings. For example:

Christianity:
- Christians believe the Bible shows that human life is special, as God created it. They may use Genesis 2:7 to show that God breathed life into Adam, and Genesis 1:27 to show that humans were 'made in the image of God', which makes them different from all other parts of God's creation.
- Christians may refer to teachings in the Bible to support the idea of the sanctity of life, and to show that life is special. One of the Ten Commandments in Exodus 20:13 is 'You shall not murder', showing that life is precious and should be preserved.

Islam:
- Islam teaches that Allah created human life, which is therefore special. Muslims may refer to Surah 4:29 or Surah 5:32, which suggest that life should not be taken as Allah created it. They may argue that Allah chooses how long each life lasts – only he decides when a life can end.

63 Sanctity and quality of life (Islam)

Answers may vary, but you may include some of the following evidence and arguments.

Arguments in support:
- Some Christians may refer to Christian teachings on compassion and helping those who are suffering. While this is not an argument to suggest they should ever take life, it does suggest that quality of life is important.
- Many non-religious believers may hold that a person's quality of life is important, and as they do not hold any religious beliefs about life being created by a divine being, they may believe that it is a person's individual choice to decide whether their life has value or quality and what action to take.

Arguments in support of other views:
- Some Christians believe that as God created all life, this is more important than anything else. They may argue that God made humans 'in his image' (Genesis 1:26) and this is more important than a person's quality of life, as only God can decide when a life should end.
- Christianity teaches that God created all life and therefore life should not be threatened in any way. Some Christians may refer to teachings such as Romans 9:20–21, which suggest that God made humanity with a given purpose and that this God-given purpose continues even when a person's quality of life is poor.
- Muslims believe that life is special as Allah created it. While they accept that quality of life is important, they do not accept the ending of life under any circumstances. They may point to teachings such as Surah 17:33, which forbids Muslims from taking life – this shows that sanctity of life is more important than quality of life.
- Muslims believe that only Allah can determine when a person's life should end, as seen in Surah 3:145, thereby showing that a person's quality of life is not more important than sanctity of life.
- Muslims believe that suffering has a purpose and that even when a person has a poor quality of life, Allah never gives them more suffering than they can cope with. Many Muslims believe suffering is a test of faith and that sanctity of life is more important than anything.

You will be awarded marks for accurate spelling and punctuation, the effective use of grammar to convey meaning and the use of a wide range of specialist terminology.

64 Abortion and euthanasia (Christianity)

Your answer must include relevant, accurate references to scripture or sacred writings. For example:

Christianity:
- Many Christians believe that God gave humans life as a sacred gift, so to take it away by 'playing God' is disrespectful to him. They may refer to Genesis 1:26, which states that humans were 'made in the image of God'.
- Some Christians may point to teachings such as 'You shall not kill' (Exodus 20:13), which suggests euthanasia is wrong as it means taking a person's life away.
- Christianity teaches that suffering has a purpose, so many Christians believe that a person should not consider euthanasia because they are suffering. They may refer to the example of Job in the Bible (Job 2:10), who suffered but did not lose his faith.

Islam:
- Islam teaches that euthanasia is wrong under all circumstances. Surah 2:156 teaches the sanctity of life, as Allah created human life. Many Muslims believe that human life has value for this reason and they may therefore argue that euthanasia is always wrong.

65 Abortion and euthanasia (Islam)

You may refer to any contrasting beliefs. Answers could include:

Christianity:
- Christianity teaches that human life is a sacred gift from God and should not be taken under any circumstances, including euthanasia. Teachings such as Genesis 1:26, which states that humans were 'made in the image of God', support this view.

- The Ten Commandments teach that murder is wrong. Many Christians view euthanasia as murder, so would use this teaching to argue that it should not happen.
- Other Christians may point to Jesus' teachings on compassion to argue that if a person is suffering, ending their life is the kinder action to take.

Islam:
- The majority of Muslims are against euthanasia because they believe that Allah created all life, so all life is sacred and euthanasia is therefore always wrong.

66 Death and the afterlife (Christianity)

For example:
- Holy books teach about the afterlife.
- Christians point to the resurrection of Jesus.
- Many of the teachings of Jesus tell of an afterlife.
- Islam teaches about the importance of judgement after death and of living life with awareness of this.
- Ideas of reward and punishment based on a person's actions during their lifetime seem fair and just.

67 Death and the afterlife (Islam)

Answers may vary, but you may include some of the following evidence and arguments.

Arguments in support:
- Many Christians believe there is evidence of an afterlife, as shown in the Bible. They may refer to Jesus' teachings, for example John 3:16 and John 11:25, which state that Jesus would be resurrected and there is an afterlife. They may refer to the story of God sending Jesus to Earth so that humanity can have eternal life with God in heaven, and the account of Jesus' resurrection.
- Muslims may refer to teachings in the Qur'an that talk of heaven being a place of reward and hell being a place of punishment after death. Many Muslims live their lives according to these teachings, in the belief that Allah will reward or punish them after death.
- Many religious people believe that the idea of the afterlife makes sense and offers comfort for those people left behind.

Arguments in support of other views:
- Non-religious believers may feel that belief in the afterlife does not make sense. They may not accept an afterlife, believing that you only have one life and should make the most of it.
- Non-religious believers may look to science to confirm and prove their beliefs in there being no afterlife. As there is no evidence of anything after death, they would argue that an afterlife is not real.

You will be awarded marks for accurate spelling and punctuation, the effective use of grammar to convey meaning and the use of a wide range of specialist terminology.

68–69 Religion and life: Contrasting beliefs (Christianity and Islam)

1 You may refer to any contrasting beliefs. Answers could include:
Christianity:
- Many Christians, especially Catholics, believe that life begins at conception and is a gift from God. Abortion in this sense is wrong, as it is the ending of a sacred life. Abortion also goes against the Commandment 'You shall not kill' in Exodus 20:13.

- Some Christians may believe that there are circumstances when abortion may be necessary. For example, if the mother's life were at risk or in cases of rape, abortion may be seen as the 'lesser of two evils' and therefore acceptable.
- Some Christians may refer to teachings from Jesus that focus on compassion. They may argue that in some cases, abortion may be the kindest action.

Islam:
- Most Muslims do not accept abortion as they believe in the sanctity of life. They believe that Allah created all life to be special; therefore it is never right to take life away.
- Many Muslims believe life begins at ensoulment, so abortion prior to this time – which is often thought to be at 120 days – may be acceptable to some Muslims.
- Some Muslims may accept abortion if the life of the mother is put at risk through continuing with the pregnancy. They may argue that the mother's life is valuable and should be recognised.

2 You may refer to any contrasting beliefs. Answers could include:
Christianity:
- Christianity teaches about the importance of stewardship, which is a God-given responsibility to care for the world, including animals. Many Christians may argue that following this teaching, as shown in Genesis when God created the animals, means being good stewards and not harming animals in any way.
- Other Christians may believe that human life is more special than animal life, since humans were 'created in the image of God' (Genesis 1:26). Therefore, using animals for medical experiments may be acceptable if it is to save human lives or further advance knowledge that would benefit humanity.

Islam:
- Many Muslims believe that animal experimentation is wrong, as Allah created all animals and humans are expected to be good khalifahs, which means protecting Allah's creation.
- Some Muslims may support animal testing for medical reasons if it is to save human life, as Islam teaches that humans are at the top of Allah's creation.

Theme C: Existence of God and revelation

Philosophical arguments for and against the existence of God

70 The existence of God (Christianity)

1 For example:
- The Design argument cannot 'prove' God definitely was the only possible designer of the universe.
- Design could be the result of evolution and not God.
- The universe could be the result of chance.
- If God designed the universe, why did he include evidence of 'bad' design, for example evil and suffering?

2 For example:
  • God is omnipotent.
  • God is omnipresent.
  • God is benevolent.
  • God is transcendent.
  • God is unknowable.

71 The existence of God (Islam)

Answers may vary, but you may include some of the following evidence and arguments.

Arguments in support:
• Many religious believers may point to evidence of design in the world, such as plants, animals or the way the world works. This suggests a designer. The concept of God being this designer makes sense.
• The Design argument offers evidence that supports Christians' and Muslims' understanding of God. It upholds God's characteristics such as his omnipotence or benevolence, in that he has the power to design the world and cares enough for his creation that he designed it to suit humans.
• Some Christians and Muslims see scientific theories of design such as evolution as supporting religious explanations for the creation of the world. For example, evolution can be seen as part of God's plan in designing the universe.

Arguments in support of other views:
• Some Christians and Muslims reject scientific theories of evolution, as their holy books do not include specific references to them. Although they still believe that God designed and created the universe, they may not support the Design argument as it contains scientific ideas they do not believe to be true.
• Some non-religious believers may argue that the Design argument is invalid and that the theory of evolution provides a better explanation of how the universe came to exist and be designed. They may see an explanation that includes reference to God as invalid.
• Many people may offer criticisms of the Design argument. For example, it does not definitely prove God is the designer; the universe may be the result of chance; if a loving God designed the universe, then why is there evidence of bad design? These arguments suggest the Design argument is not successful.

You will be awarded marks for accurate spelling and punctuation, the effective use of grammar to convey meaning and the use of a wide range of specialist terminology.

72 Miracles (Christianity)

1 **B** miracle
2 For example:
  • They show God as a greater being acting within the world.
  • They show God cares for his creation.
  • They show God wants to be involved in the world.
  • They provide humans with the comfort that God is close.
  • They offer 'proof' that God exists.

73 Miracles (Islam)

Answers may vary, but you may include some of the following evidence and arguments.

Arguments in support:
• Christianity has a long history of miracles, as seen through the many examples in the Bible. Jesus performing miracles demonstrated the power of God and helped people to have 'proof' to believe in him. Today, miracles help to inspire awe and amazement in people, as miracles cannot be explained by science.
• Christians believe that miracles support the views they hold about God, so giving strength to their beliefs. Miracles show that God is omnipotent and cares for his creation, which are key ideas in Christianity.
• Christians believe miracles help 'prove' God's existence. The laws of nature being broken demonstrate that God exists and wants to connect with humanity.
• Many Muslims accept that miracles show Allah's existence, as they cannot explain these events in any other way.
• There are various examples of miracles in the Qur'an. Many Muslims believe that miracles occurring today reinforce this and provides evidence for Allah's existence.

Arguments in support of other views:
• Some Muslims may not place great importance on miracles. They may believe that there are better ways to know Allah – perhaps through the Qur'an or his teachings – that reinforce his nature and prove his existence.
• Non-religious believers may look to explanations of miracles other than God. They may argue that miracles can be explained scientifically and they are simply everyday events that are misinterpreted as miracles.
• Some people may offer other valid explanations for miracles including medical causes, hallucinations or the result of taking drugs. These explanations may be more credible to many non-religious believers in today's scientific world.

You will be awarded marks for accurate spelling and punctuation, the effective use of grammar to convey meaning and the use of a wide range of specialist terminology.

74 Evil and suffering (Christianity)

1 For example:
  • There are two different types of evil – moral and natural.
  • Evil can challenge the existence of God.
  • Evil can question the characteristics of God.
  • Evil may be a test of faith.
  • Moral evil is the result of human free will.
2 Your answer must include relevant, accurate references to scripture or sacred writings. For example:
Christianity:
  • Many Christians believe that God sent Jesus to Earth to overcome evil and die for the sins of the world on the cross. They look to teachings such as Psalm 46:1, which teaches that God is their strength and to follow the example of Jesus.
  • Some Christians believe evil came into the world through the devil, for example when the devil tempted Adam and Eve in the Garden of Eden.
  • Many Christians believe that God is compassionate and will forgive those who are sorry for their sins, as seen in Psalm 103.

- Many Christians believe that evil and suffering are tests from God, who has a plan for everyone. Christians believe that it is how they respond to these tests, through following the example of Jesus, which determines their afterlife. They may look to the example of Job in the Bible to understand how to best respond to suffering.

Islam:

- Islam teaches that Allah is forgiving and merciful, as seen in Surah 1, although some Muslims believe that this teaching conflicts with the fact there is evil and suffering in the world.
- Muslims believe that the Qur'an teaches them to use prayer to cope with suffering. In Surah 2:153, it is taught that evil and suffering help Muslims to develop characteristics such as patience.
- Islam teaches that evil and suffering are tests of humanity – they test how Muslims respond even when life is difficult. Muslims are taught in Surah 2:155–156 to accept suffering and not question it.

75 Evil and suffering (Islam)

Answers may vary, but you may include some of the following evidence and arguments.

Arguments in support:

- Many religious believers, including Muslims and Christians, might argue that evil and suffering challenge the existence of God and their understanding of God's nature. For example, if God is omnipotent and benevolent, why does he not intervene when people are suffering?
- Non-religious believers might use evil and suffering as an argument to suggest that God does not exist. They may question why God would allow evil and suffering in the world. They may also question the characteristics that religious believers give to God (such as all-loving, all-powerful, etc.), as these characteristics are not apparent when faced with the enormity of evil and suffering in the world.

Arguments in support of other views:

- Christians and Muslims may argue that some types of evil are not God's fault and therefore he cannot do anything about them, so he can still exist. They may argue that humans using their free will cause moral evil and so God cannot intervene in this regard.
- Many Christians and Muslims believe that evil and suffering have a purpose in the world. They believe them to be a test of faith. For example, in the story of Job in the Bible and Surah 2:153 in the Qur'an, evil is needed in order to determine who deserves a reward in the afterlife. Many religious believers may argue that how individuals choose to respond to evil and suffering is a test of their faith, and that this test is part of God's plan for humanity.
- Christians and Muslims may believe that by responding to evil and suffering they can develop characteristics such as compassion and caring for others, which are key teachings in both religions. Christianity and Islam both emphasise the importance of prayer and charity work to help overcome suffering. This means many Muslims and Christians can still believe in God's existence and yet accept evil and suffering in the world.

You will be awarded marks for accurate spelling and punctuation, the effective use of grammar to convey meaning and the use of a wide range of specialist terminology.

76 Arguments against the existence of God (Christianity)

1 **B** Big Bang
2 Answers may vary, but you may include some of the following evidence and arguments.

Arguments in support:

- Non-religious believers may agree with scientific explanations for the existence of the world, such as the Big Bang theory and the theory of evolution. They may argue that God is not required to explain how the universe came to exist. Non-religious believers might also suggest that as there is evidence of these scientific theories, they are better evidence than any religious explanations.
- Some religious believers may hold that scientific arguments appear to conflict with religious argument, especially when looking at the creation of the universe. They may reject all scientific arguments and believe only the traditional arguments contained in their holy books.
- In response to scientific evidence that God does not exist, religious believers may point to evidence such as the First Cause or Design arguments, as well as evidence of miracles, which collectively strengthen their belief that God exists.

Arguments in support of other views:

- Many Christians may believe that there is no conflict between religion and science, arguing that it is possible to accept scientific theories and have a strong belief in God. They may believe that scientific theories of the origins of the universe and humanity, such as the Big Bang and evolutionary theories, reflect God's plan, and that together religion and science provide a full explanation of the universe.
- Many Muslims believe that scientific and religious explanations of the universe can work together. They may argue that there is reference to science within the Qur'an: for example, in Surah 51:47, reference is made to the idea of expansion, which supports the scientific explanation offered by the Big Bang theory. Therefore, Muslims may argue that scientific theories in themselves do not provide evidence that God does not exist.
- Many non-religious believers argue that science proves God does not exist but stress that the presence of evil and suffering in the world offers better evidence that God does not exist. If an all-loving, all-powerful and all-present God does exist, then why does he allow evil and suffering in the world? For some non-religious believers, this may be considered a stronger argument against God's existence.

You will be awarded marks for accurate spelling and punctuation, the effective use of grammar to convey meaning and the use of a wide range of specialist terminology.

77 Arguments against the existence of God (Islam)

Your answer must include relevant, accurate references to scripture or sacred writings. For example:

Christianity:

- Some Christians believe that scientific explanations of the origins of the universe and humanity, such as the Big Bang theory and the theory of evolution, conflict with religious explanations of Creation. They therefore reject all scientific explanations to accept only what the Bible says. They may refer to Genesis 1 and 2 to support their beliefs, arguing that as there is no mention of science and since the Bible is the word of God, scientific explanations are not valid.
- Many Christians believe that science and religion are not in conflict in explaining the creation of the universe. They believe it is possible to argue, for example, that the Big Bang and evolution were part of God's plan in creating the universe.

Islam:

- Some Muslims believe science contradicts religious teachings in the Qur'an about how the world was created and so respond by rejecting all scientific explanations. They may refer to Surah 32:7–8, which state that Allah created the universe and made humans out of clay. As this account does not mention scientific explanations, some Muslims will not accept them.
- Many Muslims do not see any conflict between religious and scientific explanations of the origins of the universe and humanity, and accept both explanations. They may argue that scientific explanations help explain how Allah created the universe, and that science expands and makes clearer ideas from the Qur'an. They may refer to Surah 51:47 as an example, arguing that it mentions the idea of expansion, this could be a reference to the Big Bang theory.

Nature of the divine and revelation

78 Special revelation: Visions (Christianity)

You may refer to any contrasting beliefs. Answers could include:

Christianity:

- Many Christians believe that visions are an important form of religious experience that provide a direct experience of God. They may believe that visions demonstrate the characteristics of God, such as his power and loving nature.
- Many Christians believe that visions help them to understand God better – they can be a way of developing a personal relationship with him. Many Christians see visions as confirming and strengthening their faith.

Islam:

- Some Muslims consider visions to be very important, believing they provide proof of Allah's existence. They may believe that a vision is Allah contacting them so they can understand him better. Visions therefore strengthen their faith in Allah.
- Other Muslims do not see visions as very important. For example, Shi'a Muslims do not believe visions are needed to confirm their faith in Allah.
- Sufi Muslims place great emphasis on spiritual experiences such as visions and believe they are a way of showing Allah wants to communicate with humanity.

79 Special revelation: visions (Islam)

Your answer must include relevant, accurate references to scripture or sacred writings. For example:

Christianity:

- Christians believe visions may involve the appearance of angels, saints or messengers, or they could be direct experiences of God. There are many examples of visions in the Bible, including St Paul/Saul, who was struck blind; this was enough to convince him to become a Christian.
- Many Christians believe visions help them to understand God better by connecting to him and allowing them to experience his characteristics such as omnipotence and benevolence. Reference may be made to examples such as St Bernadette and healing miracles.

Islam:

- Some Muslims place great emphasis on visions as proof of Allah's existence. Muslims may refer to Musa's vision of Allah (Surah 7:143) and the vision of Mary (Surah 19:16–20) as examples from the Qur'an that show his power and nature.
- Some Muslims do not place great emphasis on visions, believing that they are not essential to belief in Allah. While they understand that visions help to strengthen faith, faith itself means to put trust in Allah, which Muslims can do through other means, such as studying the Qur'an.

80 General revelation (Christianity)

Answers may vary, but you may include some of the following evidence and arguments.

Arguments in support:

- Many Christians argue that revelation is one way to prove God's existence and is the way he shows himself to humanity. They may argue that scripture such as the Bible and revelation through the example of Jesus show Christians how to live their lives according to God's plan, and confirms that God is real.
- Many Christians look to God's creation to show his divine nature. They believe that as God created the world, he can be revealed through his creation. Christians may refer to Romans 1:20 to reinforce their belief in God as the maker of the universe and demonstrate his powerful and loving nature.
- Revelation is very important to many Muslims. For example, many Muslims believe that Muhammad was the final prophet who brought the final message from Allah. Without this, Islam may not exist, so this is good evidence that revelation proves the existence of God.
- There is evidence of revelation in all holy books, so many religious believers place emphasis on this as proof of God's existence.

Arguments in support of other views:

- While some Christians accept that revelation proves the existence of God, they may argue that there are other, better forms of proof. They may point to miracles, where God makes a personal connection with a person, as providing better proof of God's existence.
- Some religious believers may claim that proof of God's existence is not required, as having faith means putting trust in God. God is a divine being; so many Christians believe he is transcendent and too great for humans to fully understand in any case.

- Non-religious believers might claim that religious experience is not proof of God's existence, as they do not believe in a divine being. They may offer alternative explanations for the experience of revelation, such as drug use, hallucinations or medical issues. They might argue that there is insufficient evidence of God's existence – and since God does not exist, revelation is simply people seeing what they want to see.

You will be awarded marks for accurate spelling and punctuation, the effective use of grammar to convey meaning and the use of a wide range of specialist terminology.

81 General revelation (Islam)

Your answer must include relevant, accurate references to scripture or sacred writings. For example:

Christianity:

- Many Christians believe that God is revealed through his creation of the universe. The complexities of the world as well as sources of authority such as the Bible demonstrate God's nature. They may refer to Psalms 19:1–4 or Romans 1:20 to support their views.
- Other Christians look to the example of Jesus as a form of revelation. As he is the incarnation of God – God in human form – they believe they can understand God better through Jesus' stories and teachings. They may refer to Hebrews 1:1–2 to support these views.

Islam:

- Many Muslims believe that Allah reveals himself through the natural world. As Allah created the universe and everything within it, they argue that the natural world shows what Allah is like. Many Muslims believe that only Allah has the power to create the world, and his creation shows his power and benevolence. Muslims may refer to Surah 34:50 to support this viewpoint.
- Some Muslims believe an important form of revelation is through the prophets. They accept Muhammad as the final prophet who revealed what Allah was like and received messages for humanity. Muslims may look to sources of authority such as the Qur'an to understand Allah better. Reference may be made to the Qur'an and revelations received by Muhammad.

82–83 The existence of God and revelation: Contrasting beliefs (Christianity and Islam)

1 You may refer to any contrasting beliefs. Answers could include:

Christianity:

- Many Christians believe God can be revealed through nature, as he is the creator of the universe. They believe that the complexity of the world shows God's power and love.
- Some Christians believe general revelation through nature is the basis of the Design argument that attempts to prove God's existence.

Islam:

- Many Muslims believe that Allah is perfect, so by looking at his creation they can understand him better. For many Muslims, studying the wonders of the physical universe is a good way of understanding Allah better.
- Some Muslims do not place great emphasis on nature as a form of revelation, believing that the Prophets and Qur'an reveal more about God and help to strengthen faith in him.

2 You may refer to any contrasting beliefs. Answers could include:

Christianity:

- Many Christians believe visions are important, as there are many examples of them in the Bible. They may believe that visions show what God is like by revealing his power.
- Christians may believe that visions show God's love for humanity, as it is through visions that God interacts with his creation. Many visions in Christianity have given messages to humanity such as those received by St Paul or Abraham. These prove the existence of God and help people to understand him better.
- Some Christians recognise that visions are a form of revelation, but place greater emphasis on sources of authority such as the Bible or Jesus' teachings, seeing them as better evidence of God's existence and direct sources of revelation.

Islam:

- There have been many examples of visions in Islam, including those experienced by Muhammad; so many Muslims see them as important in connecting humanity to Allah.
- Many Muslims believe visions strengthen their faith by confirming that Allah is real. They may help Muslims to understand his nature as omnipotent and benevolent.
- Some Muslims do not place great emphasis on visions, as they do not need proof of Allah's existence. They may accept that visions happen, but believe the Qur'an is a more important source of evidence of God's existence.

Theme D: Religion, peace and conflict

Religion, violence, terrorism and war

84 Peace and justice, forgiveness and reconciliation (Christianity)

Your answer must include relevant, accurate references to scripture or sacred writings. For example:

Christianity:

- Ideas of peace are promoted in the Bible through the teachings of Jesus. One example is John 16:33 ('I have told you these things so that you may have peace').
- Christianity teaches that to have peace you need justice, reconciliation and forgiveness between people. Jesus on the cross forgave those who had put him to death (Luke 23:34).
- Jesus taught 'Love your enemies and pray for those who persecute you' (Matthew 5:44) – Christians aim to put this teaching into action.

Islam:

- Islam is viewed as a religion of peace. Muslims believe Allah created a peaceful world and wants people to work for peace. Surah 25:63 promotes the idea of using words of peace towards others.
- All Muslims are seen to belong to the ummah, which is the Muslim worldwide community. They promote actions that encourage peace and living together in harmony. Surah 41:34 states that justice, forgiveness and reconciliation are important in bringing peace to all people.

85 Peace and justice, forgiveness and reconciliation (Islam)

A forgiveness

86 Violence and terrorism (Christianity)

Your answer must include relevant, accurate references to scripture or sacred writings. For example:

Christianity:

- Christianity teaches that Jesus did not use violence, and he showed through his actions and teachings the importance of peace. Matthew 26:52 provides one example of Jesus stating that violence is wrong.
- Christianity teaches that those who work for peace will be rewarded in the afterlife. Reference may be made to Matthew 5:9.
- Some Christians may be pacifists and not accept any form of violence. They may follow the example of Jesus when he was arrested (Luke 22:49–51) – he encouraged his disciples not to use violence.

Islam:

- Islam is a religion of peace and many teachings in the Qur'an, including Surah 8:61, support the idea of working for peace and not using violence.
- Islam teaches that Allah is merciful, so Muslims also try to be merciful towards others. Surah 25:63 teaches the importance of being merciful.
- Islam teaches that peaceful methods, not violence, should be used to end conflict. This can be seen in Surah 2:190.

87 Violence and terrorism (Islam)

Answers may vary, but you may include some of the following evidence and arguments.

Arguments in support:

- Many Christians and Muslims believe that although religions teach the importance of peace, there are people who do not practise these ideas and turn to violence instead. Terrorism, where people use violence, is a difficult problem to solve.
- Given the number of terrorist attacks in the last two decades and the violence of some terrorist groups, some people might argue that terrorism is the biggest threat facing the world today, especially as there is no easy solution to terrorism.
- Some people might argue that because some terrorists use religious teachings to try to justify their acts of violence, the threat posed by terrorism is far-reaching – even though the use of violence is based on misunderstandings of religious teachings.
- Some non-religious believers might argue that violent acts of terrorism carried out by minority religious groups show that religion has no place in society today. This can be a difficult view to challenge in the light of the devastation and human cost of some terrorist attacks.

Arguments in support of other views:

- Many religious believers, including Christians and Muslims, may argue that while terrorism is a major threat in terms of the devastation caused, the ideology behind such attacks is a bigger threat. They may point out that there would be no terrorist attacks based on religious teachings if people interpreted the teachings correctly – so the biggest threat is religious misunderstandings.
- Religious and non-religious believers may point to other threats in the world, such as gun crime, climate change, war and environmental pollution, as equal to or greater than the threat caused by terrorism.

- Religious and non-religious believers may argue that the media has exaggerated the threat caused by terrorism in the world today.

You will be awarded marks for accurate spelling and punctuation, the effective use of grammar to convey meaning and the use of a wide range of specialist terminology.

88 War and Just War theory (Christianity)

Your answer must include relevant, accurate references to scripture or sacred writings. For example:

Christianity:

- Some Bible teachings suggest that sometimes war is needed in order to bring about peace. Just War theory is a way of justifying the conditions under which war may be necessary. Reference may be made to Exodus 21:23–25.
- Christianity is a religion that teaches peace and avoidance of war. Many Christians may be pacifist and believe that war should never happen. Reference may be made to teachings such as John 16:33.

Islam:

- Islam is a religion of peace and supports ideas of non-violence. Surah 2:108 teaches the importance of avoiding war and making peaceful agreements.
- Some passages in the Qur'an suggest war is permitted in certain circumstances as a last resort. Surah 2:190 and Surah 4:75 state that Muslims can fight if it is to defend Islam or Allah.

89 War and Just War theory (Islam)

For example:

- War is an act of defence.
- A religious leader should declare war.
- War is a last resort.
- War will not threaten innocent lives.
- War has the support of the community.

90 Holy war (Christianity)

For example:

- Holy war is about defending religion.
- Holy war should be declared by a religious leader.
- Holy war should be a last resort.
- The intention of holy war must be to protect religious people.
- There are conditions for a holy war that must be met.

91 Holy war (Islam)

C holy war

92 Pacifism (Christianity)

Answers may vary, but you may include some of the following evidence and arguments.

Arguments in support:

- Some Christians believe that Jesus' many teachings about peace suggest pacifism is the better option when faced with war. The Christian denomination, the Quakers, is pacifist; they use Christian teachings on peace to support their argument that the use of violence can never be justified.
- Bible teachings such as 'You shall not murder' (Exodus 20:13) and 'Love your enemies and pray for those who persecute you' (Matthew 5:43–44) support pacifist views.
- One example of a Christian religious pacifist is Martin Luther King Jr, who refused to use violence to overcome injustices in the world.

- Muslims may not be pacifists, but many support passive resistance and teach about working for peace even when faced with violence. They follow the example of Muhammad and his first followers, who continued to preach the message of Allah even when faced with oppression and violence.
- Some people argue that if everyone took a pacifist stance, there would be no violence and all problems in the world could be resolved without conflict.

Arguments in support of other views:

- While Christianity and Islam both have teachings on peace, both also accept that there may be times when violence is needed. Pacifism does not work if you need to defend yourself or your religious beliefs. There have been many examples in the history of religions when violence has been used for this purpose.
- Muslims may refer to Surah 5:28 to show that sometimes violence has to be used, especially when defending their religion. They do recognise, however, that violence should only be used as a last resort.
- Many non-religious believers may feel that peace does not always work and point to examples such as terrorism in the world. They may argue that sometimes meeting violence with violence is the only way to bring peace to the world.

You will be awarded marks for accurate spelling and punctuation, the effective use of grammar to convey meaning and the use of a wide range of specialist terminology.

93 Pacifism (Islam)

Your answer must include relevant, accurate references to scripture or sacred writings. For example:
Christianity:

- Some Christians have refused to fight in wars, as they believe the Bible supports pacifism. They may refer to Exodus 20:13, which says 'You shall not murder', to support pacifist ideas.
- Jesus gave many teachings on peace and not using violence. He taught us to 'Love your enemies and pray for those who persecute you' (Matthew 5:43–44).
- The Religious Society of Friends (Quakers) is a pacifist Christian denomination. They believe they should follow teachings of peace from the Bible, such as John 14:27, and never use violence.

Islam:

- Islam is not a pacifist religion, and many Muslims accept that sometimes war and violence is necessary to defend Islam, as seen in Surah 2:190.
- Many teachings in the Qur'an and the Hadith encourage Muslims to strive for justice and resist oppression, which supports pacifism. Surah 5:28 can be interpreted as meaning a person should not use violence.

Religion and belief in 21st-century conflict

94 Religion as a cause of conflict (Christianity)

Your answer must include relevant, accurate references to scripture or sacred writings. For example:
Christianity:

- Most Christians believe that the problems of nuclear weapons outweigh any benefits of using them and so they should never be used. Bible teachings from Jesus suggest violence is unacceptable. Reference may be made to Luke 6:27–29.
- Many Christians would be concerned about the high loss of life inflicted by nuclear weapons and would not support their use. They may refer to teachings such as 'You shall not kill' (Exodus 20:13).

Islam:

- Most Muslims would not support the use of nuclear weapons, as they do not believe that innocent human life should be threatened. They may refer to Surah 5:32 to show that they should not harm God's creation.
- Many Muslims would argue that the use of nuclear weapons could not be supported by Islamic conditions of war. Muslims may refer to Just War theory, which suggests that when war is deemed necessary, it must be a last resort after all methods of peace have been tried first. As nuclear weapons are so damaging, they could not be supported. Reference may be made to Surah 25:63.

95 Religion as a cause of conflict (Islam)

Answers may vary, but you may include some of the following evidence and arguments.
Arguments in support:

- Most Christians and Muslims would be against WMD because of the high loss of life that can be caused. As WMD cause extensive damage to both human life and the environment, their use could not be justified under any circumstance.
- Christians may point to teachings in the Bible such as 'You shall not kill' (Exodus 20:13) to show that WMD should not be used, as their use would be likely to result in a huge number of casualties.
- Many non-religious believers would not support the use of WMD due to the extensive damage they cause. Although they do not follow any religious rules or believe in a divine being, they accept human life is special and should not be threatened in this way.

Arguments in support of other views:

- Christians and Muslims would not advocate the use of WMD, but may be able to justify a country having WMD if they are used as a deterrent to prevent other countries starting a war.
- Some people may argue that WMD, although dangerous, could have a positive impact in terms of defending the country that has them. A country with WMD could incur lower losses and any war might be brought to a quicker end.

You will be awarded marks for accurate spelling and punctuation, the effective use of grammar to convey meaning and the use of a wide range of specialist terminology.

96 Religion and peacemaking (Christianity)

For example:
- Donate money
- Charity work
- Volunteer
- Raise awareness
- Help to house refugees
- Work with individuals to help rebuild their lives.

97 Religion and peacemaking (Islam)

Answers may vary, but you may include some of the following evidence and arguments.

Arguments in support:
- Many Christians believe they should follow Jesus' teachings in the Bible about working for peace. Matthew 5:44 and John 16:33 suggest that everyone has a responsibility to work to bring peace to the world.
- Some Christians believe they should try to follow the example of others who have worked for peace, including Nelson Mandela, Betty Williams and Martin Luther King Jr. They may believe that this is how God expects them to live their lives and put Christian teachings into action.
- Christianity teaches that there are many ways in which people can work for peace – for example, through advocating changes in government policy, by helping individuals who are suffering, or by trying to reconcile people who are in conflict.
- Islamic teachings such as Surah 41:34 and Surah 25:63 instruct Muslims to work for peace in the world. Many Muslims believe that this is how Allah intended them to live.
- Islam has many charities that work for peace and Muslims are encouraged to follow their example and put Islamic teachings into action.
- Many non-religious believers, even though they do not follow any religious rules, may feel that working for peace is the right thing to do and actively support this idea in their lives.

Arguments in support of other views:
- Some religious believers may feel that while everyone should work for peace, only those in authority can bring peace to the world. They may believe that power is needed in order to achieve peace in the world.
- Some non-religious believers may feel that they do not have a duty to work for peace.

You will be awarded marks for accurate spelling and punctuation, the effective use of grammar to convey meaning and the use of a wide range of specialist terminology.

98–99 Religion, peace and conflict: Contrasting beliefs (Christianity and Islam)

1 You may refer to any contrasting beliefs. Answers could include:
Christianity:
- Many Christians take a pacifist approach, believing that Christianity teaches that violence is never the answer to conflict.
- Christians may refer to teachings such as 'You shall not kill' (Exodus 20:13), which can be seen to support pacifism.

- Many of Jesus' Bible teachings state that peace should be the response to violence – Jesus taught this even when he was arrested in the Garden of Gethsemane.
Islam:
- Islam is not a pacifist religion and many Muslims recognise that sometimes war is needed in order to bring about peace.
- Some Muslim teachings are in line with pacifist teachings, for example Surah 5:28.
- Islam is seen as a religion of peace and submission to Allah, so many Muslim prefer to work to achieve peace through reconciliation and not violence.

2 You may refer to any contrasting beliefs. Answers could include:
Christianity:
- Christians believe the Bible teaches them to work for peace, reconciliation and justice and not to use violence.
- Many Christians are pacifists and believe the use of violence is always wrong, referring to Bible teachings such as 'You shall not kill' (Exodus 20:13).
Islam:
- Islam is seen as a religion of peace, and many Muslims believe they have a duty to work to reconcile groups in conflict using peaceful methods.
- Islam teaches that Allah is merciful and forgives humans, so Muslims believe they should also try to be merciful. Following this teaching means not using violence and working for peace.

Theme E: Religion, crime and punishment

Religion, crime and the causes of crime

100 Good and evil intentions and actions (Christianity)

Answers may vary, but you may include some of the following evidence and arguments.

Arguments in support:
- Christianity teaches that God gave humans a duty to care for others and as all humans are special, they should try to behave in a good way towards others.
- Many Christians accept that after death, God will judge them on their actions and the way they have behaved towards others, and they believe that only good actions will help them to achieve this reward.
- Christians believe that it is wrong to cause suffering to others. They are taught that actions such as charity work, caring for the environment and helping other humans in the world are part of the way God wants them to live their lives.
- Muslims are taught (Surah 76:30–31) that intentions and actions are equally important, and that Allah judges a person on both to determine their afterlife.

Arguments in support of other views:
- While Christians recognise the importance of performing good actions, they also recognise that suffering can lead to good; for example, the pain of losing a loved one can teach people to be stronger and more compassionate. Most Christians believe it is wrong to cause suffering to others, and that you should try to support a person who is suffering.

- Some religious and non-religious people may believe that while it is wrong to carry out bad actions, sometimes it may be the kindest thing to do. For example, if a person is homeless, doing something that is not considered morally right by religious rules (such as stealing food for them) might be the 'lesser of two evils' if it ends their suffering.

You will be awarded marks for accurate spelling and punctuation, the effective use of grammar to convey meaning and the use of a wide range of specialist terminology.

101 Good and evil intentions and actions (Islam)

Your answer must include relevant, accurate references to scripture or sacred writings. For example:
Christianity:

- Christianity teaches that a person's actions will determine their afterlife. If a person does something for the wrong reason – for example, helping an elderly person across the road because they want to be perceived as a good person – this would be considered a bad intention. Reference may be made to Romans 2:6–8.
- Christianity teaches that God wants Christians to perform good actions and live their lives according to his rules. They believe that helping others, for example through charity work, will enable them to be rewarded in the afterlife. If they perform a good action and their intention is to do this for the right reason, this will help them to go to heaven. Reference may be made to Acts 14:22.

Islam:

- Muslims are taught that their intentions and actions are equally important; for example, one teaching from the Hadith is: 'verily actions are by intentions and for every person is what he intended', suggesting that Muslims need to be aware of both.
- Islam teaches that after death, Allah will judge Muslims on both their intentions and their actions in life. They believe Allah is always watching, so will know both; this is supported by Surah 76:30–31.

102 Reasons for crime (Christianity)

C equality

103 Reasons for crime (Islam)

Your answer must include relevant, accurate references to scripture or sacred writings. For example:
Christianity:

- Christianity teaches that punishment is needed to achieve justice. Christians believe it is important for a victim to gain retribution for what has happened to them. This follows examples in the Bible of gaining justice, as seen with Amos in Isaiah 5:24 and Isaiah speaking out for justice in Isaiah 58:6–7.
- The Bible teaches in Romans 13:1 that every person should follow the laws of the country in which they live. When these rules are broken, this teaching also suggests that there should be an appropriate punishment.

Islam:

- Islam teaches that Allah behaves in a just way and so Muslims should too. This includes expecting an appropriate punishment when a crime has been committed. This teaching is found in Surah 4:26–28.
- Muslims have a code of conduct known as Shari'ah law, which was established to build a peaceful society as Allah intended. Muslims believe that punishment is needed in order to maintain order and control when crimes have been committed.

104 Types of crime (Christianity)

Your answer must include relevant, accurate references to scripture or sacred writings. For example:
Christianity:

- Christianity teaches that murder is always wrong and against the Ten Commandments. The Bible teaches, 'You shall not kill' (Exodus 20:13), showing that murder is wrong.
- Jesus reinforced the teaching of murder being wrong in the New Testament when he said, 'You shall not murder, and anyone who murders will be subject to judgement' (Matthew 5:21).

Islam:

- Murder is seen as a very serious crime in Islam and is punishable by death in any Islamic country that has the death penalty.
- The Qur'an teaches in Surah 6:151 that all life is sacred and should never deliberately be taken, showing that murder is wrong.

105 Types of crime (Islam)

Answers may vary, but you may include some of the following evidence and arguments.
Arguments in support:

- Christians may argue that as 'You shall not kill' (Exodus 20:13) is one of the Ten Commandments, murder is one of the worst crimes possible. They consider life sacred, as God created it, so it should not be taken under any circumstances.
- Some Christians may support the use of the death penalty (the most severe punishment) for the crime of murder, as murder is seen as the worst crime that can be committed.
- Islamic teachings state that life is sacred and should not be taken (e.g. Surah 6:151). For this reason, in some Islamic countries the crime of murder can carry the death penalty, showing it is the most serious crime.
- Non-religious believers may view murder as a horrific crime, as the life of another person has been taken and no one can make up for this loss. They may support strong punishments for this crime because of the terrible impact on the victim and their friends and family.

Arguments in support of other views:

- Many Christians believe that all crimes are wrong. While murder is a horrific crime, Christians may see other crimes such as hate crimes, theft or rape as equally wrong.
- Most Muslims believe murder is a terrible crime, but in some Islamic countries the death penalty is also used to punish other offences such as homosexuality and adultery. This suggests that these crimes are viewed as equally bad as murder, as they receive the worst punishment.

You will be awarded marks for accurate spelling and punctuation, the effective use of grammar to convey meaning and the use of a wide range of specialist terminology.

Religion and punishment

106 Punishment (Christianity)

Answers may vary, but you may include some of the following evidence and arguments.

Arguments in support:

- Many Christian teachings support ideas of forgiveness and educating criminals to improve their behaviour, e.g. Galatians 6:1. Many Christians therefore agree that reformation is the most important aim of punishment, as it allows the criminal time to reflect on their crime, recognise why it is wrong and try to change their behaviour.
- Some Christians may argue that humans have a duty to help others, which includes helping those who have done wrong and committed crimes. Giving criminals a chance to change while also receiving a fair punishment is an important idea of justice.
- Islam teaches that Allah is forgiving and merciful, so Muslims believe they should try to apply this teaching to their lives. Surah 4:26–28 teaches the importance of giving someone a chance to change their behaviour when they have done wrong.
- Many non-religious believers may argue that those who have done wrong deserve a chance to change, although not for religious reasons. They may believe that happiness is important and that people should be encouraged to better themselves.

Arguments in support of other views:

- Many people, both religious and non-religious believers, may find it hard to accept a person being given a chance to change, especially if they have committed a crime such as murder. If a criminal has taken the life of a loved one, it may be very difficult to offer forgiveness towards them and accept that they may be able to continue with their life as normal after punishment.
- There are many other aims of punishment, including protecting society, retribution and deterrence, which are equally important to reformation; both religious and non-religious believers may feel that if there is a risk the offender will commit the crime again or may not take the opportunity to change, these are more important aims.

You will be awarded marks for accurate spelling and punctuation, the effective use of grammar to convey meaning and the use of a wide range of specialist terminology.

107 Punishment (Islam)

Your answer must include relevant, accurate references to scripture or sacred writings. For example:

Christianity:

- In Christianity, God is seen as just and Christians believe that when a crime has been committed, it is important to achieve justice. This means that the person who has done wrong should be given an appropriate and fair punishment for the crime they have committed. Reference may be made to Exodus 21:24 ('an eye for an eye, a tooth for a tooth').
- Jesus taught the important of forgiveness and agape love, and he forgave those who put him to death on the cross. This could be taken to mean punishment should allow the offender time to change their behaviour, be educated and reform.
- Christianity teaches that one aim of punishment is to ensure that the person recognises what they have done wrong and repents for their sins. This is seen in Colossians 3:25, which talks about repaying for wrongs you have done.

Islam:

- Islam teaches the importance of reformation as an aim of punishment. Many Muslims believe criminals should be forgiven, as Allah is forgiving, and should be given the opportunity to try to change their behaviour. Reference may be made to Surah 4:26–28.
- Islam teaches that when a crime has been committed, people in society need to feel safe. The criminal therefore needs an appropriate punishment for their crime in order for justice to be gained. Reference may be made to Surah 4.

108 The treatment of criminals (Christianity)

For example:

- It is wrong.
- It can be seen as getting revenge.
- Jesus taught about the importance of forgiveness.
- Punishment is better as it gives justice.
- All life is sacred and deserves respect as God created it.

109 The treatment of criminals (Islam)

For example:

- Criminals should have a fair trial.
- Criminals should not be tortured.
- Prisons should be habitable.
- Criminals should not receive corporal punishment.
- Criminals' human rights should be upheld.

110 Forgiveness (Christianity)

Your answer must include relevant, accurate references to scripture or sacred writings. For example:

Christianity:

- Many teachings in the Bible show that forgiveness is important. For example, Mark 11:25 teaches, 'If you hold anything against anyone, forgive him.'
- Christians believe God is forgiving towards humans and wants them to be forgiving towards each other. This is taught in Ephesians 4:32.
- Forgiveness is important in Christianity, as Jesus died on the cross to bring forgiveness to the world. Christians believe that God wants them to forgive those who do wrong to them by following Jesus' example. Reference may be made to Luke 6:37.

Islam:

- Muslims believe that Allah is merciful and forgiving, and so Muslims should try to be too. This is taught in Surah 64:14.
- Islam is seen to be a religion of peace, and in order to achieve this many Muslims believe that forgiveness is needed. Many Muslims believe that Allah intends for people to live peacefully together and that forgiveness allows the ummah to achieve this. Reference may be made to Surah 64:14.

111 Forgiveness (Islam)

Answers may vary, but you may include some of the following evidence and arguments.

Arguments in support:

- Christianity teaches that people should forgive one another when they have done wrong. Christianity teaches that after death, God will forgive those who repent, and Christians believe they should apply this idea of forgiveness to their own lives.
- The Bible teaches that Jesus died on the cross to forgive the sins of the whole world. Christianity teaches Christians to try to forgive, even when it is difficult.

Many believe that God helps them to do this, as seen in teachings such as Ephesians 4:32.
- In Islam, Allah is seen as merciful and forgiving, as seen in Surah 64:14. Muslims believe they should try to follow this example as well as the example of Muhammad by being forgiving towards others when they do wrong.
- Many non-religious believers support ideas of being forgiving, believing it is important to try to work together with others to live in harmony and peace.

Arguments in support of other views:
- There may be some examples where forgiveness is difficult for both religious and non-religious people. For example, if a loved one is murdered it may be difficult, if not impossible, to forgive the offender who committed this crime.
- While there are many religious teachings on forgiveness, it may be more difficult to put these into practice when a crime has been committed. Saying sorry and actually moving on and forgiving someone may take time and patience.

You will be awarded marks for accurate spelling and punctuation, the effective use of grammar to convey meaning and the use of a wide range of specialist terminology.

112 The death penalty (Christianity)

Your answer must include relevant, accurate references to scripture or sacred writings. For example:
Christianity:
- The overall message from Christianity is to love and forgive others. Capital punishment can be seen to go against this teaching, as it is taking the life of another person, which many Christians view as murder and therefore wrong. The Bible teaches, 'You shall not murder' (Exodus 20:13).
- There are many teachings from Jesus where revenge is seen as wrong; for example, in Matthew 5:38–39, Jesus says: 'If anyone slaps you on the right cheek, turn to them the other cheek also.' The death penalty can be seen as taking revenge.
- Most Christian Churches have spoken out against the death penalty, believing it goes against the sanctity of life argument – life is special because God created it. Reference may be made to Genesis 1 to support this view.

Islam:
- While some teachings in the Qur'an support the death penalty, it is not the only punishment available in the Qur'an – so other punishments could be used instead of the death penalty when a serious crime has been committed.
- There are many differences in opinion over how and when the death penalty should be used within Islam. Some Muslims believe that the death penalty is controversial and should not be supported, while Shari'ah law is not always clear on its use.

113 The death penalty (Islam)

Answers may vary, but you may include some of the following evidence and arguments.
Arguments in support:
- Many Christians believe love and forgiveness are more important than revenge; as capital punishment goes against this, they would therefore see it as wrong.
- Many Christians believe that capital punishment is wrong, as it does not respect the sanctity of life (that all life is sacred because God created it).

- Some Muslims may not support the death penalty because Shari'ah law scholars do not agree on how or when the death penalty should be applied.
- Many Muslims point out that although the death penalty is one possible punishment given in the Qur'an, it is not the only one. Others can be used that would be less severe, and therefore some Muslims do not support the use of the death penalty.
- Non-religious believers, such as humanists, generally do not support the death penalty as they believe murder is wrong. There is also the possibility of making a mistake and an innocent person being put to death.

Arguments in support of other views:
- Some Christians may support the use of the death penalty for the most serious crimes. The Old Testament supports this in Genesis 9:6 and Jesus in the New Testament never taught that the death penalty was wrong.
- In the past, the Christian Church supported the death penalty; for example, in the Middle Ages it was used when some Christians challenged the Church's authority.
- Some Muslims support the use of the death penalty, as Sahih Muslim 16:4152 suggests it can be used for the crime of murder and for Muslims who refuse to perform their Islamic duty. The Qur'an supports this – it allocates the death penalty for the crimes of rape, homosexual acts and apostasy (renouncing one's religious beliefs).
- Some non-religious believers may support the use of the death penalty, as they may believe that the most serious crimes – for example, murder and rape – deserve this punishment.

You will be awarded marks for accurate spelling and punctuation, the effective use of grammar to convey meaning and the use of a wide range of specialist terminology.

114–115 Religion, crime and punishment: Contrasting beliefs (Christianity and Islam)

1 You may refer to any contrasting beliefs. Answers could include:
Christianity:
- Many Christians do not support corporal punishment, as they believe all humans have rights; these include the right to not be harmed.
- Christianity teaches life is sacred as God created it, and the use of corporal punishment appears to contradict this teaching.
- Christians believe that punishment should be appropriate to the crime – this does not mean it has to be a physical punishment.
- Christianity teaches about the importance of forgiveness and reformation – this can be achieved through peaceful means such as imprisonment and education rather than physically harming a prisoner.

Islam:
- Islam is a religion of peace, so many Muslims would not support the harming of criminals.
- Most Muslims believe that all life is special as Allah created it – corporal punishment is not in line with this belief.
- Many Muslims believe it is important for a person to be given a chance to reform when they have done wrong, so corporal punishment is not necessary.

2 You may refer to any contrasting ways. Answers could include:

Christianity:

- Some Christians believe the use of the death penalty for the most serious of crimes is acceptable. This is a view promoted in the Old Testament.
- Some Christians will support the death penalty as the Christian Church in the Middle Ages used it for those who challenged the Church's authority.
- Many Christians believe life is special and that using the death penalty goes against this belief.
- Many Christians would argue that Christianity teaches the importance of forgiveness, which the death penalty does not account for.

Islam:

- Some Muslims support the death penalty for the most serious crimes, as this is what the Qur'an teaches.
- Many Muslims today might argue that although the death penalty is one possible punishment, it is not the only one, and that other, less severe punishments should be considered instead.
- Muslims believe that all life is sacred as God created it – this leads some Muslims to believe the death penalty is wrong.

Theme F: Religion, human rights and social justice

Human rights

116 Prejudice and discrimination (Christianity)

For example:

- Humans were created equal by God.
- Agape love.
- Sources of authority teach equality between races.
- Jesus/Muhammad taught it was wrong.
- The golden rule of treating people how you want to be treated.

117 Prejudice and discrimination (Islam)

Your answer must include relevant, accurate references to scripture or sacred writings. For example:

Christianity:

- Christians believe that all humans are equal as they were all made 'in the image of God' (Genesis 1:26), so racial discrimination is wrong.
- Christians follow the example of Jesus, who treated all races equally and gave teachings such as 'do to others what you would have them do to you' (Matthew 7:12).
- There are many teachings in the Bible, such as Galatians 3:26–28, which suggest there should be equal treatment and respect between different races.

Islam:

- Surah 49:13 teaches that Allah created all humans equally.
- Muhammad taught in his final sermon the importance of treating all people equally; the Hadith says 'All people are equal... as the teeth of a comb.'
- All Muslims are seen to belong to the ummah, which includes people from many different racial groups, so racial discrimination goes against this idea.

118 Equality and freedom of religious belief (Christianity)

Your answer must include relevant, accurate references to scripture or sacred writings. For example:

Christianity:

- Many Christians believe that God created everyone to be equal. For example, Galatians 2:6 teaches that God does not show favouritism. Freedom of expression should be supported so that people can put this teaching into action.
- Christian teachings promote human rights, which includes freedom of expression. For example, Matthew 7:12 and Matthew 25:40 show this is important.

Islam:

- Islam teaches that religious freedom is important. Surah 2:25–27 supports this view.
- Muslims believe that Allah created all people equally, although not the same. Differences between people are not important, as shown by Surah 30:22.

119 Equality and freedom of religious belief (Islam)

Answers may vary, but you may include some of the following evidence and arguments.

Arguments in support:

- The majority of Christians support human rights, as they believe God created all humans equally. Many Christians accept Jesus' stories, such as the Parable of the Good Samaritan, which show that humans should stand up for others when their rights are denied.
- Christians want to follow the example of Jesus, who treated everyone the same – including women and outcasts such as lepers, Gentiles and criminals.
- There have been many examples of Christians standing up for the rights of others. For example, Martin Luther King Jr inspired others by the way he put Christian teachings such as 'do to others as you would have them do to you' (Matthew 7:12) into action. The civil rights movement in the USA happened because many individuals took a stand against racial oppression together.
- Islam teaches that Allah created all humans equally, although not the same. Teachings such as Surah 30:22 support the view that differences do not matter and that standing up for human rights is important.
- Many Muslims believe they should follow the example of Muhammad, who tried to treat all people fairly, and that everyone has a duty to help others when their rights are denied.
- Many non-religious believers believe that every person should be treated fairly, so would stand up for others whose rights were denied.

Arguments in support of other views:

- Some people – both religious and non-religious – may be reluctant to stand up for the rights of others if they are afraid of retaliation for doing so. For example, Martin Luther King Jr was assassinated because he was standing up for the human rights of black Americans.
- Some religious and non-religious believers may feel that people in authority have greater power to stand up for human rights. They may argue that it is not up to individuals within society to defend human rights, as only those in government and positions of influence can bring about change when human rights are denied.

You will be awarded marks for accurate spelling and punctuation, the effective use of grammar to convey meaning and the use of a wide range of specialist terminology.

120 Social justice (Christianity)

Answers may vary, but you may include some of the following evidence and arguments.

Arguments in support:

- Christians believe they have duty to work for social justice, as this reflects the example Jesus set and Bible teachings such as 'Love your neighbour as yourself' (Mark 12:31).
- Christianity teaches that God made all humans to be equal, therefore everyone deserves equal and fair treatment. Christians believe they have a duty to stand up for the rights of others when denied.
- The Christian Church works to raise awareness of social injustices and to overcome them through charity and volunteer work. Many Christians work to help others in this way.
- Many Muslims believe they have a duty to work for social justice in the world, as Allah created all humans and everyone is entitled to human rights, which includes social justice.
- The Five Pillars of Islam promote ideas of justice through Zakah (charity).
- Many non-religious believers feel they should work to campaign for social justice in the world, as they believe all people are important.

Arguments in support of other views:

- Some people may feel that social justice is the responsibility of governments and charities, believing that individuals cannot make a significant difference.
- Some people may feel that those facing social injustice need to work to help themselves as well as receiving help from others.

You will be awarded marks for accurate spelling and punctuation, the effective use of grammar to convey meaning and the use of a wide range of specialist terminology.

121 Social justice (Islam)

Your answer must include relevant, accurate references to scripture or sacred writings. For example:

Christianity:

- Christianity teaches that God created all humans, so everyone is equally important.
- Teachings from Jesus such as Mark 12:31 show the importance of helping others.
- The Bible teaches that humans have a responsibility to help those less fortunate. Teachings such as Proverbs 19:17 and statements of beliefs from the Church of England and Catholic Church reflect these ideas.

Islam:

- The Qur'an teaches Muslims they should work for social justice. Surah 7:157 talks of the importance of bringing equality to the world.
- Islamic practices such as Zakah show the importance of duty in helping others through charity work. Reference may be made to Surah 7:157.
- Muslims are taught that Allah is watching their actions, and that selflessly helping others will help them to get to heaven in the afterlife.

Wealth and poverty

122 Responsibilities of wealth (Christianity)

For example:

- Educate others
- Food banks
- Charity work
- Volunteer work
- Give money.

123 Responsibilities of wealth (Islam)

Your answer must include relevant, accurate references to scripture or sacred writings. For example:

Christianity:

- Christians believe they should follow Jesus' example in showing care and compassion for others. Luke 3:11 talks of sharing what you have with others.
- The Parable of the Sheep and the Goat teaches Christians to help others and that they will be judged on their actions in the afterlife. Reference may be made to Matthew 25:31–46.

Islam:

- Muslims believe they need to develop the right attitude to wealth, which includes helping others through paying Zakah – giving 2.5% of their annual wealth to charity. Surah 2:177 teaches the importance of giving wealth.
- Islam teaches that all Muslims are part of the ummah and that as Allah made them equally, they should care for and support each other. This can be achieved through helping those facing poverty. Surah 2:110 tells Muslims to be 'regular in charity'.

124 Exploitation of the poor (Christianity)

A human trafficking

125 Exploitation of the poor (Islam)

Answers may vary, but you may include some of the following evidence and arguments.

Arguments in support:

- Christianity teaches that all humans are equal as they were 'made in the image of God' (Genesis 1:26). Many Christians believe it is wrong to exploit people and that everyone has a responsibility to prevent it and to work to help those affected by it.
- Christianity teaches the importance of looking after each other. Christians follow the teachings and example of Jesus, who told us to 'love your neighbour as yourself' (Mark 12:31).
- Islam teaches that Allah made all humans and that everyone is therefore special. They believe in the sanctity of life argument, which suggests that Muslims have a duty to prevent the exploitation of others.
- Many Muslims believe they should help those who are being exploited. These beliefs are reflected in the duties of the Five Pillars; for example, Zakah requires them to give 2.5% of their annual wealth to help the poor and needy.
- Many non-religious believers feel it important to prevent the exploitation of the poor, as they believe that all human life is valuable and should be protected.

Arguments in support of other views:

- Some people may hold the view that only those in authority can work to prevent the poor being exploited. They may feel that individuals cannot provide the resources and time needed to achieve significant change.
- Some people may feel that those being exploited have to stand up for themselves. While help and support can be given, the poor also need to make sure they do not allow themselves to be exploited, in order to improve their own situation.

You will be awarded marks for accurate spelling and punctuation, the effective use of grammar to convey meaning and the use of a wide range of specialist terminology.

126 Poverty and charity (Christianity)

Your answer must include relevant, accurate references to scripture or sacred writings. For example:
Christianity:
- Christianity teaches that helping the poor and needy gains favour with God. Christians look to teachings such as Deuteronomy 15:10.
- Christians follow the example of Jesus, who worked to help the poor. In Luke 6:20 he says 'Blessed are you who are poor for yours is the kingdom of God', showing that the lives of poor people are valuable and that they deserve support when needed.

Islam:
- Charity and helping the poor is seen to be important in Islam. Muslims give 2.5% in Zakah every year (which is one of the Five Pillars) to help the poor and needy. Surah 2:110 may be referenced.
- Surah 2:177 teaches the importance of caring for others, especially those who are poor. Muslims believe that through helping the poor, they gain favour with Allah.

127 Poverty and charity (Islam)

Answers may vary, but you may include some of the following evidence and arguments.
Arguments in support:
- Many Christians and Muslims believe that support should be given to those in poverty, but that this should not be relied on. They believe that those experiencing hardship need to be proactive in looking for ways to help themselves.
- Many people – both religious and non-religious – feel that emergency relief can be provided when needed, but that people should learn to cope with their situations and be willing to try to support themselves when opportunities arise.

Arguments in support of other views:
- Christians believe they have a duty to care for God's creation; this includes looking after others. Proverbs 14:31 teaches that helping the poor is a way of honouring God.
- Christianity teaches that God created all humans to be equal, so when there is inequality and people are struggling, people should work to support each other.
- Islam teaches that helping others brings favour with Allah and that Muslims have a duty to try to support those living in poverty. Muslims give 2.5% of their annual wealth in Zakah to help achieve this.
- Many Muslims believe that charity work may provide emergency relief for those in hardship. Some Muslims may carry out voluntary work in deprived areas, in order to support others to better their situation.

You will be awarded marks for accurate spelling and punctuation, the effective use of grammar to convey meaning and the use of a wide range of specialist terminology.

128–129 Religion, human rights and social justice: Contrasting beliefs (Christianity and Islam)

1 You may refer to any contrasting beliefs. Answers could include:
Christianity:
- Christianity teaches that all humans – both men and women – are equal, as they were all made 'in the image of God' (Genesis 1:26).
- Christians follow the example of Jesus, who did not discriminate between men and women.
- Catholics only allow men to hold positions of Church authority – such as bishop, priest, deacon and pope. This is because they believe these roles represent Jesus, who was male.
- The Protestant Church allows female bishops, which is one sign of equality between men and women in the Church.

Islam:
- Islam teaches that men and women were made equal by Allah although not the same – they were given different roles that are seen to complement each other.
- Men are seen to be the providers and protectors of the family, while women have the role of raising the children and looking after the home.
- In his final sermon, Muhammad taught about the importance of treating everyone equally.

2 You may refer to any contrasting beliefs. Answers could include:
Christianity:
- Most Christians believe all people of all religions should be free to express their faith and practise their religion.
- Some Christians believe all religions are equally valid.
- Some Christians believe only Christianity contains the 'true' message, so while they respect other religions, they believe they have a duty and responsibility to share their faith with others.
- Some Christians believe that Christianity in today's world is at threat from secularisation.

Islam:
- Most Muslims believe that all believers of all religions should be free to practise their religion freely.
- Some Muslims believe that Allah will favour all righteous people and therefore it does not matter what religion a person belongs to.
- Some Muslims believe that Islam is the one true faith and it is a duty to lead others to Allah.

Theme G: St Mark's Gospel I

130 John's preparation for Jesus' ministry

1 **B** Messiah
2 For example:
- John prepared the way for the ministry of Jesus.
- John began preaching about God and Jesus.
- John baptised people in the River Jordan.
- John gave messages about Jesus.
- John is a servant of God.

131 Jesus' baptism and temptation

1 **C** 40 days
2 Your answer must include relevant, accurate references to scripture or sacred writings. For example:
   - The idea of the Trinity is shown through God as Father, Son and Holy Spirit.
   - The voice of God is heard, the spirit descends through the representation of the dove and the Son of God is baptised.
   - Jesus' baptism by John shows the truth of the prophecy of Jesus as Messiah.
   - Jesus is publically recognised by John as the Son of God.
   - Jesus is accepted as the one they have been waiting for.
   - The baptism of Jesus represents Jesus identifying with sinners.
   - Jesus had no sin and yet was baptised.
   - Reference can be made to Mark 1:9–11.

132 Miracles of Jesus I

1 For example:
   - Faith in Jesus is needed for the miracles to happen.
   - The power of God is shown.
   - Recognition of Jesus as the Son of God.
   - Faith means putting trust in God.
   - It is recognised that only Jesus could perform these miracles.
2 Your answer must include relevant, accurate references to scripture or sacred writings. For example:
   - They demonstrate he is the Son of God.
   - Through healing the sick, as in the paralysed man in Mark 2:1–12, Jesus shows the power of God.
   - They give Christians today hope.
   - God wishes to connect with humanity, which is shown through stories such as Jairus' daughter in Mark 5.
   - They show that faith is needed to accept God and Jesus.
   - In the rejection at Nazareth in Mark 6:1–6, the people did not have faith.

133 Miracles of Jesus II

Answers may vary, but you may include some of the following evidence and arguments.
Arguments in support:
- Many Christians believe that miracles such as healing the sick and feeding the five thousand show that God is able to break the laws of nature and perform actions that normally would not be possible.
- Miracles are visible and in the examples in the Bible many people witness them, which gives them greater credibility. When miracles are performed in front of crowds, it is harder for them to be disputed and alternative explanations found.
- Miracles show the power of God, as science cannot explain how they could have happened any other way. Christians find their strength and belief in God increased by the accounts of the miracles of Jesus.

Arguments in support of other views:
- Some Christians now may find accepting the miracles of Jesus difficult, as when these events occurred society was very different and less was known about science. It may be possible today to find alternative explanations for these miracles.

- While Christians do not doubt the power of God, as they were not present to witness the events from the Bible and they were recorded so long ago, some Christians may look to other sources of authority and revelation to strengthen their faith, rather than emphasising the miracles of Jesus.
- Non-religious believers may argue that the miracles performed by Jesus, as detailed in the Bible, may not have occurred. As they hold no belief in God or religion, they may suggest that there are alternative explanations for these occurrences that people at the time did not understand.

You will be awarded marks for accurate spelling and punctuation, the effective use of grammar to convey meaning and the use of a wide range of specialist terminology.

134 Caesarea Philippi and the transfiguration

1 **C** transfiguration
2 Your answer must include relevant, accurate references to scripture or sacred writings. For example:
   - It is one of the first recognised events where the disciples accept Jesus as the Messiah.
   - As they now know who Jesus is, this makes it easier for Christians today to understand and recognise him in this way.
   - This event shows Jesus accepting who he is as the person who is sent to Earth to die.
   - Jesus recognises his purpose in saving the sins of the whole world. This helps Christians today to accept this purpose too.
   - Reference can be made to Mark 8:27–33.

135 Passion prediction and James and John's request

For example:
- Jesus wanted to prepare the disciples for his death.
- Jesus wanted to help his disciples understand his sacrifice.
- Jesus wanted the disciples to know why he had to die.
- Jesus wanted to prepare the disciples for their role after his death.

136 The story of Bartimaeus

1 For example:
   - Jesus of Nazareth
   - Son of David
   - Son of God
   - Rabbi
   - Son of Man
   - Messiah
2 Your answer must include relevant, accurate references to scripture or sacred writings. For example:
   - Son of God was a name only given to Jesus after his death. This recognises his role as being God and yet being Jesus. It reinforces the words used after Jesus' baptism, as given in Mark 1:9–11.
   - Rabbi is a name of respect given to Jesus, as seen in Mark 10:46–52. It is a Jewish term used for a teacher. It shows the authority Jesus was seen to have as well as the teaching he gave.
   - Jesus saw himself as the Messiah, as seen in Mark 8:27–33. This reflects the idea of Jesus being chosen. His disciples recognise him but not his name after Caesarea Philippi.

137 The entry into Jerusalem

1 For example:
- He is seen in front of people and is not afraid.
- It is seen as a celebration.
- He rode on a donkey to show simplicity.
- His entrance contradicts with what is expected from the King of the Jews.
- His significance is recognised.
2 Answers may vary, but you may include some of the following evidence and arguments.

Arguments in support:
- Some Christians may find the many names confusing, as some of the ideas are contradictory. They may believe that in order to be able to share faith with those outside of Christianity or explain ideas to young children, having one name may help avoid confusion.
- Some Christians may believe that it would be easier to have one idea to understand and relate more easily to Jesus. Jesus being human is the reason why many Christians feel close to Jesus, as they can understand the normal life he lived and the teachings he shared.

Arguments in support of other views:
- Many Christians believe that the many titles Jesus is given reflect the many ways he is seen to people. For example, Son of God recognises who he is in being both divine and human, while Messiah recognises his purpose in coming to Earth to die on the cross to atone for the sins of the whole world.
- The many names show the authority and respect Jesus commanded. They also reflect the contradictions that the person of Jesus is – for example, being divine and yet born to a human mother.
- Many Christians may recognise the complexity of the character of Jesus, with the names reflecting this. He is given authority and a status above that of normal humans, and his having many names demonstrates this.
- Non-religious believers may argue that the statement is irrelevant, as they do not believe in God or Jesus.

You will be awarded marks for accurate spelling and punctuation, the effective use of grammar to convey meaning and the use of a wide range of specialist terminology.

138 The Last Supper

Your answer must include relevant, accurate references to scripture or sacred writings. For example:
- Some Christians, such as Catholics, believe in transubstantiation – that the bread and the wine become the physical body and blood of Jesus. They may make reference to Mark 14:22–24.
- Some Christians, such as Protestants, believe the bread and wine are symbolic and that they are shared in remembrance of the sacrifice of Jesus. They may make reference to Mark 14:22–24.

139 Jesus in Gethsemane and the trial

1 A Judas
2 For example:
- The prophecy about Jesus came true.
- One of the disciples betrayed Jesus there.
- Jesus was betrayed with a kiss.
- The Garden of Gethsemane was where he was arrested.

- Gethsemane was where Jesus prayed for the final time with the disciples.

140 The trial before Pilate, the crucifixion and burial

1 For example:
- The body was given to Joseph.
- The body was wrapped in linen.
- The body was placed in a tomb.
- A stone was rolled against the tomb entrance.
- There was no time to anoint the body.
2 Your answer must include relevant, accurate references to scripture or sacred writings. For example:
- Some Christians see the death of Jesus as a divine sacrifice. It represents God's love for humanity. Jesus' sacrifice repaired the relationship between God and humanity that was broken because of the actions of Adam and Eve in the Garden of Eden.
- It is a victory of good over evil. The death of Jesus (Mark 15:33–40) meant that a sacrifice was made.
- It is the price to be paid by humanity – in order for the sins of humanity to be forgiven Jesus had to die.

141 The empty tomb

For example:
- The women went to anoint the body of Jesus.
- The stone had been rolled from the entrance to the tomb.
- A young man dressed in white was sitting on the right-hand side.
- The young man told them Jesus had gone.

Theme H: St Mark's Gospel II

142 The Kingdom of God I

1 For example:
- It was prophesised by Jesus at the start of his ministry.
- It explains how Christians should gain eternal life with God.
- It unites all Christians in their shared beliefs.
- It brings all Christians together as a community.
- It tells Christians how they should individually respond to God.
2 You may refer to any contrasting beliefs, e.g. from Catholic, Orthodox and Protestant traditions. Answers could include:
- The Kingdom of God can be understood as yet to come.
- It is the future life given as a reward after death.
- It shows Christians how they should live their present life to achieve eternal life.
- The Kingdom of God can be a personal inner state.
- It is understood as being in a person's heart.
- It is an individual's inner acceptance.
- The Kingdom of God can be understood as a community.
- Christians hold shared beliefs in the Kingdom of God.
- It unites Christians who accept the teachings of Jesus.

143 The Kingdom of God II

Your answer must include relevant, accurate references to scripture or sacred writings. For example:
- Jesus' parables help Christians understand how to achieve entry into the Kingdom of God; the teachings of Jesus make it clear that you need to accept it like a child; you need to accept it with trust and gratitude (Mark 10:15).

- Jesus' parables help Christians understand how the Kingdom of God is both in the present and the future; the Parable of the Sower shows the link between living life and achieving it in the future; it tells that a person needs to respond individually in order to gain entry to the Kingdom of God (Mark 4:1–9).
- Parables help Christians understand the nature of the Kingdom of God; the Parable of the Mustard Seed shows the growing nature of the Kingdom of God; it reflects that it is like a community that starts small and continues to expand (Mark 4:30–32).

144 Jesus' relationships: Women

For example:
- Jesus' attitude is seen as revolutionary and different to traditional teachings.
- Jesus demonstrated ideas of equality.
- Jesus set a new example.
- Jesus showed that all people were made in the image of God.
- Jesus' treatment set the standard for positive treatment of women.

145 Jesus' relationships: Gentiles and tax collectors

Your answer must include relevant, accurate references to scripture or sacred writings. For example:
- Jesus treated people such as Gentiles or tax collectors differently to those who followed traditional attitudes; Jesus did not discriminate against any group in society; his actions demonstrated Christian principles in practice (Mark 7:25–26).
- Jesus began to challenge traditional stereotypes; he showed that all people were made in the image of God; he demonstrated that it was important to care for all God's people with love (Mark 2:16–17).
- Jesus set the example for others to follow; by healing the child of a Gentile he was showing people how to behave; he was showing that God's love was for everyone and he died for the sins of everyone (Mark 7:25–26).

146 Jesus' relationships: The sick

Answers may vary, but you may include some of the following evidence and arguments.
Arguments in support:
- Christians believe it is important to follow the example of Jesus. Jesus treated all people equally in the miracles he performed.
- Treating people equally and in a fair manner are key teachings, not only given by Jesus but through all teachings within Christianity.
- Christians believe that God wants them to help others, as shown through the greatest commandment in Mark 12:28–34 – to love one another.
Arguments in support of other views:
- Some people in today's society may not deserve to be treated equally, for example if someone has hurt others and broken rules such as 'you shall not kill' they deserve to be treated differently.
- Some people in today's world need more help than others and so would need to be treated differently (for example, those who are disabled).
- All people should be treated fairly, but this does not mean that treatment should be equal; Jesus taught about the importance of helping others but this could be achieved in different ways.

- Non-religious believers may argue that it is right to treat people equally, as this is fair. They may not agree with following the example of Jesus, as they are unlikely to accept ideas about religion. They might argue that the idea of treating people equally comes from society.
You will be awarded marks for accurate spelling and punctuation, the effective use of grammar to convey meaning and the use of a wide range of specialist terminology.

147 Faith and discipleship I

For example:
- It seems unfair to exclude some people.
- It is hard to adopt the attitude that only Christians may be saved when there are other religions that teach similar ideas.
- It could encourage prejudice and discrimination.
- Some Christians believe it is not just about belief but also about actions and behaviour.
- Most Christians respect those from other faiths as well as people with no faith.

148 Faith and discipleship II

1 For example:
- It meant giving up all aspects of life.
- It meant leaving your family.
- The disciples faced prejudice and discrimination.
- The disciples were mocked as they tried to share the message of Jesus.
- It meant living a simple and humble life.
2 Answers may vary, but you may include some of the following evidence and arguments.
Arguments in support:
- Jesus told the disciples that they would be rewarded with eternal life and their rewards would be over one hundred times more than what they had given up.
- Being a disciple was a privileged role, as they had the opportunity to learn directly from Jesus, which would have been considered an honour.
- The example of Peter shows how important the role of being a disciple was and how others looked to him for leadership after Jesus' death.
Arguments in support of other views:
- There were many challenges to being a disciple, including giving up your home, possessions and family, which would not have been easy.
- Being a disciple was a difficult life as the disciples were ridiculed for following Jesus and mocked and treated badly, which could have made them wonder whether it was worth it.
- The example of Peter shows how difficult it was to be a disciple – his denial of knowing Jesus shows the challenge he faced in being a loyal disciple.
- Non-religious believers may argue that as they place no importance on religion or ideas of God and Jesus, the statement is irrelevant to them. They may argue that at the time, being one of Jesus' disciples would have been a position of importance, but it is not relevant to their worldview today.
You will be awarded marks for accurate spelling and punctuation, the effective use of grammar to convey meaning and the use of a wide range of specialist terminology.

Notes

Notes